Praise for *Four Steps to Financial Security for Lesbian and Gay Couples*

"Harold Lustig gives us the financial strategies we need to overcome the many ways lesbian and gay couples are unfairly treated under the laws."

—THE HONORABLE CAROLE MIGDEN
California State Assembly

"In my work with thousands of lesbian and gay couples, I have found finances to be a leading cause of death of happy relationships. This book is a source we have long needed and can use."

—REV. MICHAEL S. PIAZZA
Senior pastor, Cathedral of Hope, Dallas

"Understanding insurance, financial matters, and estate planning issues are critical to basic security for most lesbian and gay couples. *Four Steps to Financial Security* offers simple advice and suggests important steps that most couples can take to protect each other, obtain financial security, and rest a little easier."

—KATE KENDELL
Executive director, National Center for Lesbian Rights

"At long last, money advice we can actually use! *Four Steps* is the only personal finance book a gay family needs."

—PAULA LANGGUTH RYAN
Prosperity advisor and author of *Bounce Back from Bankruptcy*

4 STEPS

TO

FINANCIAL
SECURITY

FOR

LESBIAN

AND

GAY COUPLES

Harold L. Lustig

FAWCETT BOOKS

THE BALLANTINE PUBLISHING GROUP • NEW YORK

A Fawcett Book
Published by The Ballantine Publishing Group

Copyright © 1999 by Harold L. Lustig
Foreword copyright © 1999 by Kelly Bonnevie

www.randomhouse.com/BB/

Library of Congress Cataloging-in-Publication Data
Lustig, Harold L.
   Four steps to financial security for lesbian and gay couples /
Harold L. Lustig—1st ed.
      p.   cm.
   Includes bibliographical references and index.
   ISBN 0-449-00249-7 (tr : alk. paper)
   1. Gay men—Finance, Personal.   2. Lesbians—Finance, Personal.
3. Unmarried couples—Finance, Personal.   I. Title.
HG179.L87   1999
332.024′0664—dc21   98-45371

Cover design by Kristine V. Mills-Noble
Cover photo © William Westheimer/The Stock Market
Text design by Ann Gold

Manufactured in the United States of America

First Edition: June 1999
10 9 8 7 6 5 4 3

TO ALEX AND STEPHANIE,

MY PARENTS,

FOR LIFE'S RICHES YOU HAVE GIVEN ME.

Contents

Acknowledgments

This book wouldn't have been possible without the support and willingness of many friends in the gay and lesbian community and from the financial and legal professions.

First, I would like to express my gratitude to Metropolitan Community Church for welcoming this nice Jewish boy from Manhattan into your arms and introducing me to the gay community in San Francisco. If it weren't for the Sunday evening "Gospel and Praise" services on Eureka Street, I would still be living a sheltered life and this book might never have been written.

Without the guidance and enthusiasm of my agent, Mike Larsen, this book would still be just a great idea. Mike's own wonderful book, *How to Write a Book Proposal*, was an immense help to me.

Maria Duerr, my editor, worked with me on every word in every chapter to ensure that the book would be accessible and enjoyable.

Tax laws seem to change as quickly as the page turns. Larry Pon, CPA, guided me through the income tax law maze and read every chapter. Bobby Schneider, CLU, ChFC, also read every chapter and made sure my insurance and estate law facts were correct.

I want to thank Kate Kendell at the National Center for Lesbian Rights for her willingness to support this project and review what I had written, and for introducing me to her friends around the country. I am also indebted to Shannon Minter at NCLR and Betsy Johnsen at AIDS Legal Referral Panel in San Francisco for their time and help.

Considering how little time all of us have to spare, I want to thank Elizabeth Ann Bird, Jack Teeters, Emily Doskow, David Gellman, Fred Hertz, Suzanne Marelius, Michelle Zavos, Jeanine Pow, Kelly Bonnevie, Cheryl Dalton, Moira Leigh, Rebecca Covell, Laura Gray, Randy Knepper, and Bill Young for their help with the legal issues.

When it came to charitable trusts and the more sophisticated end of estate planning, Myron Greenberg, Phil Temple, and Robert Margetic provided invaluable assistance.

I want to acknowledge Joe Re at Octameron Associates for his help on the section about financing children's education.

Social Security rules and regulations have always baffled me; Dan Fortuno, formerly at AIDS Benefits Counselors in San Francisco, and Phil Curtis at AIDS Project of Los Angeles helped me see the light.

Mike Crifasi, Max Brougher, Lori Novy, Bernita Lipsey-Watson, Margaret Murphy, Albert Browning, and Dick Gariepy provided insights and help on the different insurance areas.

I want to thank Jacque Chambers at the AIDS Project of Los Angeles, Kym Hopwood, and Jackie and Jim Spahr for helping me understand the rules in managing the high cost of health care.

In the area of bankruptcy and credit repair, I couldn't have done it without Martha Simon, Paula Langguth Ryan, Angela Valenti-Romeo, and Robert Burns.

Deborah Rhoades, Scott Wilbanks, and Gloria Grening Wolk provided information on viatical settlements.

Nancy Veith and Patricia C. Drivanos, CFP, lent their expertise in the area of estate planning for people with short life expectancies.

Many people served as readers and told me what wasn't clear. I would like to thank Deborah Behrens, Kathy Erion, Keith Millay, Chuck Cole, Susan Cain, Christine Kongol, Susan Ellis, Anne Krivellis, Jo Mitchell, Fern Leaf, Judy and Kim Moon-Moore, Roger Moore, Kevin Schaub, Jackie Sutton, and Elizabeth Fernloff for their enthusiasm and support.

I am just beginning to understand that the process of writing a book is like having a third partner in a relationship. I would like to thank my wife, Rindy, for her understanding and acceptance of all the time I spent with the computer and this book instead of with her.

And last but not least, I want to thank my clients, who saw me through this project and shared their lives with me. Thank you for all that I have learned in working with you—this is really your book.

Foreword

By Kelly Bonnevie

(Founding partner and litigator at the Boston area law firm of Wilson, Marino & Bonnevie, P.C., Ms. Bonnevie has litigated a number of high-profile cases where issues relating to sexual orientation were involved.)

I hope reading this book scares you. By this I mean that I hope Harold Lustig's stories scare you into taking steps to protect yourself and your loved ones. Those of us in the legal and financial professions who work with gay men and lesbians have horror stories to tell; some of mine even appear in this book. Despite the progress the gay and lesbian community has made in recent years, there are still areas where the courts and the laws don't protect us in the same way they protect other people.

The good news is that with some forethought and planning you can ensure that your wishes are respected with regard to what happens to your home, your bank accounts, and even your body in the event of illness or death. As Harold Lustig so clearly puts it, there are ways to protect yourself when the law doesn't. Unfortunately, many gay men and lesbians don't take those steps, whether out of fear, confusion, or sheer inertia. The consequences, as you will read, can be tragic.

Harold Lustig has written a book which helps eliminate the fear and confusion. While no one likes to think about future disability, the end of a relationship, or death, a little planning now can make a big difference later. Relying on his many years of experience in the field of financial planning, Harold helps readers begin to chart a course which makes sense for their particular situation. In easy-to-understand language, he explores the issues and helps us sort through the different options. Whether you are single, in a committed relationship, planning a family, dealing with a chronic illness, or dreaming of a comfortable retirement, you should be planning now to ensure your future financial security. *Four Steps to Financial Security* raises the difficult questions of love and money and shows us how to build a sense of financial and emotional security in our lives.

What I like about Harold's approach is his ability to apply traditional, mainstream financial planning concepts to the unique needs of the gay and lesbian community. Harold isn't gay, and I think his perspective as an "outsider" proves beneficial here. Because gays and lesbians don't enjoy the same benefits married couples often do, professionals working with this population sometimes need to be creative (e.g., in executing living-together agreements). In other cases, our financial strategies can and should mirror traditional financial planning (e.g., we all need to save for retirement). Harold's ability to incorporate traditional, time-tested financial planning concepts with innovative strategies addressing contemporary issues (like those involving people with AIDS reentering the workforce) makes this book critically important.

A nationally recognized expert in the field of financial planning, Harold has done much of the thinking for us already. In doing so, he has come up with some viable strategies for preserving our assets and protecting our loved ones.

This is a timely book written by a financial expert who understands the special legal and financial issues of the gay and lesbian community. I am certain *Four Steps to Financial Security* will prove to be an invaluable tool for gay men and lesbians, and I will be recommending it to my clients. I hope reading it scares them into action.

Introduction

*Whatever you can do, or dream you can, begin it. Boldness has
genius, power, and magic in it. Begin it now.*
                                        —Johann Wolfgang von Goethe

F inancial security is probably one of the greatest concerns for
lesbian and gay couples. It certainly ranks right up at the top
for the straight community. But lesbians and gays face the additional challenge of being subject to adverse laws and social discrimination. This situation can be to your benefit if you use it as an
incentive to plan ahead—something straight couples often put off
because they don't have to think about discrimination. In fact, you
may find that by using the right financial tools in the right way, you
actually have advantages over legally married couples in many areas.

The financial planning process can be shrouded in confusion and
misinformation. This book is not intended to be the last word in financial planning. It is not a workbook—there are few worksheets,
and no exercises or forms—but it does provide you with the names
of other books that serve that purpose and are specifically focused
on the gay community. It is not an investment book—no stocks,
mutual funds, or life insurance companies are mentioned by name.
What the book will do is help to light the way, show you what's possible, and give you the concepts to achieve financial security. It will
also give you the tools you need to reduce your taxes, increase your
wealth, and protect what's yours. In spite of adverse laws, you *can*

have what you want. But you have to be proactive and use at least three of the Four Steps.

Often, it's easier to understand complex financial and legal concepts if they are illustrated by stories about people like ourselves. In this book you will meet gay and lesbian couples who are struggling with situations very similar to yours. They have discovered that it's possible to have financial security—and so can you. You'll find out how they overcame the obstacles in their way and you'll learn specific actions to take from Step-by-Step instructions in almost every chapter.

"Who is this guy and why should I listen to him?" you ask. That's a fair question. Yes, I'm straight. And yes, I'm in a legally recognized marriage. "So, who's he to tell me what to do?" you may be wondering. "In fact, why is this straight guy even writing this book for us?"

Here's my story:

In 1991, I moved from Manhattan to the Castro district in San Francisco, into my then girlfriend's apartment. We lived next door to Metropolitan Community Church. Who could resist the music wafting into our living room from the chapel only a few feet away? Every Sunday night, we went to the "Gospel and Praise" service. As I am Jewish, we also started attending the Castro's gay synagogue, Sha'ar Zahav.

When Rindy and I decided to get married, the rabbi at the synagogue wouldn't perform an interfaith marriage. Interestingly enough, same-gender marriages were okay, but not interfaith ones. So we had a traditional Jewish wedding at MCC. They took the cross down and we put the *chuppa* up—a first for the Castro. Before the wedding, my mother and I were walking in the Castro. My mother, bless her soul, said, "Aren't there any normal people here?" I replied, "They're all normal. It's you and I who aren't!"

As I looked around the community as a financial planner, I realized that here was a large group of people whose financial planning needs were going unserved. My friend Aaron had just lost his lover to AIDS. He complained bitterly about how his partner's family came in and took everything they shared. He was to have the same experience more than once over the next few years. Sharna Sutthern, then the minister at MCC Golden Gate, told me the same story about other couples on a number of occasions. I kept hearing it over and over. I knew there was a better way. So I began to focus my financial planning services for the gay community.

When I was asked to speak on the subject of financial planning for this "new emerging market" to an insurance group in Florida, I went to the library and discovered that there was a dearth of material on the subject. Someone once said, "If you really want to learn about a subject, either teach it or write a book on it." Having already taught seminars on financial and retirement planning, I decided to write a book.

The Four Steps I propose are really quite simple: Plan, Plan, Plan; Protect What's Yours; Think Community; and Use Unconventional Wisdom and Take Action. If God could create the world in six days, you can achieve financial security in four steps. You might need a stepladder for each step, but this book is here to provide you with that first boost up.

Use this book to prepare yourself when you speak with your financial advisor. Tell him or her what you want. Financial professionals—both straight and gay—are capable of helping you achieve your goals, and many of them are in the community or are gay-friendly. Just make sure they understand lesbian and gay legal and financial issues in your state.

When you have finished the book, I invite you to tell me how you used the concepts in it and what you accomplished. I'd love to hear from you at hllustig@aol.com. My Web site, www.foursteps.com, provides updates to critical issues in the book, provides current articles by other advisors on financial and legal issues relevant to your financial security, and links to financial information and resources.

4 STEPS
TO FINANCIAL SECURITY
FOR LESBIAN AND
GAY COUPLES

PLAN, PLAN, PLAN

You have an advantage over legally married couples in that you must be proactive if you want to achieve and maintain financial security. The first step then is to plan and then plan some more.

There are five chapters in this section. Chapter 1 examines twenty-one financial myths that can make you poor and stresses the importance of planning ahead. Chapter 2 provides an overview of the basic principles of financial planning. When broken down into its component parts, financial planning becomes a manageable task. You'll learn the important questions that you and your partner need to address in creating your financial plan, and you'll find out how to choose a financial planner. In chapter 3, you'll learn how to avoid the "estate nightmare," the loss of your property to relatives or to taxes that can hit your partner after you die if you don't know how to transfer your assets correctly. You will discover, in chapter 4, that you have some distinct income tax advantages that straight friends in legally recognized marriages don't have. Since more lesbian and gay couples are having children now than in the past, chapter 5 shows you how to finance your child's college education whether in the near or far future.

Throughout this section and the rest of the book, you will also find critical retirement planning concepts that will help protect you, your lover, and your family.

CHAPTER 1

Twenty-one Myths
That Can Make You Poor

The great enemy of the truth is not the lie—
deliberate, contrived and dishonest—but the myth—persistent,
persuasive and unrealistic. —John F. Kennedy

Everyone has the right to live with financial security. In a society
rife with discrimination, misleading financial information, bi-
ased retirement distribution rules and estate tax laws, and
ever-changing investment and insurance vehicles, gay and lesbian
couples face many challenges as they strive to reach this goal. To
achieve financial security, it is vital that you and your partner understand the key issues and have a plan.

Any of twenty-one commonly held myths could prevent you
from realizing this security. This chapter identifies those myths
and the major obstacles that you must overcome to protect yourself
and your family. Perhaps the biggest myth is that gay and lesbian
couples are always at a disadvantage compared to their straight
counterparts.

**Myth #1: I'm young, healthy, and in a solid relationship, and
I have great group benefits and save regularly. I don't have
to do financial planning.**
Not true. Think about the following:

- How long will your money last if your employer downsizes and you're out of a job?
- If your partner was hit by a drunk driver, how would your lifestyle, financially speaking, change?
- Are you paying more taxes than you should?
- If you were unable to work, what would you live on when your disability expired?
- How do you want your money to be used after your death?

Myth #2: I am in a committed relationship. I don't need a domestic partnership agreement.
Get serious. Gay divorce can be just as ugly as straight divorce. Think of a domestic partnership agreement as a prenuptial or nuptial agreement.

Myth #3: Married couples pay less in income taxes than gay couples with the same income.
This is actually one area where you fare better than straight couples. In financial planning circles, this is known as the gay couple bonus or the marriage penalty. You pay less in taxes than straight married couples with the same income who file jointly.

Myth #4: My partner and I have had a commitment ceremony and we are registered as domestic partners with our city. We now have rights like other married people.
Not true. Until lesbian and gay couples have the right to legally marry, nothing has changed for you. Many states have passed laws saying that they will not recognize out-of-state same-sex marriages. The federal Defense of Marriage Act, passed in 1996, provides that same-sex marriages will not be recognized for any federal purpose—federal income tax, Social Security benefits, pension distribution laws, etc. Until the law recognizes and allows same-gender marriage, you must do financial and estate planning to assure your security.

Myth #5: We can afford to send our daughter to a state college, but we will never qualify for financial aid for her to attend an expensive private school.

Whoa! Let's not be hasty. This is an area where you may have an advantage over straight couples, if there is only one custodial parent in your household.

Contrary to popular belief, financial aid is based on "need," which is not to be confused with being "needy." Just because you can afford a state school does not necessarily mean you cannot qualify for financial aid for a more expensive private school.

Myth #6: We won't need as much money when we retire as we do now.

Too many Americans subscribe to this fallacy, and the consequences hit gay couples particularly hard. Often, because of estrangement from your relatives, you cannot count on help from them. Many of you are cut off from your inheritance. And many gay and lesbian couples don't have children who can provide emotional and financial support. (There can be similar problems when you are dealing with disability.)

Myth #7: Because we are not married, I can't receive my partner's pension, 401(k), or IRA proceeds.

Partly true and partly false. If your partner dies before his or her retirement, you may be out of luck. Some plans have *no* provision for passing proceeds to anyone other than a married spouse. Retirement plans that are funded entirely by the employer typically fall into this category. Life insurance can help solve this problem before and after retirement.

Myth #8: I will lose my group health insurance benefits if I take early retirement because of disability.

Not true. Any employer-sponsored plan for twenty or more employees must comply with the Consolidated Omnibus Budget Reconciliation Act (COBRA) continuation requirements. COBRA allows you to continue your health insurance for up to eighteen months after leaving your job.

If you are disabled or become disabled during the first sixty days of electing COBRA, you may also be eligible for Omnibus Budget Reconciliation Act (OBRA) benefits. OBRA coverage works like COBRA, costs more, and extends your benefits for eleven more months. If the Social Security Administration certifies that you are disabled, then these two programs guarantee that your health insurance will continue for twenty-nine months prior to your becoming eligible for Medicare.

Group life insurance can also be converted to individual life insurance, if you must leave your employment because of disability.

Myth #9: My partner has domestic partner benefits at work. I will be protected by COBRA if his employment is terminated.
This is incorrect. Spouses in legally recognized marriages are protected, but since federal law does not recognize your relationship, you are not protected in the same way. Should your partner's employment be terminated, you will have no coverage unless the insurance carrier has special provisions.

Myth #10: I don't have to worry about retirement income. I will collect my disability insurance as long as I live.
Many people collecting disability benefits other than Social Security Disability Insurance (SSDI) are going to be blindsided by this one. Almost all individual and group disability benefits expire at age 65. Some individual plans expire sooner. This means that when your policy expires, your income stops. Also at age 65, SSDI may convert from disability income to retirement income at a reduced level, 85 percent of which is currently taxable.

Myth #11: If we sell our house, which I own, we are entitled to a $500,000 exemption just like married couples.
You are entitled to a $250,000 exemption every two years on capital

gains taxes for a primary residence that you have lived in for two of the last five years. If each of you owns a 50 percent interest in the house, then it's $500,000.

Myth #12: I have AIDS but have no symptoms. If I wait to start medical treatment, I will receive a larger viatical settlement than people with symptoms.
Under a viatical settlement agreement an individual sells all of the death benefits in his or her life insurance based on his or her life expectancy.

If you are thinking about selling your life insurance and are holding off trying the new drugs because you think you will get a larger settlement, forget it! Viatical settlement companies factor in a longer life expectancy in their offer whether you are on the drugs or not.

Viatication can be appropriate for any terminal illness—including breast cancer, hepatitis C, and prostate cancer—when people have no other resources or need additional cash. And remember, not everyone can afford or tolerate the new drugs.

Myth #13: Viatication is tax-free.
Tax legislation signed by President Clinton made viatical settlements tax-free at the federal level effective January 1997, but only in certain situations. If the payment does not meet the requirements of the Health Insurance Portability and Accountability Act of 1996 (HIPAA), it won't be tax-free. The law essentially says that payment must be for long-term care for someone who is terminally or chronically ill. If the person is chronically ill, that person must be expected to die within twenty-four months.

Myth #14: I'm too young to need life insurance.
True, you don't need it. But once you see what you can do with life insurance, you will be amazed. You can use your policy to accumulate tax-free dollars that can supplement your retirement income on a favorable tax basis. Some life insurance policies can even be

invested in mutual funds during your lifetime, enabling you to build your nest egg free of capital gains taxes.

Myth #15: As a gay person, I cannot buy life insurance and name my partner as beneficiary.
This depends upon the state where you live. Some states, such as California, allow anyone to be your beneficiary. Other states, such as New York, require an "insurable interest," generally defined to mean a blood relative, spouse, or business partner.

Myth #16: I have breast cancer, so I can't get health insurance.
Don't bet on this. Some states have high-risk pools to help individuals who are otherwise uninsurable.

Myth #17: I have HIV, so I can't buy life insurance.
Not entirely true. There are insurance companies that issue a kind of policy known as graded death benefit insurance. Such policies can be used by people who are living with cancer, AIDS, heart disease, or any other terminal illness. Applying for them generally does not involve medical questions or blood or urine tests.

Myth #18: We've been together for years. We don't have to worry about who will handle the money and take care of our children if one partner dies.
Wrong, wrong, wrong! State intestacy laws, which stipulate how property is distributed when a person dies without a will or trust, do not recognize lesbian and gay relationships. If you assume that these laws apply to you, you will make a tragic mistake. In addition, not all states allow adoption by same-sex partners. If your state does not, you may have a serious problem if one of you dies.

Myth #19: We've been together for years. Our families understand us and will help the survivor.
This is probably the most tragic assumption lesbian and gay couples make. Death does strange things to people. Old loyalties disappear

and estrangement resurfaces. Many partners have lost everything because they thought their loved one's family would respect his or her wishes. But you can protect yourself no matter what anyone's family thinks.

Myth #20: Joint ownership with right of survivorship is all I need to ensure that my partner will receive our house if I die.
This should be true, but it may not always be true. Family members of the deceased who want property have challenged many gay survivors. Usually the challenger claims that your partner made a casual decision, not one that he or she really wanted to make. Many courts have accepted this argument.

Myth #21: There is little or no financial difference when a partner, rather than a married spouse, dies.
Actually, there is a very big difference. This is where the pedal hits the metal, where political disenfranchisement hits the pocketbook. Retirement plan payments may continue if your partner has already retired, but everything can be lost if death occurs before retirement. (For married couples, payments continue.) Social Security doesn't protect the surviving partner. Joint property can be taxed differently for you than for married couples. You need to have documents proving how much each partner actually contributed.

On the other hand, you have a major advantage over straight couples who wrongly assume there is no urgency about doing financial and estate planning: Because you don't have the luxury of making false estate assumptions, you have an opportunity to be better prepared for the future.

HOW TO TAKE CONTROL OF
YOUR FINANCIAL LIFE

Lesbian and gay couples can easily fall victim to financial misinformation. This chapter has shed light on the most common financial myths that confuse people and cause them to make serious mistakes. By becoming familiar with these myths you can avoid these mistakes and even enjoy financial advantages that straight couples do not have.

In the next chapter, you will learn the basic principles of financial planning that will serve as the foundation for the rest of the book. In the following chapters, you will find out how to plan for your future so that you can have many of the benefits that legally married couples take for granted.

Would you like to take control of your financial future? This book will give you the tools to overcome financial and social hurdles and take control of your money.

CHAPTER 2

How Financial Planning
Can Help You

In preparing for battle, I have always found that plans are
useless, but planning is indispensable.
                    —Dwight D. Eisenhower

Jenny was concerned about her and her partner Cathy's financial situation. "Paycheck to paycheck, it never changes," she lamented.

Cathy nodded her head in agreement. "I know. No matter what we do, it's always the same. I earn more money, nothing changes. We budget and we still can't save. How will we send Julian to college?"

"It's a good thing we live in a good school district. Julian can stay in the public school system," Jenny added.

"And how will we get by if I lose my job?" Cathy continued. "You know how volatile the catering business at the hotel can get. The tips are great but it gets crazy sometimes. I really need to think about another job."

"Thank goodness we have my credit cards. We can always use them if we run into a money crunch or I get sick. And don't forget the twenty-eight hundred dollars in your IRA, we can always use that," Jenny tried to reassure her partner.

Cathy and Jenny have been together for four years. They live in Cathy's house in Laureville, Maryland. Cathy, 37, is the catering director for a large hotel in Baltimore. Jenny, 32, teaches in a private school. Both learned in previous relationships how difficult joint accounts can be, so they decided to maintain separate checking accounts but share income and expenses. Although they are happy with their present arrangement, they worry about the future. Will they be able educate Julian? How will they afford retirement if they are living paycheck to paycheck?

To get a handle on their financial affairs, they attended an adult education class on financial planning. The seminar was informative but it focused on planning for singles and married couples.

The instructor did, however, ask a question that helped Cathy and Jenny realize why financial planning might be useful for them.

The instructor asked if anyone would try to drive to Seattle without a road map. An easy question—"Of course not," members of the class responded. "If you would use a road map to get where you are going by the easiest and most efficient route," the instructor asked, "why wouldn't you use a road map to reach your financial goals?"

Then she asked the class what was the best way to get to a specific address in Seattle. "Fly," everyone said. "Is that the only thing you'd have to do to get there?" she said. "To get to the Seattle address from here, you would need to take the elevator to the first floor, drive to the airport, walk to the check-in counter, fly to Seattle, shuttle to the house, and walk up the driveway." Her point was that achieving your goals, like traveling, requires the integration of different activities. Cathy and Jenny agreed to work with a financial planner who understood the needs of lesbian and gay couples.

Your financial plan is the first step in achieving financial security. In the process of preparing a comprehensive written plan, you will create a road map to follow for the future.

Your financial plan must be monitored regularly. Changes in tax laws, investments, family situations and definitions, inflation, and debt and savings patterns will affect how and when you reach your goals. Financial planning is an ongoing process and entails looking at all aspects of your life, examining your goals, and determining the best way to reach them.

WHAT IS FINANCIAL PLANNING?

Sound financial planning takes a holistic approach to your financial situation. The process covers a wide spectrum of areas relating to your present security and future well-being, and has three phases: planning, implementing, and monitoring. Your financial plan should include an analysis of your situation and needs as well as specifics on how to achieve your goals. A plan that is not implemented is basically useless. Plans that become a living process can help you achieve your goals.

Conventional wisdom states that financial planning incorporates six activities.

- Identifying your financial position
- Estate planning
- Protection planning
- Investment planning
- Income tax planning
- Retirement planning

As a financial planner and advisor working with lesbian and gay couples, I believe that there is another element that is key to goal achievement. I call this seventh area the psychology of money in relationship, or what happens when people in a relationship deal with financial issues together. An excellent resource and a good place to begin learning about this last area is *Money Harmony: Resolving Money Conflicts in Your Life and Relationships*, by Olivia Mellan.

Let's review each of the traditional areas of financial planning.

Financial Position

The first step in the financial planning process is to gain an understanding of your present financial position. Like many people, Cathy and Jenny do not understand where they stand with respect to their assets, liabilities, income, and expenses. They need to start with an examination of the three elements that make up their present financial position: **net worth**, **cash flow**, and **cash reserve**.

Net worth is the difference between everything you own and everything you owe, or, to use accounting language, your assets less your liabilities. Your assets fall into three main groups. The first category includes **liquid assets**, which are everything that can be converted to cash easily without significant loss to the principal. This category includes savings accounts, money market funds, and treasury bills. The second category is **investment assets**, which generally include your long-term investments. Stocks, bonds, mutual funds, IRAs, and company retirement plans fall into this category. Your home may be a great investment, but if you live in it, it falls into the third category, **personal assets**. Personal assets include your home, furnishings, skis, art, auto, jewelry, and so on.

Cash flow is an accounting of all of your sources of income and expenses. The difference between income and expenses is the amount you have to invest for the future. Since Cathy and Jenny are living paycheck to paycheck, they either have negative cash flow and are using their credit cards to balance the budget (this sounds like the government!) or they are barely breaking even.

An exercise that you might find helpful is to track every expense for a thirty-day period to see where your money is really going. The hardest part is tracking what you do with the cash that comes out of the ATM. Think of this as a consciousness-raising experience or, if you have counted calories, as a money calorie counting exercise.

After doing the counting exercise, divide your expenses into the following categories:

- **Committed expenses:** housing, food, clothing, transportation, education, insurance
- **Investment outlays:** retirement plan contributions, regular savings
- **Taxes:** withholding, estimated payments, Social Security
- **Discretionary expenses:** dining out, hobbies, gifts, entertainment, vacations, home improvements, car repairs

I guarantee that after you see the results you will be spending less. Many times, even taxes can be reduced by this kind of awareness. If you think this process is impossible or nothing will change, read *Your Money or Your Life: Transforming Your Relationship with Money and Achieving Financial Independence*, by Joe Dominquez and Vicki Robin.

Cash reserve is money that is readily available for emergencies or unexpected opportunities that are not in your budget, such as sudden unemployment, an auto accident or repairs not covered by insurance, medical expenses, and trips. The amount of cash reserve you have will depend upon your and your partner's job stability, insurance, and lifestyle. A good rule of thumb is to try to have a cash reserve large enough to cover three to six months of expenses.

Cathy's IRA is not a cash reserve, it is a long-term investment. Jenny's credit cards represent not cash reserve, but liabilities. Cathy and Jenny need to start saving on a regular basis to build a cash reserve. They agree to dine out less and deposit their newfound savings by monthly direct deposit into a money market account with checkwriting privileges. They will also start paying off their credit cards with the highest interest rate first. Cathy agrees to obtain a credit line on the house in case they need money for an emergency. Financial planning will help them find the dollars to save.

QUESTIONS TO HELP YOU GET STARTED

• Where do you stand today?
What is your net worth after subtracting all of your liabilities?

Exactly how much cash is readily available in case of an emergency? Don't count your ability to borrow easily— credit cards, equity loans—that's not a cash reserve.

How much discretionary income do you have after meeting fixed expenses?

How much can you comfortably afford to save and invest for the future? Having identifiable goals makes saving much easier.

• **What do you hope to accomplish?**

What would you like to accomplish in twenty years? In five to ten years? How about the next year?

Who would provide support if one of you is incapacitated and unable to work for several years? If your partner were disabled, would you pay off his or her credit card debt incurred prior to the relationship?

What are you taking for granted that you haven't discussed?

• **How can you reach your goals?**

How much time do you have to achieve your goals and how much money will you need to invest?

How well will you be able to afford the twenty-five or thirty years of unemployment that is known as retirement?

• **What if you break up?**

Who keeps the house? How do you divide the property you have been sharing?

Do you have a written agreement for dividing your property?

These are important questions for you and your partner. Answer them separately and compare your findings, or do them together. Whatever you do, do them! You might be surprised by the results. For Cathy and Jenny, this was the first time they had shared their hopes, wishes, and dreams. They discovered assumptions each was making about the other that didn't work for them.

Estate Planning

As a lesbian or gay couple, you need to understand how estate tax law affects you. You don't have to be an expert, but you will be in a better position to protect yourself against unfair treatment if you have a handle on the basics. This area is so important that six chapters in this book address different aspects of this issue and show you how to protect yourself.

Estate planning is usually defined as the process of transferring a lifetime of accumulation to someone else—your lover, children, relatives, charity—at death. Too many people in the United States don't plan. For them, estate planning is the process of transferring property to the IRS. A broader definition includes what you do with your assets during your lifetime as well as at death.

The American Bar Association has said that over 70 percent of people over the age of 65 don't have a will. Is this true for you? How current is your will? Does it apply to your present situation? Does it confirm your home ownership intentions?

Protection Planning

Protecting yourself against the unexpected, also known as risk management or insurance planning, is a vital element in financial planning. Think of insurance as a way to counteract the economic consequences of unexpected change. If you don't adequately prepare for risks in life, you could wipe out your life savings, suffer a loss in the quality of your living, or even worse, die prematurely.

Insurance generally covers life, health care, loss of income, custodial care, and property and casualty (coverage for your home, car, boat, etc.). (Specific chapters in the book address the first four areas. The area of property and casualty is beyond the scope of this book.)

Life insurance is probably the single best weapon you have in your financial and estate planning arsenal because it is inexpensive, easy to put in place, legal, and guaranteed. Let's take a look at its many uses.

Survivor income: Life insurance has traditionally been used to provide for people who depend on you for income: your partner, children, parents, nieces, and nephews. You pay for life insurance whether you buy it or not. If you don't have coverage, your family pays by loss of lifestyle if you die uninsured.

Children: No one likes to think about the death of his or her child, but it does happen. Many times when a child dies, financial devastation follows the emotional devastation—parents stop working, families break up. The purpose of insurance coverage on children is to protect you from that financial devastation. If you tie the insurance into solving other goals, such as education funding, it becomes more palatable.

Debt payment: Life insurance can be used to pay off your debts—a mortgage, credit card debt, school loans, college expenses for your partner or children.

Estate taxes: Life insurance can be used to "prepay" future estate taxes for pennies on the dollar. It can also be used to create a fund that will replace dollars lost to estate taxes.

Charitable contributions: Life insurance can be used to create a substantial gift for a small investment. Cathy can create a future gift of $100,000 for her favorite charity by investing as little as $25 a month.

If she makes the charity the owner of the policy, the premium is tax-deductible. If she owns the policy and changes the beneficiary in the future, it's not. If she has an old policy and gives it to a charity, the cash value accumulation in the policy is income tax deductible.

Business protection: When a business owner dies, the business also dies if there is no written plan to continue it. Life insurance can be used to fund an agreement that enables a business to survive. Life insurance can provide the money for the surviving business partner to buy the deceased owner's interest in the business from the estate. It's best to consult a life insurance broker knowledgeable in business continuation plans for help in this area, as there are a number of different strategies that may apply to you.

Group insurance: Many employees have used group life insurance to protect their families.

Investment Planning

An almost endless array of investment alternatives is available today. Here are some important questions to consider: What are your short- and long-term goals? Do they include having an adequate cash reserve, buying a house, educating a child, retiring early, or just having enough retirement income? If you do not have enough "liquidity" (cash or the ability to convert to cash easily and quickly) and you do not have disability insurance, life insurance, or long-term-care insurance, then investments are not for you. Until you've protected the basics, investments are too great a risk.

There are other investment questions you will need to address. How do you pick the right investments for your goals and time frame? How well do you sleep at night when the stock market drops? What is the right investment mix to protect you against inflation and recession?

Income Tax Planning

Intelligent tax planning can be a powerful part of protecting and building your assets. Cathy and Jenny don't mind paying their fair share of taxes; they just don't want to pay more than they have to. As a lesbian couple, they have a number of advantages over their straight friends. They can, for example, take advantage of the difference in their tax brackets to lower their total income taxes.

Tax-deferred investments can help build assets. And employee benefit plans can be used by lesbian or gay couples in ways that are not applicable to married couples.

Retirement Planning

A visit to the bookstore or library will provide you with a plethora of books on retirement planning, IRAs, 401(k)s, pension plans, and the like. The problem is that these books may not address your issues:

- How can you create a tax-deferred, tax-free income to supplement your other retirement income?
- How can helping to meet the needs of the community help you increase your retirement income?
- What happens to the money in your retirement plan if you die before retirement? How can you avoid the "gay penalty" on retirement plans?

CHOOSING A FINANCIAL ADVISOR

We all know that one of the best ways to find a doctor, dentist, or accountant is by referral. The same is true with your financial planner.
It is essential that whomever you choose be familiar with the estate
planning issues of lesbian and gay couples. Cathy and Jenny sought
to meet a qualified financial advisor through a seminar. This can be
an effective way to check out an advisor.

When meeting a new advisor, be direct and speak the truth
of who you are and what's important to you. Ask the person for referrals from other lesbian and gay couples. Be sure that you are
comfortable with this person. You are embarking on a long-term relationship. Ask about credentials and how this person or firm will be
compensated.

How Do You Identify
a Real Financial Planner?

There is no best education program or single credential for financial
planners. While planners are not salespeople, they may offer to sell
you products as you implement your program. (Buying a particular
investment or insurance vehicle is not part of the planning process,
though it may come later.) People who are practicing true financial
planning will disclose fees, risks, and conflicts of interest up front.
They will also provide their credentials and their regulatory filing.

Who Regulates Investment Advisors?

If the person or the firm you are working with is giving investment
advice and managing more than $25 million, they must register
with the Securities and Exchange Commission (SEC) as a Registered Investment Advisor (RIA). This is not a credential but a
yearly registration. They must also provide you with Part II of the
"ADV" (Application for Investment Advisor Registration) within
forty-eight hours of your becoming a client. Part I includes financial
information about the advisor or the firm and Part II discloses what
the advisor or firm charges and how it operates. Both parts are filed

with the SEC. The SEC does not regulate fees or determine the quality of the advisor or the advice.

Accountants, attorneys, teachers, and engineers are exempt from filing with the SEC if they are giving investment advice incidental to their specialty. But top professionals or the firms they are associated with will register.

The Uniform Securities Act (USA) is the model law that governs the regulation and registration of investment advisors at the state level. Under the USA, it is unlawful for any person to transact business in a state as an investment advisor or representative unless that person is registered with the state or exempt from registration. Investment advisors are exempt from registering with the state if they manage more than $25 million in assets, have had fewer than six clients in the previous twelve months, have no place of business in the state, or only have clients who are other investment advisors, broker-dealers, and/or financial institutions.

What Credentials Should Your Financial Advisor Have?

There are a number of designations that the financial planning industry uses to indicate education programs planners have completed. Having the designation does not mean that the planner is top-notch, but it helps identify the serious financial advisor.

Chartered Financial Analyst (CFA) is a designation from the Association for Investment Management. This three-year program is particularly appropriate for money managers and stock analysts and is focused on investment analysis.

Certified Financial Planner (CFP) is the designation issued by the International Board of Standards and Practice for Certified Financial Planners to applicants who complete an exam, agree to abide by the code of ethics, and follow a program of continuing education.

Certified Public Accountant (CPA) is a designation regulated by the board of accountancy in each state. CPAs must pass a two-and-a-half-day comprehensive examination and meet state licensing requirements. CPAs who are serious about financial planning will either become a Personal Financial Specialist or obtain the CFP designation.

Chartered Life Underwriter (CLU) is a designation offered by the American College. A CLU has at least three years' experience in insurance and has completed a ten-course program and passed an exam in each course. CLUs who are doing financial planning will generally also get the Chartered Financial Consultant designation or the CFP.

Chartered Financial Consultant (ChFC) is a designation offered by the American College. There is a ten-part exam or, for applicants who are also CLU, a three-part exam.

Personal Financial Specialist (PFS) is a designation issued by the American Institute of Certified Public Accountants to applicants who complete a comprehensive examination and have received letters of reference from clients and colleagues. CPAs who have personal financial planning experience and pass the exam can qualify for this designation.

Registered Representatives (RR) do not necessarily do financial planning. They are generally securities salespeople who have passed a series of securities exams and are registered with a broker-dealer. Registered representatives and broker-dealers are regulated by the National Association of Securities Dealers.

Registered Investment Advisor (RIA) is an individual or a broker-dealer who has registered with the SEC and who manages more than $25 million. States are responsible for regulating and auditing all others. The SEC does not approve RIAs in any way.

How Are Financial Advisors Compensated?

There are a number of ways that financial advisors and planners are compensated. Let's look at the alternatives:

Assets under management: Some advisors will charge a percentage of the total amount of assets that they manage for you. In addition they may charge a flat fee for developing a financial plan or an investment policy.

Flat fees: Some planners are paid an annual retainer for all planning work. The fee could stay the same from year to year, or it could be reduced because the job gets easier, or it could increase if the estate and assets under management are increasing.

Commissions: Some planners believe that commissions are more fair than fees, as they question whether the client is receiving value for annual fees. They also believe that annual fees on top of fund-management fees can make investing too expensive.

Fee plus commissions: Some planners will charge an assets-under-management fee plus commissions on products, such as disability or life insurance, because there isn't an adequate choice of insurance products without sales charges. Others separate the planning process into several components and charge a flat fee for the planning plus commissions for implementation. They may receive a **wrap fee** for no-load assets under management. A wrap fee is an annual percentage charge based on total investments. Financial planners with the larger firms such as American Express Financial Advisors and Merrill Lynch work on a fee-plus-commission basis.

Fee offset: Some planners will offset fees with commissions only when they use products structured with commissions. Planners who are transitioning from commissions to fee-only may use this method.

Hourly fees and caps: Some planners charge a flat hourly rate for the time they spend with you or the time they spend working on your program. Other planners will charge by the hour and have a cap on the total fee.

Hourly fees plus asset-based fees: Some planners will charge an hourly fee for a comprehensive plan and/or an annual money-management fee. Others will charge a flat fee for the initial program and then receive asset-based fees as a percentage.

Fee cap: Some planners will work on an hourly basis and also receive asset-based fees. They may estimate the time it will take to complete an initial plan and then limit the maximum charge.

It really doesn't matter which method of compensation your

financial advisor is using, as long as you know in advance what it is and have an agreement.

What Can a Financial Planner Really Do for You?

When the stock market took a serious nosedive in October 1987, people who didn't have an advisor to talk them through the correction fled the market. I remember one client who invested in September and told me he was losing $11,000 per month, which wasn't actually true. His investments went down by that much in the month the market corrected. By "holding his hand" during a very rough time, I helped him stay with his investments and make a profit six months later.

The best job your planner or advisor can do for you is help you identify your goals and then help you stick to your plan. One of the biggest mistakes people can make is failing to stay with their investments when the market goes down. It's not easy. How would you feel if you woke up one morning and found that your $10,000 investment was worth $7,200? Living your plan can be tough. Having the support and guidance of a skilled financial planner can help tremendously.

THE LAST WORD

The key to reaching your goals is to identify them, develop a plan to achieve them, and *stay on course*. The financial plan and the insurance and investment portfolio you construct to execute that plan should answer three basic questions: what is the money for, who is it for, and when will it be needed? Your financial advisor's job is not to guess the ups and downs of the market but to ask the question what has changed—in your life and in the economy—and be your long-term partner to help you get results.

When working with a financial planner, make sure you get an initial letter or written agreement that includes how you will be charged and a copy of the ADV or the state filing.

CHAPTER 3

Avoiding the Estate Nightmare

All money nowadays seems to be produced with a natural homing for the Treasury.
—Prince Philip, Duke of Edinburgh

Harry and Marc are not rich by San Francisco Bay Area standards. They live comfortably in Harry's house in San Rafael, a small suburban town north of San Francisco. The house is now worth $400,000. Harry also owns a summer cottage near Lake Tahoe that he owned previously with his first lover, John, who died four years ago. John had enough insurance to pay off the mortgage, so Harry owns the cottage free and clear.

For twelve years, Harry has enjoyed his job as a per diem nurse with a local registry because it gives him a choice about when and where he works.

Harry's older brother has objected to his lifestyle for years. The brother believes Harry is living in sin and has no right to the wealth he has accumulated.

Marc, Harry's partner of three years, is a gardener and has been working with the same company for almost ten years. He feels like an owner but knows he is not. Other than his credit union account, an IRA, and health insurance, Marc has no property except for a Harley-Davidson. Being handy with the hammer and shovel, Marc does all the repairs and landscaping in the house he shares with Harry.

Harry wants to make sure Marc receives his property, without interference from his brother, should he die. He wants to put Marc on the deed to the house. Although he does have life insurance for Marc to pay off the mortgage, neither of the men has a will. Harry is also concerned about estate taxes because he knows that Marc doesn't have any money. He wants to know the best way to plan his estate in case either he or Marc dies.

ESTATE PLANNING
FOR THE LIVING

In the previous chapter, you learned that estate planning is the process of transferring a lifetime of accumulation to someone else upon your death. It is also the process of arranging your affairs to help you achieve financial security while alive.

The tools many estate planners take for granted don't always work for gay and lesbian couples. Too often, I have heard of couples going to an advisor or an attorney and paying lots of hard-earned cash only to find out that their estate plan would not work for them. So let's start with the basics.

During your lifetime, estate planning can help to:

- Protect your loved ones
- Reduce your income taxes
- Avoid capital gains taxes
- Maintain control of your assets
- Protect you in the event of incapacity
- Provide supplemental retirement income

The more you know about two areas of estate law—how property transfers and how estates are taxed—the better equipped you will be to protect yourself and to make sure your partner receives what you intended without family interference. Estate planning is too complex and critical to do yourself. You must use a qualified, community-oriented estate planner.

HOW PROPERTY TRANSFERS AT DEATH

Imagine, for a moment, all of your property falling into four buckets. All of your real estate is in one bucket; your bank accounts, investments, personal property, and business interests are in another; your life insurance, IRAs, and retirement plans at work are in the third bucket; and any trusts you may have established during your lifetime or after your death are in the fourth bucket. When you die, the contents flow from these buckets through a giant funnel, as in the illustration on the next page.

On the way to the opening at the bottom of the funnel is a spigot. Out of the spigot pours your estate expenses: federal estate taxes, state inheritance taxes, final medical bills, debts, funeral costs, legal fees, appraisal fees—and the list goes on. What comes out at the very bottom—what your heirs receive—is generally a lot less than what went in. If your assets are not in the right bucket, even more comes out of the expense spigot and less from the bottom. If you have no will and have not provided for your partner via the other buckets, everything you own will go out the spigot and down the drain. Laws that protect married couples do not protect you and your partner. You have to be proactive in closing the spigot with every financial decision you make.

The purpose of estate planning is to help close the spigot. How you hold your property or designate what will happen to it when you die will determine whether you have a flood or a drip. You control the spigot.

When a person dies, property can transfer to his or her life partner by one of four means: **probate**, **title**, **beneficiary**, and **trust**. Let's use Harry and Marc's situation to take a look at the facts about each method.

Probate: All property that transfers by means of a will goes through a court proceeding called probate, and part goes out the spigot. At death, proof must be shown that the will is authentic, was properly signed, and meets all the requirements of the state in which the person died. If your partner dies without a will, the court

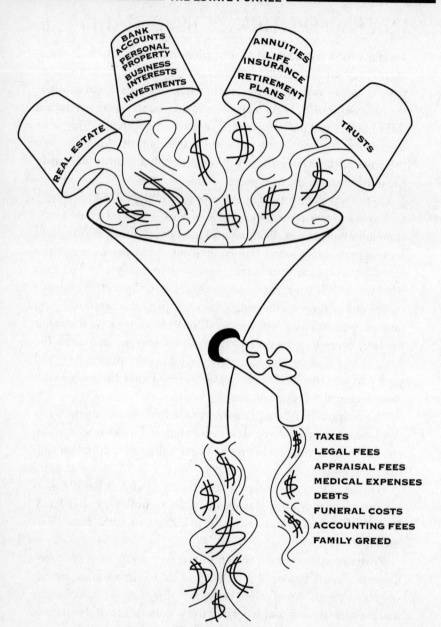

will determine who will inherit his or her property—and it won't be you.

The probate process can take twelve to eighteen months to complete. It can be expensive, but costs can be reduced if you plan ahead. If you do not plan, a considerable amount of your estate can go out the spigot. If your estate, for example, is worth $300,000, then $15,000 in fees and state taxes alone can easily be lost. Furthermore, assets are tied up while the process continues. If Harry leaves everything to transfer by probate, Marc will not be able to manage the property, make business decisions, or access Harry's investments until the estate is closed. He could be rich on paper but destitute in reality.

Probate is public. Through a formal probate hearing, Harry's brother can challenge Marc's right to Harry's property—and make Marc's life a nightmare—based on what he learns from the public records. There are other ways to transfer property that are private and less expensive. A will, however, is important and necessary.

Title: Property that you own with someone else can transfer by title directly to that person. The cottage in Tahoe transferred directly to Harry at John's death because Harry was on the deed as the "joint owner with right of survivorship." The key benefit of **joint tenancy** is the "right of survivorship." When one tenant dies, his or her share automatically goes to the survivor(s) listed on the deed without going through probate. As a lesbian or gay couple it is important that you have a current will in addition to title transfer arrangements to help avoid challenges from unhappy relatives.

Beneficiary: When a person is designated as the beneficiary on an insurance policy, annuity, IRA, 401(k), or other retirement plan at work, the proceeds pass directly to that person without going through probate.

Many states have adopted laws that allow you to designate a beneficiary on stocks, bonds, mutual funds, or brokerage accounts without going though probate (see Appendix G). These designations are called **transfer-on-death** or **TOD** designations. It costs nothing to create a TOD beneficiary. It is easy to establish a TOD designation and easy to claim the assets under it. Most important for you is that it is private and fast. All the beneficiary needs is proof of death in the form of a death certificate.

Another form of beneficiary designation is a **payable-on-death** account, or **POD**. This designation is found on bank, savings and loan, and credit union accounts. An account with a POD designation will pass directly to the designee with proof of death of the depositor. If Marc puts Harry on his credit union account as the POD beneficiary, Harry will receive the proceeds of the account immediately after Marc's death, without going through probate, and at no cost. Harry, however, would have no access to the account during Marc's life unless he was also a co-owner.

POD accounts are easy to establish and cost nothing. When you fill out the signature card at the bank or credit union, name the person you want as your beneficiary. You can change this at any time.

Trust: Property that is owned by a trust will pass directly to the beneficiary of the trust without going through the probate process. A trust that is established during your lifetime is called an inter vivos trust, or **living trust**. If you can change the beneficiary and add property or take it out of the trust at any time while you are alive, it is a "revocable" living trust. These trusts do *not* avoid federal estate tax but they do avoid probate costs. However, drafting the trust instrument and retitling property that is contained in the trust can entail significant legal fees.

You can be the trustee as readily as anyone else can. Your lover can be the "successor trustee" as well as the beneficiary or one of the beneficiaries. If you are incapacitated, your co-trustee can manage the assets in the trust without a conservatorship or a court process. Since trusts are designed to last a long time, a corporate trustee, such as a bank, that is familiar with your situation, goals, and concerns should be considered as co-trustee or successor trustee.

Not everyone needs a living trust. People who have small estates or the majority of their assets held in life insurance, IRAs, annuities, TOD accounts, and employer-sponsored retirement plans might not need a living trust. If your beneficiary has independent means, you might not need a living trust. Check with your attorney.

HOW ESTATES ARE TAXED

Most people behave as if the IRS should get the biggest portion of their estate when they die. By not planning, you'll lose more money to taxes than is necessary. Taxes differ from state to state—some states have inheritance taxes that are imposed on the recipient of an estate *after* distribution, while others follow the federal tax structure and tax the estate *before* distribution.

In some states, transfers between unmarried partners at death are taxed differently than transfers between spouses. Transfers may be treated as gifts and taxed, and as a result your partner could receive only 85 percent or 90 percent of your property. (Life insurance can be used to make up the difference or provide the survivor with the cash to pay taxes.) The implications of state tax statutes must be discussed with your attorney or estate planner. I will focus here on the federal rules.

When a person dies, everything he or she owns or controls is included in the gross estate. The tax is due within nine months of the date of death, in cash. The IRS does not accept real estate, stocks, bonds, jewelry, or art—just a check, if you please. Here is how the estate tax is calculated on the federal level:

ESTATE TAX CALCULATION

GROSS ESTATE	$_____
Less: Debts	(_____)
Administration expenses	(_____)
Losses during administration	(_____)
Equals: Adjusted gross estate	_____
Less: Marital deduction	(_____)
Charitable deduction	(_____)

Equals: Taxable estate	\$_____
Times: Rate from tax table (Appendix A)	
Equals: Tentative tax	(_____)
Less: Unified credit	(_____)
Gift taxes paid after 1976	(_____)
Foreign death tax credit	(_____)
Tax on prior transfers credit	(_____)
State death tax credit	(_____)
Equals: Net estate tax	\$_____

Let's define some of these terms in more detail.

Gross Estate is everything you own on the day of your death. This includes property that you may own outside the United States. If there are any strings on property that you have given away, such as the right to change a beneficiary or the right to designate when a property can be sold or not, then the law says you own it. Your gross estate includes:

- **Liquid assets:** cash, stocks, bonds, mutual funds
- **Real estate:** residence, home, vacation homes, time-shares, rental property, land
- **Personal property:** art, jewelry, clothing, furnishings, cars, yacht
- **Business interests:** closely held stock, partnerships, sole proprietorships
- **Life insurance:** your own or payable to your estate
- **Retirement benefits:** IRAs, pensions, 401(k) plans, 403(b) plans

Debt is deducted from the gross estate and includes anything you owe: mortgages, credit card debt, or personal loans. Some states, like California, do not deduct debt but instead tax the gross estate.

The **marital deduction** is where lesbian and gay couples lose out. A legally recognized married couple is entitled to an unlimited marital deduction for spouse-to-spouse transfers. With proper planning, a married spouse can leave his or her partner an estate worth any amount and limit or avoid tax consequences completely. You and your partner cannot.

Charitable gifts that are bequests to charity are deducted from the gross estate and are for the full amount of the value of the property transferred to the charity. The charity must be operated exclusively for religious, charitable, scientific, literary, or educational purposes, or to foster amateur sports competition or the prevention of cruelty to children or animals.[1]

TABLE 3.1
ESTATE TAX THRESHOLD

Year	Unified Credit Exemption Equivalent
1999	$650,000
2000–1	675,000
2002–3	700,000
2004	850,000
2005	950,000
2006 & after	1,000,000

The **unified credit** is a dollar amount allocated to each taxpayer that can be applied to the gift tax and estate tax.[2] In 1999 the unified credit is equal to $211,300. This amount increases per the Taxpayer Relief Act of 1997 as follows: $220,500 in 2000 and 2001;

1. *1998 Tax Facts 1 On Life Insurance,* The National Underwriter Co, 1998 Edition, Question 763, page 823.
2. *1998 Tax Facts 1 On Life Insurance,* The National Underwriter Co, 1998 Edition, Question 766, page 833.

$229,800 in 2004; $326,300 in 2005; and $345,800 in 2006 and thereafter. This amount corresponds to *the unified credit exemption equivalent*, which is listed in table 3.1. Think of the unified credit exemption equivalent as the amount you can transfer to your lover, children, or anyone for that matter, tax-free during your lifetime or at your death.

The largest item that is deducted from the tentative tax to arrive at the estate tax due is the unified credit. In some instances you may receive credits that will lower the federal estate tax—including foreign estate taxes paid on property in other countries, taxes on prior gift transfers, and credit for state inheritance or estate taxes.

Gifts are another area that requires extra planning. An individual can give $10,000 not subject to gift tax to an unlimited number of people each year. A married couple can give $20,000 in one spouse's name. Since you or your partner can give up to $10,000 to each other or as many other people as you wish each year, you have significant planning opportunities to avoid estate and gift tax consequences at your death.

OTHER ESTATE PLANNING ISSUES

There are six other areas that you must be concerned with that married couples do not have to worry about.

Sharing Existing Real Estate

Harry wants to put Marc on the deed to the house as a co-owner. Given that Harry's house is worth $400,000, this title change will constitute a $200,000 gift to Marc. Do you think Harry realizes that that's what he is doing?

Since they are a young couple, Harry's putting Marc on the deed as a co-owner may invite another problem. Gifts are permanent and hard to get back. When I started to write this chapter, I heard of a case where one partner put the other on the deed to her house. The new owner stole from her employer, was caught, arrested, and sued. A lien was put on the house. The original owner effectively lost her house. It doesn't have to be this way.

There is another potential tax time bomb in Harry and Marc's arrangement. Harry's annual payments for the mortgage principal, interest, and taxes exceed $20,000. In the eyes of the IRS Harry is paying more than his $10,000 gift exclusion per year for Marc's benefit. If either person is audited, the bomb could explode with unexpected gift taxes.

A **property agreement** (also called an **equity share agreement** or **property sharing agreement**), can solve all of Harry and Marc's problems without creating a tax problem in the future. This document can be used to answer questions dealing with death, disability, splitting loss or profits on a house sale, and separation. The agreement can solve the gifting problem by stating that Marc's labor on the house repairs and landscaping is "consideration" for his share. ("Consideration" is a legal term for payment.)

For a young couple, this is a viable alternative to transferring an ownership interest too early in the relationship. The document can be drafted to answer any what-if question that could arise between two people concerning shared property. Unlike a domestic partnership agreement, this document deals only with property issues. It can also be used between parent and child or between strangers.

Buying Real Estate Together

For many people, real estate is the single biggest asset they will buy. This is as true for lesbian and gay couples as it is for straight couples. How you title your property is more important for you than for straight couples because of homophobic judges and greedy relatives who may not approve of your lifestyle. You have three choices: **sole ownership**, **joint tenancy**, and **tenancy in common**.

When only one person in the relationship is named on the deed, only that person is the recognized legal owner. If you are buying property together, this is a bad idea. When the sole owner dies and there is no will, the property will *not* go to the surviving partner.

If the sole owner sells the property the other partner may not be legally entitled to any profits. If the relationship breaks up and there are no supporting documents, deeds, or written agreements, the non-owner may lose out completely.

The only time it is a good idea to put one name on the deed is if that person truly owns the house, puts up the down payment, and makes the mortgage payments. If you do go this way, then consider discussing an equity share agreement with your attorney.

When your intention is to share the property ownership equally and for both partners to have full right to use the entire property, then **joint tenancy with right of survivorship** should be considered. When one partner dies, the survivor will automatically own the whole property. (If there is an out-of-date will saying the property goes else-where, however, you could be creating a real problem. *With lesbian and gay couples it is essential that all documents say the same thing!*)

Joint tenancy can be used only when the house will be owned equally and when each of you will have full use of the property. When there is more than one owner or unequal shares, consider holding title as tenants in common. With **tenancy in common**, each owner owns his or her portion exclusively. Had Harry and John owned the house in Tahoe as tenancy in common, then John's half would have gone to Harry through his will. If John had had no will, Harry would not have received John's half of the house without a property agreement. Tenants in common do not have right of sur-vivorship. With tenancy in common, an owner can sell his interest to anyone, not necessarily his partner.

No matter how you decide to hold title to your real estate, it is essential that you have a written agreement. Because state laws dif-fer in this area, you must see an attorney who understands lesbian and gay legal issues and the real estate laws of your state.

Statutory Rights

If there is no will memorializing Harry's intentions or other means of transferring property, then, unlike married couples, Marc has no legal right to Harry's property. It does not matter how long lesbian or gay partners have been together or how friendly they think their family or state domicile is. Marc has no right to any property of Harry's unless he is a co-owner and there is legal documentation that says he has a right to the property or there is a will or trust.

Intestacy Laws

State intestacy laws were designed to provide for inheritance where there is no will. *They do not protect you as a couple.* If you and your partner have been together for thirty years and your partner dies without a will, a trust, or a property agreement and you are not a joint owner of your property with right of survivorship, you will have no legal right to ownership or inheritance. Your partner's children, parents, siblings, and relatives will receive his or her property—you will not.

Community Property

States that have community property laws do not protect you. These laws only apply to legally recognized married couples within that state.

Joint Ownership and Taxes

Jointly owned property is taxed differently for lesbian and gay couples than for married couples. The tax treatment is more onerous for you. The tax law presumes that half the property belonged to the person who died when a spouse dies. When one of you dies, the law presumes that the deceased owned 100 percent unless the survivor can prove that he or she paid for half or some other portion of the property. The advantage of joint property is that the property will pass *automatically* to the survivor, which is not the case with tenants in common.

If Harry gives half the house to Marc and dies before filing a gift tax return or signing an equity share agreement, the IRS will assume that the whole property was Harry's. In estates larger than $650,000 (1999), this could become a very expensive problem. When determining how to own property, you need to answer three questions: how do you split the property (equally or unequally), where do you want your portion to go after your death, and what is the size of your estate?

Step-by-Step Instructions for Harry and Marc

1. Harry and Marc go to an attorney familiar with gay and lesbian legal issues who does substantial work in estate planning.

2. Harry and Marc provide the attorney with a list of everything they own. The list includes: who owns each item, current value, cost, description, location, and an indication of where it goes should either of them die.

3. Harry and Marc have the attorney draft a will and powers of attorney (financial and medical) for each partner.

4. Marc names Harry as the payable-on-death (POD) beneficiary of his credit union account.

5. Marc updates the registration form at the Department of Motor Vehicles by adding Harry as the transfer-on-death (TOD) beneficiary of his Harley. Harry does the same with his car's registration.

6. Marc names Harry as the beneficiary of his IRA and his retirement plan at work.

7. Harry has a revocable trust drafted under the laws of Nevada listing himself as trustee and Marc as successor trustee. He puts the cottage in Tahoe in the Nevada living trust with Marc as the beneficiary.

8. Harry's attorney drafts a living trust for California. Harry transfers the title to his house in San Rafael to his California trust. Harry is the trustee and Marc is the successor trustee and beneficiary.

9. Harry and Marc sign an equity share agreement that spells out what happens to the house they are sharing should Harry die, sell the house, or dissolve their relationship. Marc's payments in the form of labor are enumerated and

valued. The agreement addresses every what-if question that could occur between them.

10. Marc buys a life insurance policy on Harry to pay estate taxes and settlement costs. (Chapter 6 discusses how to buy life insurance if you live in a state that does not permit same-sex couples to purchase life insurance.)

11. Marc also buys a life insurance policy on himself and lists Harry as the beneficiary. This will help to replace his economic contribution to their relationship should he die.

ESTATE TAX PLANNING

Once the size of your estate exceeds the unified credit equivalent exemption (see Estate Tax Threshold table, page 35), you have a taxable estate. You can solve the estate tax problem in either of two ways: by replacing the loss to the estate created by estate taxes or by reducing your estate for tax purposes. Because planning for the large estate is beyond the scope of this book, I will give just a brief overview of each strategy.

Estate Tax Replacement

Life insurance can be used as a means to pay estate taxes either on a discounted dollar basis or as a replacement vehicle. Since life insurance can be purchased for pennies on the dollar, it is, in effect, a method of paying taxes with "discounted" dollars since the premium is always less than the death benefit. The life insurance can then be used to pay the tax or to replace the dollars that were used to pay the taxes. Harry could buy life insurance to solve his future estate tax problem.

Reducing the Size of Large Estates

If you have an estate larger than the unified credit exemption equivalent and want to lower the estate taxes, you can use planning techniques that reduce the size of your estate. The following strategies can be used and must be addressed with your tax advisor and estate-planning attorney: grantor retained income trusts (GRITs), charitable lead income trusts (CLITs), and family limited partnerships (FLPs). By combining these techniques with charitable remainder unitrusts and life insurance trusts, you can achieve substantial estate tax savings. To do this, you will need the expertise of an attorney who specializes in tax and estate planning for unmarried couples.

SUMMARY

The way you can avoid the estate nightmare is to be prepared. Title your property so that it passes to your partner or heirs without going through probate. Always have a current will to avoid state transfer laws that don't protect you, to confirm your intentions, and to transfer property you might have left out of a trust, if you use one. If you don't prepare, your relatives will get what you or your partner should receive when one of you dies.

Probate is expensive, time-consuming, and public. Consider the following alternatives:

- Beneficiary designations
- Payable-on-death designations (POD)
- Transfer-on-death designations (TOD)
- Joint ownership with right of survivorship
- Equity share agreements
- Revocable living trusts
- Gifts

Remember, when it comes to property, if you prepare, you can protect your family.

CHAPTER 4

Reducing Taxes, Increasing Cash Flow

. . . a democratic government is the only one in which those who vote for a tax can escape the obligation to pay it.
—Alexis de Tocqueville

Sally and Jan live in Park Slope, Brooklyn, and love it. They bought a cooperative apartment together a few years ago, using part of Jan's inheritance for a down payment. Sally is paying the mortgage and started to take the tax deduction for the interest expense when Jan went back to school.

Sally's fashion design business in Manhattan is just beginning to get national recognition. She decided to start the business rather than deal with the double discrimination she'd encounter in the corporate world for being a woman and a lesbian, and felt she could do better on her own in a straight male-dominated world. Since she majored in fashion design, she wanted to take advantage of her education and skills.

Jan, her partner of six and a half years, is a Ph.D. student at New York University and works part-time in the school library. She also takes care of their two children and does Sally's bookkeeping. They had intended to adopt only one child, but when the agency called and told them that Freddy's sister, Sarah, needed a home, they agreed. Sarah's adoption isn't finalized yet.

Sally owns $25,000 worth of R. J. Reynolds stock that her

grandmother gave her when she was born. Granny helped raise her and has supported her all along. Sally wants to get rid of the stock, since Granny just died from emphysema, and also because she is a nonsmoker. No way does she want to continue to own a piece of the company that helped kill her favorite grandmother.

Sally thinks she is paying too much in taxes. Jan, on the other hand, is paying very little tax since she earns just under $12,000 a year working in the library. Sally would like to pay her for child care but isn't clear about the tax consequences. Jan would like to quit her job and devote her entire time to raising the kids, focusing on her school work, and helping Sally with her business. They wonder if their ideas are possible.

INCOME TAXES AND YOU

We are about to look at strategies that lesbian and gay couples can use to help reduce their taxes. When it comes to income taxes, you have some definite advantages over married couples. This chapter will show you how to use them. The key is to think of yourselves as a unit rather than two single tax filers, even though you will not be filing a joint return.

As an unmarried couple, you can take advantage of the difference in tax brackets between the two of you. When a married couple has a difference in tax brackets, the person in the lower bracket tends to raise the overall taxes by increasing the level of taxable income. When *you* have a difference in brackets, the person in the lower bracket can actually help lower the overall taxes. Because you cannot file a joint income tax return, you escape the "marriage penalty." The sum of the taxes of two single people is less than the taxes a married couple would pay on the same income. The savings can amount to several thousand dollars.

This chapter covers both personal and business strategies that will enable you to take advantage of the loopholes and reduce your taxes. But first we will review the basics of how taxes are calculated. If you use a software package to do your taxes, remember these programs are *not* as good as expert advice that applies to your specific situation. The program only calculates the numbers, it does not plan.

HOW TO DETERMINE YOUR TAXABLE INCOME

When it comes to tax planning, it is very helpful to understand the difference between marginal tax and effective tax, particularly with respect to your situation. Before we start playing with tax brackets, let's look at how taxes are calculated.

INCOME TAX CALCULATION

GROSS INCOME	\$_____
Less: Adjustments	(_____)
Equals: Adjusted Gross Income (AGI)	_____
Less: Deductions	(_____)
Exemptions	(_____)
Equals: Taxable income	_____
Times: Rate from tax table	_____
Equals: Tax liability	_____
Less: Tax credits	(_____)
Plus: Other taxes	_____
Equals: Net tax	_____
Less: Payments	(_____)
Equals: Refund or **Tax due**	\$_____

Let's define the key terms in more detail.

Gross income includes every source of income that you receive unless it is specifically exempted by the tax code. It includes salary, dividends, capital gains, business income, rental income, partnership income, prizes, awards, tips, gambling winnings, strike benefits, a portion of Social Security benefits, disability income paid by your employer, and more. If you put effort into obtaining the income, such as filling out a sweepstakes form or lottery ticket, then the winnings are taxable. Gifts received are tax-free to the recipient.

Adjustments are deductions from gross income: allowable amounts contributed to traditional IRAs, contributions by self-employed persons to pensions; profit-sharing plans and employer retirement annuities; alimony (but not child support); and unreimbursed work-related moving expenses.

Adjusted gross income (AGI) is a critical number between gross income and taxable income. The higher your AGI, the less your itemized deductions will be. The only way to really lower your AGI is to lower gross income or to increase adjustments. The secret is to find ways to change the character of your income so that it is either tax-deferred or tax-free or to shift it to the partner with the lower income.

AGI is important to your tax calculation because many deductions and credit phase-outs are based upon this number. For example, if your AGI is greater than $126,600 in 1999, a portion of your itemized deductions are "phased out." As Sally's income rises, she must find ways to shift income to Jan or the children or else she will start losing her deductions.

The following percentage limitations are used in calculating itemized deductions:

- Medical expenses must be greater than 7.5 percent of AGI.
- Certain itemized deductions must be greater than 2 percent of AGI.
- Charitable contributions are limited to 50 percent of AGI for cash or 30 percent of AGI for appreciated property.
- Casualty loss must be greater than 10 percent of AGI.

Taxable income is the magical number we are trying to reduce. This is the amount that your taxes are based on. Sally's taxable income is $100,000; Jan's is $10,000. There is room to maneuver here if they think as a unit and "leverage" or take advantage of the difference in their tax brackets.

WHAT YOU NEED TO KNOW ABOUT TAX BRACKETS

There is a difference between tax brackets and effective tax rate. Your tax bracket is the tax rate on the last dollar earned. **Effective tax rate** is the tax you actually pay divided by taxable income. As of this writing, there are five tax brackets: 15 percent, 28 percent, 31 percent, 36 percent, and 39.6 percent. The levels are based on filing status and amounts of taxable income.

If Sally's taxable income is $100,000, she would pay 15 percent on the first $25,750, 28 percent on the next $36,700, and 31 percent on the balance up to $130,250 (based on 1999 federal income tax rates). Sally would pay a total of $25,778 in federal income taxes. Her tax bracket is 31 percent and her effective tax rate is 26 percent ($25,778 divided by $100,000). (When you do the calculation, you use either a tax table or work with your accountant.)

Now we will see how Sally and Jan can take advantage of strategies that are generally not available to married couples. In so doing they will be able to increase their cash flow and have more spending or saving dollars available.

PERSONAL STRATEGIES FOR REDUCING TAXES

Bunching

One way to reduce income taxes is to "bunch" your itemized deductions. If your and your partner's adjusted gross incomes are the same or very close, you might consider whether you are better off splitting your itemized deductions or bunching them.

If you are both in the 28 percent bracket and your total itemized deductions are $10,000, you would each have $5,000 in itemized deductions. If you bunched all of your deductions and took them on your partner's 1040 income tax return and you took the standard deduction, you would have total deductions of $14,250 using 1998 tax tables. Bunching strategy must be reviewed in light of the practicality of incurring the expenses—check your cash flow.

The standard deduction for 1998 was $7,100 for married couples filing jointly, $6,250 for heads of household, and $4,250 for singles. You obviously fare better than married couples by $1,400 or 20 percent ($4,250 times two less $7,100). But it gets much better than that: one of you can file itemized and the other standard. Married couples cannot do that.

Mortgages

Since there is a large difference between Sally's and Jan's income, they have been taking all of their mortgage interest deduction on Sally's tax return. Many couples will change who takes the mortgage interest deduction from year to year depending upon who needs it. This is illegal and a tax time bomb. The person who is liable for the loan is the one entitled to the interest deduction. Beware of advice that says otherwise. If you are audited, this could get very expensive.

Sally's income is approaching the threshold, and her deductions will be reduced when she passes it. Sally and Jan want to refinance their mortgage and use strategies that help pay it off faster. When they refinance, it may make sense to have Sally as the debtor, as she needs the larger deduction. But if Sally's AGI exceeds $126,600 (1999 rate), her itemized deductions will phase out. As Sally's AGI approaches the phase-out, she should find ways to shift income to Jan. Remember, if you think as a unit rather than as two individuals you will stretch your dollars further.

If you decide to refinance, seriously consider doing an equity share agreement if you don't have a domestic partnership agreement that addresses shared property. (In addition to reducing income taxes, however, you must also consider gift taxes.) Your financial advisor can help you decide what's best for the two of you.

Charitable Contributions

Sally should make all the charitable contributions using her checkbook, since deductions at 31 percent are worth more than deductions at 15 percent. Jan can reimburse Sally, and they can bank the extra tax savings or make bigger gifts. If you do a spreadsheet at the beginning of the year showing your projected income and expenses, you will have a map to follow when deciding who should write the checks.

If you have appreciated stock or mutual funds that you want to keep, consider following Sally and Jan's strategy. Give the stock or the mutual fund to the charity rather than the cash you were going to give. Then take the cash that was going to go to the charity and buy a new position in the same or a different investment. The advantage of this strategy is that you will raise the cost basis of the investment so that when you sell later, you will pay less taxes. If the stock or mutual fund goes up from your new cost, your gain will be less when you sell it. If it loses value, you may have a tax-deductible loss from the new cost basis whereas before you might have had a smaller gain.

Sally and Jan each pledged $100 a month for fifteen months to their church, for a total of $3,000. Since Sally has the R. J. Reynolds stock, she gives $3,000 worth of the stock to the church as her gift. She and Jan now buy a mutual fund that has no tobacco stock by having $200 a month transferred from their bank account to the fund.

What have Sally and Jan accomplished? They got rid of a future capital gains tax as well as a stock they hated to own. They raised their cost basis on a new investment and they got a tax deduction. Their out-of-pocket expense is the same but their taxes are lower. Less dollars to the IRS, New York State, and New York City; more dollars to them.

There is another hidden benefit. Since the stock was originally given to Sally by a living person rather than through an inheritance, she avoids Granny's cost basis. When you sell an investment that you received as a gift, the gain is based on the cost to the person who gave you the gift. In contrast, investments that pass at death "step up" in value so that the cost basis is the value on the date of death, when property transfers. By making a charitable gift of the stock, Sally doesn't even have to address the cost basis issue.

Shifting Assets

Another way that partners can leverage the difference between tax brackets is to shift their assets. People who are in the 28 percent or higher tax bracket pay capital gains tax at 20 percent on sales of assets held over twelve months,[1] while people in the 15 percent bracket pay capital gains tax at 10 percent.

Sally is in the 31 percent bracket and Jan is in the 15 percent bracket. If Sally gives her stock to Jan, Jan will then be able to sell the stock at a maximum tax rate of 10 percent instead of Sally's 20 percent. If the stock is worth $22,000 ($25,000 less the $3,000 gift to their church) and Granny's original cost was $2,000, Sally and Jan will save $2,000 by this transfer and sale ($20,000 of capital gains at 10 percent instead of 20 percent will save $2,000 in dollars lost to taxes). Married couples cannot do this. Sally can spread the transfer of the stock to Jan over two years, since she is allowed to give $10,000 per year gift-tax-free to as many people as she wants. This amount is indexed for inflation per the Taxpayer Relief Act of 1997.

Adoption Tax Credits

Sally and Jan can also take a tax credit up to $5,000 of qualified adoption expenses. The expense can be incurred or paid over several years, but the credit is limited to $5,000 per child and is taken in the year the adoption becomes final. If Sarah were a child with special needs, the maximum tax credit would be $6,000 for quali-

1. Per IRS Restructuring and Reform Act of 1998

fied expenses. Freddy is not eligible because he was adopted prior to when the law became effective in 1997. Had Freddy been adopted after 1996, the maximum tax credit would have been $10,000 for both children ($5,000 per child). After December 31, 2001, the only tax credit allowed will be for adoption expenses for a child with special needs. If you are adopting a foreign child, talk to your accountant or tax advisor because the rules are a little different.

Tax credits are different from tax deductions. A **tax credit** is a dollar-for-dollar savings against taxes. A $5,000 tax *deduction* would save $1,550 in taxes ($5,000 times 31 percent). A $5,000 tax *credit* would reduce taxes by $5,000.

The credit allowable for any tax year is phased out for taxpayers with an AGI of over $75,000, and is fully eliminated when AGI reaches $115,000. This area calls for expert help from your tax advisor.

Head of Household versus Single Rates

If Sally files as a head of household rather than as a single person, she will pay less in taxes. Calculating the tax the long way again, it looks like this: 15 percent of the first $34,550; 28 percent of the next $54,600; and 31 percent of the balance of $10,850, for a total of $23,750. Sally's effective tax rate has dropped from 26 percent to 24 percent. If the nonbiological mom or both parents adopt the child, then both parents can file as head of household and both will pay less taxes. This strategy is also not available to married couples. But check with your accountant first.

You may be able to file as head of household if you are not legally married on the last day of the year and you have paid more than half the cost of keeping up a home for you and a qualifying person for more than half the year. If you qualify to file as head of household, your tax rate usually will be lower than the rates for single taxpayers or married taxpayers filing separately. You will also receive a higher standard deduction than if you file as single or as married filing separately.

Dependents

You may also be able to claim your partner as a dependent for an extra exemption. To claim someone as a dependent if the person is not related to you, that person must:

- be a relative or live with you for the entire year
- have income less than the personal exemption for the year, unless he or she is a child (in 1999, the exemption is $2,750)
- receive 50 percent or more of his or her total support from you
- not file a joint return if she or he is a spouse
- be a U.S. citizen or a resident of Canada, Mexico, or the United States

Suppose you are taking care of your lover who has AIDS. The amount of your lover's income (along with other factors) will determine whether you can claim him or her as a dependent. You must discuss this with your accountant or tax advisor. Some local laws may prohibit claiming adults as dependents.

Is this the best way to go? Generally the test is too rigorous for most people. Another strategy is to look at your relationship through the eyes of your business or see if there is some legitimate business enterprise you could create for the two of you. If you have a business and can treat your partner as an employee, then you can do what married couples have a tougher time doing—shift income.

BUSINESS STRATEGIES FOR REDUCING TAXES

If, like Sally, you own a business, there are a number of ways you and your partner can tie your personal goals to the business and reduce your taxes. One strategy is for Sally to hire Jan and pay her as an employee of the business. Jan would then be eligible for all of the benefit programs that Sally has established for her employees.

With Jan as an employee, Sally can do some serious income shifting. Let's take a look at six areas where these strategies can apply: dependent care, group insurance, retirement plans, bonuses, leasing, and borrowing.

Employer-Provided Dependent Care Services

The value of dependent care services provided by an employer with a written plan for dependent care is generally not included in the employee's income if the dependent is younger than 13 or is physically or mentally incapable of self-care, or is a spouse who is physically or mentally incapable of self-care. Freddy and Sarah qualify because both are less than 13 years old. This means that if Jan is an employee of Sally's business, $5,000 of her income is not included as gross income until the youngest child becomes 13 years old.

Sally is too highly compensated to qualify for this benefit herself, but she can pay Jan at least $5,000 more without incurring additional income taxes while she is eligible for the dependent care benefit. Dollars that are not going to taxes can be saved or invested. The $5,000 would be tax-deductible as an expense to Sally's business.

Group Insurance

As an employee of the business, Jan can now be in the group health insurance plan. Sally can then deduct 100 percent of the premium as a business expense. For Jan, the cost of the insurance is not taxable income. This differs from employer plans with domestic partner benefits. While group insurance is tax-free to the employee, domestic partner benefits are taxable.

If you work for an employer that has a domestic partner benefit and your partner does not have health insurance, consider the company plan versus outside plans. It is always good to check out the tax cost of the domestic partnership plan and compare that to an individually purchased health plan, which may cost less. If you are lucky enough to work for an employer that has domestic partner benefits, then the value of the additional cost over an individual plan is taxable income to the employee partner. Your employer will report this amount on your W-2.

Another benefit of the group health insurance plan may be the inclusion of life insurance for all employees. The first $50,000 of life insurance that is part of an employer-paid benefit plan is tax-free to the employee. This tax provision enabled Sally and Jan to have life insurance that was paid for with dollars deductible to the business. Since the cost of life insurance is not normally tax-deductible, this benefit is a tax windfall for the couple who can use it.

Retirement Plans

The term **qualified plan** applies to all forms of retirement plans where the contribution is exempt from current taxation. Qualified plans that businesses may offer include 401(k)s, profit-sharing plans, pensions, simplified employee pensions (SEPs), and SIMPLE IRAs.

Sally decides to install a profit-sharing plan, since she doesn't know if she will be able to sustain her success year after year. The company will now fund retirement plans for both Sally and Jan, as well as for Sally's other employees, using tax-deductible dollars. As the business grows and becomes more successful, Sally will be able to offer other retirement plans. If you have a business, see your accountant, as a more in-depth treatment of business retirement planning strategies is beyond the scope of this book.

Bonuses

At the beginning of the new year, Sally gave Jan a new title because of her expanded duties—executive assistant—and a raise which brought her into the 28 percent tax bracket. Sally also decided to give her a bonus in the same year that the adoption happened to become final. Sally can do this because bonuses can be done selectively. Unlike qualified plans, other employees do not have to be included.

Because Sally's income is too high to benefit from the tax credit for adoption expenses, Jan should write the check for adoption expenses even if Sally has to give her the money. A $5,000 tax credit is the equivalent of $17,857 in additional income on the federal return for someone in the 28 percent bracket ($5,000 divided by 28 percent). At the end of the year Jan received a $10,000 bonus effectively tax-free because she had qualified for adoption expenses which enabled her to get a tax credit for $5,000 of those expenses.

Leasing Between Partners

This strategy only works when one partner has a business or is self-employed, the other partner is in a lower tax bracket, and they have approval by their tax advisor that this strategy is appropriate for their situation because of special IRS rules.

Let's suppose that Sally wants to get a $30,000 car for business use. Jan could take part of the remaining portion of her inheritance and buy a car, which she then leases to Sally's business. The lease payment is tax deductible to the business and taxable income to Jan. Since Jan is now in the leasing business, her accountant would show her how to depreciate the car on her tax return. The difference between Sally's tax deduction for the business expense and Jan's actual tax rate for the lease income is money that is not spent on taxes by the couple.

If Jan does not have enough money for the car purchase, Sally could give her $10,000 income-tax-free as a personal gift.

If you do this, be sure that you document your agreement spelling out the terms of the lease and that there is a bona fide business need.

Borrowing

Let's suppose that Sally's accountant tells her she is better off buying the car rather than leasing it. She could borrow the funds she needs from Jan. Like the lease strategy, this works best when one partner is in a higher tax bracket and has a business or is self-employed.

Let's say Jan's money is in a bank money market account and let's assume that banks are currently lending money at 15 percent for

60-month loans. Sally could borrow the money from Jan and pay her 12 percent. Jan will earn more than she could in a conservative investment.

The couple will save costs and taxes. Sally saves 3 percent on interest for the loan she is not paying (15 percent at the bank versus 12 percent with Jan) and 3 percent of the interest expense in taxes (deductible at 31 percent for Sally but taxable to Jan at 28 percent). Sally could also reduce her self-employment tax (15.3 percent in 1999) depending on the level of her income, as the interest is deductible.

If you follow this strategy, you should have a written loan agreement spelling out the terms of the loan, set a reasonable rate of interest, and have documentation on how you arrive at the interest rate.

Step-by-Step Instructions for Jan and Sally

1. Sally and Jan meet with their accountant, who amends their last three tax returns to head-of-household status. They will receive a refund for each year and invest the refunds for Freddy and Sarah's college fund.
2. At the beginning of the year, they do a spreadsheet of their expected income and expenses.
3. Since they have decided to "bunch" their deductions, Sally and Jan pool their income. Sally writes the checks for charitable gifts.
4. Sally transfers the ownership of $3,000 worth of stock to their church.
5. Sally and Jan make a commitment to save $100 each and every month by a bank transfer into a mutual fund without stock from tobacco companies.
6. Sally gives Jan money for adoption expenses and Jan pays adoption expenses.
7. Jan takes the tax credit in the year the adoption is finalized.

8. Sally's fashion design business hires Jan as an executive assistant doing bona fide work for the business.

9. In the year that the adoption is finalized, Jan gets a nice bonus from her new employer.

10. Jan joins the company's group health plan and cancels her private plan.

11. Sally gives Jan $10,000 worth of her R. J. Reynolds stock in December and another $10,000 worth in January.

12. Jan sells the stock while she is still in the 15 percent tax bracket and pays 10 percent capital gains tax.

13. Sally and Jan take the savings in capital gains tax and spend it on a vacation in the Caribbean by themselves.

A WORD OF CAUTION

Do all these strategies apply to everyone? No. Expert financial and tax advice is essential, and you should use the approach, whether personal or business, best suited for your particular situation. If, for example, one of you has bad credit or no credit and you need a car, the other partner can borrow or lease it for you depending on the particulars of your situation. Here, too, your tax advisor can guide you.

And remember, once you and your partner think and operate as a unit, you must protect yourselves with written agreements, since there are no marital laws to protect you.

CHAPTER 5

Investing for the Future: Funding College Expenses

The only fence against the world is a thorough knowledge of it.
—John Locke

Penny and Roni have been together eight years. They have two daughters: 17-year-old Sami, Roni's daughter from her previous marriage, and 3-year-old Michelle. Penny is Michelle's biological mother and Roni adopted her shortly after she was born.

Penny works as a "permatemp" and manages the programming design team for a successful computer company in Silicon Valley. The money has been good and the hours are flexible, but she doesn't have stock options or lucrative benefits like permanent employees. She does have a health plan and a meager 401(k). Now she would like a permanent position. Roni is a teacher in the state school system. Her job is secure but the pay is so-so. She does tutoring on the side to help generate extra money.

They are beginning to think about how to pay for Sami's and Michelle's college expenses. The cost of a private college for Sami could exceed $100,000, and by the time Michelle is ready for college in fifteen years, it could exceed $200,000. Roni's ex-husband's support payments have been sporadic at best. He has promised to help with Sami's education, but Penny doesn't fully trust him since he has not always kept his word.

Sami has been looking forward to college for years and now it's only a year away. She has saved $18,000 from gifts from her bat mitzvah and other gifts from her relatives. She loves gymnastics and is hoping that it may help her to qualify for a college scholarship. Roni doesn't want her to spend the thirty hours a week working out that a scholarship would require, but is tempted by it because she thinks a partial scholarship would reduce the amount of tuition they would have to pay. Penny doesn't think they have enough money for an expensive school with a competitive team.

Penny and Roni have thought about taking out a second mortgage on their house to help pay for Sami's college expenses now and Michelle's in the future, but they don't want to wipe out their retirement income paying it back, nor do they want to go deeper into debt. Roni has $42,000 in her credit union account; she owes $8,200 on her car and another $2,600 in credit card debt. They don't know the best way to save for a tuition expense in the future. They do know that they don't want to work forever.

LOOKING AHEAD

The purpose of this chapter is twofold: to introduce you to some basic principles essential to all investing strategies, and to show you how to apply these strategies to fund higher education for your children.

Because there are many good investment books out there, this chapter will focus on investing as a tool specifically for saving for college. While the story we are following here is about paying for the education of children of lesbian and gay couples, you can also adapt some of these strategies if you or your partner plans to return to school at some point in the future.

The first section of the chapter is a primer on certain investment basics. The second section gives you a thorough overview of the financial aid process.

Funding a college education is similar to purchasing a home. If you were going to buy a house, would you pay the full amount with your own cash? Of course not—you'd get a mortgage and pay it off over time. You can do the same with a college education. If you think of college expenses as similar to buying a house, then you plan not for the whole amount but for the down payment, the portion you must pay at the beginning. The critical question is to find out what your **estimated family contribution (EFC)** requirement would be. Once you know your level of contribution, then funding becomes more manageable. This section will cover in detail how to determine your EFC.

The final part of the chapter covers which investment strategies work best when financial aid may make the difference in college choice.

Let's begin by looking at some basic principles.

INVESTING FOR THE LONG TERM

Long-term investing is generally for goals that reach five or more years into the future. Long-term investing requires that you accept a certain amount of risk in order to be rewarded with higher investment returns. Appendix C provides an exercise that will help you determine your tolerance for risk. Try it—it will help you put together your investment program.

There are two strategies that apply to any investment program: dollar-cost averaging and asset allocation.

Dollar-Cost Averaging

As you know, the best investment strategy is to buy a winning stock at its low point and sell it at its high point. If you were clever enough to have invested in a company like Microsoft when it started, you would be a millionaire by now. But picking a winner at its low point and selling it when it's high isn't so easy for most of us. If you're like me, you might not have the time to do the research or the stomach to ride out the ups and downs of the market; so you turn to mutual funds and let someone else handle it. Fortunately, there is an easy way to get into the market and still avoid the emotional trauma when it plunges.

Dollar-cost averaging (DCA) is a method for gradually moving money into stocks or stock mutual funds. DCA is an alternative way of investing that helps you buy into the market by investing a fixed amount on a regular schedule, whether the market is at its low point or its high point. This method reduces the risk of losing money if the stock market takes a major downturn. If you put all of your money in the market at one time and stock prices plummet, you will be devastated. If, on the other hand, you've been investing small amounts over time, you probably won't feel too bad.

DCA also provides a discipline for investing. If you establish a rigid plan with the same amount coming out of your checking account or your paycheck every month, you won't spend your money before you save it. And, by doing it through direct deposit, you can skip the roller-coaster emotions that go with deciding when, where, and how much to invest. DCA can help you achieve your goals by helping you stay on course.

Asset Allocation

Asset allocation is the process of dividing your investments into categories. It uses a disciplined and systematic approach to looking at your investment objectives to help you and your advisor sort through thousands of investment alternatives in a meaningful and logical way. It is best used for long-term planning (five years or longer).

Investments have certain common characteristics. First, there is a degree of uncertainty in predicting the future. There are simply too many variables and unknowns in the financial world to predict the future with certainty. Next, there is a correlation among securities in a category—similar securities tend to move up and down in price together. Intelligent diversification using different categories of investments can help protect a portfolio against many investment risks. How you allocate your investment dollars far outweighs the potential effects of individual security selection and attempts at timing the market (guessing when the price of securities will change).

Asset allocation analysis usually depends on four major criteria: your financial objectives, time horizon, risk tolerance, and your present financial situation. Planning for a future college expense or retirement planning are financial objectives for many people. Time horizon is the amount of time until the money is needed. If the period is short-term (under five years) you may not have the tolerance for short-term losses. Assets with less risk are used in the short term, while growth assets that tend to fluctuate in value are used in long-term planning.

Risk tolerance is how well you handle risk and the swings in investment value as you seek higher returns. An asset allocation analysis will have a number of questions to try to measure your tolerance for risk. Most approaches assign a risk profile such as conservative, moderate, or aggressive to the investor.

Your present financial situation will have a direct effect on your risk tolerance profile. Roni and Penny feel that they are in a stable financial situation and can tolerate more risk over the long term.

Three other factors that can affect an asset allocation plan: taxes, transaction costs, and historical performance. If you are using the asset allocation analysis for tax-deferred investments (IRAs, retirement plans, annuities, life insurance cash values), then taxable capital gains are not a consideration. If not, then taxes will have an impact. Costs can be a factor in the form of transaction fees. Historical performance is generally a poor indicator of future performance. It is important to remember that past performance does not guarantee future performance.

An easy method to use to determine how long it will take your money to grow is to use the *Rule of 72*. If you take the interest rate on an investment or a growth rate you hope to achieve and divide it into the number 72, you get the number of years it takes the dollar to double in value.

$$\frac{72}{\text{GROWTH RATE}} = \text{Number of years in which money will double}$$

If you invested the same amount in a certificate of deposit, a mutual fund, and the same mutual fund in a tax-deferred account such as an IRA, you would see a dramatic difference in the time it takes your investment to double. A CD earning 6 percent less taxes at

28 percent will take 16.7 years to double in value (72 divided by 4.32 percent), but a mutual fund growing at 10 percent less taxes will double in 10 years. If the mutual fund were in an IRA or other tax-deferred investments, then it would take 7.2 years to double in value.

Later in the chapter we will discuss the use of tax-deferred investments to save for future college expenses. When it comes to compound interest, tax-deferral can give you a significant edge over the long term. A 3 percent increase in return rate over a fifteen-year period will generate 50 percent more money at the end of that period. The use of asset allocation to determine your portfolio mix and dollar-cost averaging can help minimize investment risk for your long-term financial objectives.

PLANNING FOR COLLEGE

Penny and Roni have bought into three common misconceptions about funding for higher education. The first is that financial aid is only for the poor or the needy. The second is that a partial scholarship will reduce the amount they need to spend on their child's tuition. And finally, they think that because they can only afford to send their child to a state school, they will never qualify for an expensive private school.

Financial aid is available from a variety of programs funded by federal, state, university, and private sources. According to the booklet "What You Need to Know about Financing Your Children's Education" from American Express Financial Advisors, in the 1997–1998 school year, 61 percent of all the funding for college came from family and nonsubsidized loans. Another 20 percent came from subsidized loans, and 19 percent from grants and scholarships. Grants and scholarships are gifts of money that do not have to be repaid. Federally subsidized loans must be repaid at relatively low interest rates after the student has completed his or her education.

Because financial aid conditions change rapidly, Sami should contact the financial aid offices of the schools that she is considering as soon as possible. She should also consult the book *Don't Miss Out: The Ambitious Student's Guide to Financial Aid*, by Anna and Robert Leider. It is published annually and provides up-to-date information on obtaining financial aid. It is a must-read for Sami and anyone thinking about undergraduate or graduate education.

Roni and Penny learned that Sami has an advantage over children of legally married couples. Because Penny has not adopted her, she has only one custodial parent, Roni. This means that Penny's income and assets will not be included in determining their estimated family contribution (EFC) for most state schools and some private schools. If Roni and Penny were a legally married couple or Penny had adopted Sami, both parents' assets would go into the calculation and their EFC would be higher.

They also discovered that money in the name of the custodial parent(s) has a smaller impact on their estimated contribution than money in the name of the student (discussed in greater depth on page 68). Then they found out that consumer debt has no impact on the financial aid formula.

Once you've determined what your estimated family contribution is, no matter how expensive the school is, the balance can come from financial aid if the student qualifies for the school. Roni and Penny's out-of-pocket expenses will be the same wherever Sami goes. The student loans that she receives will then have to be paid over time, just like a mortgage. Partial scholarships don't reduce your contribution; they reduce the school's portion of the financial aid package. They may help your child's admission if the school has to spend less in financial aid. The moral of the story is, if you are trying to get a scholarship, try to get one that will cover the full cost.

The chart on the next page illustrates how much Roni and Penny would contribute toward their daughter's college cost. Three different schools are illustrated assuming their estimated family contribution (EFC) is calculated at $5,000. In this example, Sami is receiving a $3,000 scholarship from her gymnastics club because she is such a good athlete. The amount of financial aid will differ by school but Roni and Penny's out-of-pocket expenses will remain at $5,000.

TABLE 5.1
PARENTAL CONTRIBUTION AFTER NEED ASSESSMENT

College	Cost of Attendance	Estimated Family Contribution	Scholarship	Financial Aid
A	$20,000	$5,000	$3,000	$12,000
B	$12,000	$5,000	$3,000	$4,000
C	$8,000	$5,000	$3,000	$ 0

Calculating Your Estimated Family Contribution

Don't Miss Out describes three methods used by schools to assess your level of contribution: the **Federal Methodology**, the **Simplified Need Test**, and the **Institutional Methodology**. The Federal Methodology and the Simplified Need Test serve all federal programs, most state programs, most collegiate programs, and some donor programs. The Institutional Methodology serves some state programs, some collegiate programs, and some private donor programs.

The Federal Methodology has the largest impact on most students. The Simplified Need Test may be used by parents whose adjusted gross income (AGI) is below $50,000 and who file a 1040-EZ or 1040-A or who do not file a return at all. This methodology does not include assets.

The more expensive schools primarily use the Institutional Methodology. The main difference is that it has more questions—concerning the value of your house, your retirement assets, and your partner's income and assets—if both of you are legal parents. The Institutional Methodology is more subjective and will vary from school to school depending upon who has the money and wants your child to attend.

The Federal Methodology is legislated and has little room for negotiation. The Institutional Method is not legislated, so there is some room to negotiate with the school. The financial aid package can vary from school to school.

The two worksheets below provide the basic steps to determine the amount of your EFC and are based on the Federal Methodology. Congress changes the formula every four to five years when it reauthorizes the Higher Education Act. It also may revise the percentages every year or make other rule changes, so you must be in touch with the financial aid office where you plan to apply. *Don't Miss Out* is issued every September to reflect current HEA authorization percentages and rule changes that could affect your family's contribution. (If you are doing the calculation for an independent student or yourself, *Don't Miss Out* provides the appropriate tables and steps.)

ESTIMATED FAMILY CONTRIBUTION
PARENTS' CONTRIBUTION FROM INCOME
(for Dependent Students)

1. Adjusted gross income	$_____
2. Nontaxable income	_____
3. IRA, Keogh, 401(k) payments	_____
4. Total Income	_____
LESS:	
5. Allowances	(_____)
6. Income protection allowance (from Appendix B-1)	(_____)
7. Employment expense allowance	(_____)
8. Parents' available income	$_____

Adjusted gross income is from your prior year's federal income tax return. If you are filing for financial aid for the 1999–2000 school year, you would use your AGI from the tax year 1998. Since college is generally a four-year proposition, Roni might be able to do some income shifting to improve her aid calculation for Sami's later school years.

Nontaxable income includes the parents' untaxed Social Security benefits, Aid to Families with Dependent Children (AFDC), child support, earned income credit, workers' compensation, disability payments, welfare benefits, tax-exempt interest, housing, and food and living allowances for military, clergy, and others.

Allowances include federal and state income taxes you paid, Social Security taxes you paid, and child support paid by you for another child.

Employment expense allowance is currently 35 percent of the working parent's income or $2,800, whichever is less. If the student is working, this is called the Income Protection Allowance and is limited to $2,250.

ESTIMATED FAMILY CONTRIBUTION
PARENTS' CONTRIBUTION FROM ASSETS
(for Dependent Students)

1. Cash and bank accounts $_____

2. Other investments   _____

3. Business net worth allowance   _____
   (from Appendix B-2)

4. **Total assets**   _____

5. Asset protection allowance (from Appendix B-3)   (_____)

6. Discretionary net worth (line 4 less line 5)   _____

7. **Contribution from assets**   _____
   (line 6 times 12%)

8. Parents' adjusted available income   _____
   (line 8 from worksheet on page 66, plus line 7)

9. Parents' contribution (from Appendix B-4)   _____

10. Number in college adjustment   _____

11. **Contribution for each student** $_____
    (line 9 divided by line 10)

The **asset protection allowance** is the amount of assets the government feels a family needs and is derived from the table in Appendix B-3. There is no Asset Protection Allowance for a dependent student's own assets. A parent's assets are taxed at 5.6 percent for student aid, but the dependent student's assets are taxed at 35 percent.[1] The $18,000 in Sami's account becomes a $6,300 contribution to college costs. The same $18,000 in Roni's name becomes a mere $1,008. The way the college looks at it, the more investments there are in the child's name, the lower the amount of need. Then you will pay more out of pocket.

Let's go through the steps:

Step-by-Step Instructions
for Roni, Penny, and Sami

1. Prior to Sami's applying for admission, Roni and Penny calculate their estimated family contribution so they have an idea of how much money they will need for her college education.

2. Roni and Sami learn as much as they can on the real cost of attending each school. They gather information on tuition and fees, books and supplies, housing costs, food expenses for both the school plan and eating out (sodas, snacks, fast-food meals), transportation, and miscellaneous expenses (clothing, health insurance, CDs, etc.).

3. Once they know what each school will cost, they compare it to their estimated family contribution to determine approximately how much aid they will need.

4. Sami and Roni discuss the schools to apply to. In making their selection, they consider each school's ability to meet their financial need.

5. During the second week of January of the year she will start

---

1. If you are applying for the 1999–2000 school year or beyond, the percentages may have changed with the reauthorized Higher Education Act.

school, Sami applies for both admission and financial aid to each school she is considering. She only applies to schools where her qualifications would place her in the upper 25 percent of the applicant pool, as she believes that standing will have a significant impact on her financial aid package.

6. Sami and Roni complete the Free Application for Federal Student Aid (FAFSA) for federal aid and submit that.

7. Sami and Roni also complete the College Scholarship Service Financial Aid PROFILE (CSS PROFILE) and any supplemental state and/or college financial aid form.

8. Realizing that it may cost more in application fees, Sami applies to the level of schools she wants in pairs. This way if she is accepted to a school at one level, she can compare financial aid packages among competitors and leverage one against the other.

9. Roni gets Sami's permission to use her savings to help pay for her first year's family contribution. This improves her picture for financial aid for the next year, since each year's application is based on the assets as of the date of filing the application.

10. Because consumer debt is not accounted for in the EFC calculation, Roni switches her credit union savings to a stock and bond portfolio, which she then borrows against by taking a loan on "margin" to pay off her car. To reduce her reportable assets for the next year's financial aid application, she pays off her credit debt with her savings.

11. Realizing how planning for college expenses can be complicated and the rules can change every few years, Roni and Penny seek the help of a financial planner who specializes in college planning for their future needs.

12. Learning that some parents treat the financial aid office poorly and that the life of a financial aid administrator might not be a happy lot, Roni and Sami send thank-you notes to the financial aid administrator and her staff.

INVESTMENT STRATEGIES TO FUND COLLEGE FINANCING IN THE FUTURE

Roni and Penny would like to send Michelle to a private school when she is ready. They have seen the projections that show private schools may cost $200,000 in fifteen years. Based on their experience with Sami, they think that they will have to provide about 60 percent of Michelle's college expenses. To reach that goal, they must save $292 per month (assuming their money grows at 10 percent every year net after taxes). There are a number of investment strategies they can use. Let's take a look at the pros and cons of each of them.

Education IRA

An **Education IRA** can be created to pay qualified education expenses for a designated beneficiary. Contributions are limited to $500 per year per beneficiary. Penny and Roni can put $500 per year together into an Education IRA only if each one's AGI is less than $95,000. In the years that Roni's AGI exceeds the limit, Penny can contribute the full $500.

Contributions to an Education IRA are not tax-deductible but can be distributed tax-free to the beneficiary for qualified education expenses, which include postsecondary school tuition, fees, books, supplies, equipment, and certain room-and-board expenses. Qualified education expenses do not include elementary or secondary school expenses. Distributions not used to pay qualified education expenses are taxable to the beneficiary.

Roni and Penny's problem is that $500 per year for fifteen years will not make a dent in their education funding need. If we assume a 10 percent growth rate, in fifteen years they will have accumulated approximately $15,050. Also, the Education IRA will work against them should they want to apply for financial aid in the future as it will be in Michelle's name.

Uniform Gift to Minors Account
versus the Roth IRA

A **Uniform Gift to Minors Account (UGMA)** allows the contributor or donor to invest funds in the child's name but with someone else, usually the parent, as the custodian. When the child reaches legal age (majority), he or she receives the money. Even if the child becomes involved in gangs and drugs and doesn't go to school, the money still goes directly to him or her at legal age.

Many times, UGMAs are established by grandparents who want to put money aside for their favorite grandchildren. This is exactly what Penny's parents want to do for Michelle. They are approaching retirement and would like to put $4,000 per year into an UGMA for Michelle. But because an UGMA is included in the financial aid formula at 35 percent, it can work against you when applying for financial aid.

A **Roth IRA** may be a smarter strategy than an UGMA for Michelle.[2] Her grandparents can each put $2,000 into a Roth IRA with Penny as the beneficiary. When Michelle is ready for college, they should pay the money directly to the school so it won't affect Penny, Roni, and Michelle's financial aid calculation. The money in a Roth IRA accumulates tax-deferred and, as long as it's been in the account for at least five years and Michelle's grandparents are over the age of 59½, will be distributed to them tax-free. Or, if Penny's parents die, the proceeds will pass income-tax-free to Penny from the Roth IRA.

If we assume a 10 percent growth rate on their investments, Penny's parents will have approximately $120,000 in fifteen years. Again, since this is a tax-deferred investment for a long period, they can invest as aggressively as is comfortable for them.

2. A Roth IRA permits individuals to make a nondeductible contribution of up to $2,000 per year. Contributions can be made beyond age 70½, and husbands and wives can contribute irrespective of contributions to other retirement plans either spouse may have. It accumulates tax-deferred and is distributed tax-free if the owner is over the age of 59½ and the account has been held for five years, or after the owner's death or the owner is disabled.

State Savings Plans and Prepaid Plans

A number of states have some form of state-sponsored tuition savings.[3] **Prepaid tuition plans** allow you to buy up to four years of tuition at today's prices, either in installments or as a lump sum. The benefit with this arrangement is that your college cost is guaranteed. While these plans were great when tuition inflation was 10 percent, now that they are increasing at approximately 5 percent, these plans may be no match for the stock market.

Many of the new **state savings plans** are state-run investment plans that invest in stock or bond portfolios. You decide how much to contribute and the state pays you a return based on the investments it chooses. Unlike an Education IRA, a Roth IRA, or your own savings plan, you cannot, under federal law, choose the investments. Some state plans invest only in bonds while others use mutual funds.

These plans are exempt from state taxes and are tax-deferred at the federal level until the student is ready for college. At that point, distributions are taxable to the student for both federal and state taxes at the child's bracket, which could be only 15 percent. In some states, you get a state income-tax deduction for contributions. In other states, the distributions are income-tax-free. If your child does not go to college, funds can be transferred to a sibling. If there is no sibling, most plans penalize you if the funds are not used for college expenses. These plans differ from state to state.

While prepaid plans guarantee the cost of colleges in your state or at colleges that your state has contracted with in other states, savings plans do not provide any guarantees and could lose money if the market crashes. If you are thinking about either a state savings plan or a prepaid plan, you must ask several critical questions. If we move, how much will we get back? What penalties will we have if we do not use the funds?

There is an alternative to state plans at this time that should be considered. At this time schools in Canada are a good buy because

3. Stephanie Gallagher, "A Winning Way to Save for College," *Kiplinger's Personal Finance Magazine,* May 1998.

the Canadian dollar is very weak compared to the U.S. dollar. While Canadian schools don't qualify for need-based aid they do qualify for U.S. subsidized loans and you do get tuition tax credits.

Life Insurance Products

Two types of life insurance products do not currently appear in the financial aid formula using the Federal Methodology: **annuities** and **life insurance**.

ANNUITIES

The Internal Revenue Code defines an **annuity** as a series of periodic payments resulting in the liquidation of a principal sum. Although an annuity is a contract with a life insurance company, it is the opposite of life insurance. **Life insurance** is designed to create an estate upon the insured's death. An annuity is designed to create an income which can be distributed during a person's lifetime, a fixed period of time, or as a fixed amount. If it is paid for a lifetime, it can also be paid as a joint and survivor benefit with a reduced amount for the second person.

There are basically two types of annuities: immediate and deferred. An **immediate annuity** begins to pay the income to the beneficiary during the first year, but deferred annuities do not begin to make distributions for at least a year. Because of tax benefits, we'll focus on deferred annuities. Money can be invested in a **deferred annuity** either as a lump sum or on a flexible basis. Some plans allow the owner to accumulate funds in the deferred annuity to age 90 or beyond before they must start distributing a periodic income. Funds can be invested in a deferred annuity to accumulate and then be withdrawn when needed.

The tax treatment on annuities is different than for mutual funds. While annuities accumulate on a tax-deferred basis, distributions are taxable at your tax bracket. There is no capital gains treatment. And if the owner withdraws funds before age 59½, there may be a premature withdrawal penalty just like a traditional IRA. Funds coming out of a deferred annuity are taxed on a last-in-first-out

(LIFO) basis. The last dollar to go into the plan is presumed to be the profit and will be fully taxable until all of the profit is used up. So, if you put $10,000 into a deferred annuity that grows to $25,000 and then you take out $7,000, the full $7,000 will be taxable in your tax bracket.

It has been argued that deferred annuities are less desirable than mutual funds because the latter have better tax treatment. It's really all relative to what your goals are. If your goal is to accumulate funds for retirement or college, and to benefit from tax-deferral, then deferred annuities could be for you.

Private schools using the Institutional Methodology may consider your annuities. They will look at your age and if the funds are for retirement or are an accumulation and shelter vehicle. The money you have accumulated in deferred annuities may or may not go into their calculation, depending upon whether it is part of your retirement cash flow needs or just for tax-deferred accumulation.

Deferred annuities can be fixed or variable. A **variable annuity** (VA) is an annuity where the underlying investments are mutual funds. If Roni and Penny use a variable annuity to accumulate funds for Michelle's education, they will not receive any 1099s for interest, dividends, or capital gains earned by the variable annuity, as it is a tax-deferred investment. And it is not reported on the federal method. When they take distributions from the variable annuity, however, they will pay taxes at their tax bracket instead of capital gains tax.

LIFE INSURANCE

Certain types of life insurance can be used to accumulate funds on a tax-deferred basis and then distributed as a loan tax-free. If you have a need for life insurance, it can serve a double purpose. Since both Roni and Penny need additional life insurance to protect Sami and Michelle if they die prematurely, they can use the insurance for survivor protection and as a place to accumulate tax-deferred funds.

If you are lucky enough to have a parent or parents who can establish a Roth IRA for your children, then consider the following strategy as an alternative. If your parents are healthy and cooperative, buy an investment-type of life insurance on their life. If their life expectancy is shorter than the number of years until you will need the money for college, you could have a significant windfall because the proceeds from a life insurance policy are paid income-tax-free.

This strategy can also be carried out another way. Since your parents can give up to $10,000 per person, they can give the money to your child, who can then buy the insurance on their lives. This way the child has the investment and is the beneficiary.

Step-by-Step Instructions
for Roni, Penny, and Michelle

1. Roni and Penny do an EFC calculation based on their combined incomes and assets, realizing that the factors will probably change by the time Michelle is ready for college.

2. Roni and Penny decide to try to save for the full college cost, since they may not qualify for financial aid. They will try to save $575 per month together.

3. The partners open an Education IRA and have $42 per month deposited directly into it for investment in a moderately aggressive growth mutual fund.

4. Since Penny will be over 59½ when Michelle is in her second year of college, she starts a Roth IRA to which she will contribute $2,000 per year.

5. In working with their insurance broker, Roni and Penny agree to purchase an additional $100,000 of investment-type life insurance. They will contribute $100 per month each over the cost of that insurance for their college savings fund.

6. Roni invests $150 per month on a dollar-cost-averaging basis in a moderately aggressive mutual fund. The money comes from her checking account and goes directly to the mutual fund.

7. Once a year they meet with their financial advisor and review their college-funding program for Michelle.

SUMMARY

If you think of college as a mortgage-type expense, you have a better chance of sending your child to the school of your choice. You'll get your best chance of obtaining financial aid by knowing how the college financial aid game is played. The proactive student and parent have a better chance of getting aid than those who wait and hope for the best.

If you take charge of your financial aid campaign, you can:

- Increase the amount of aid you are eligible for
- Enhance your chances of receiving all the aid you are eligible for
- Improve the composition of your aid with more grants and fewer loans
- Have a major advantage over your competition who don't understand the financial aid process

STEP 2:

PROTECT
WHAT'S YOURS

This step covers two key areas: insurance and legal documents. Chapter 6 starts off with a discussion of how to use life insurance to provide tax-favored investment opportunities as well as protection. Then, in chapter 7, you'll find out how to buy life insurance when you have a serious medical condition such as HIV/AIDS or breast cancer. Chapter 8 tells you what you need to know about disability insurance, and chapter 9 offers guidance on obtaining health insurance when you have a history of serious medical problems. This chapter also covers long-term-care insurance.

The last chapter in the section provides information about legal documents that can protect you when marital laws don't. Since each state and jurisdiction can have different statutes, this is one area where it's important to work with an attorney well-versed in the legal issues of the lesbian and gay community where you live. Do not try to go it alone.

CHAPTER 6

Building and Transferring Wealth with Life Insurance

If a man doesn't believe in life insurance, let him die once without it. That will teach him a lesson. —Will Rogers

Jeffrey, 46, is a systems engineer. He works both at home and at his employer's offices in Redwood Shores, a suburb of San Francisco. He earns $96,000 a year. Walter, his partner of nine years, is a 41-year-old research analyst for a small East Bay investment firm, where his salary is $35,000. They are both avid golfers. In fact, they met while vacationing in Palm Springs.

Jeffrey and Walter moved to the Bay Area from Boston two years ago, after Jeffrey's mother died. He had been taking care of her after she developed diabetes and ulcerative colitis. After she died, Jeffrey and Walter couldn't see any reason to stay. Now they are building a new house, which they will own jointly, in the Oakland Hills, overlooking San Francisco Bay.

Jeffrey netted $200,000 from the sale of his house in Boston and plans to put it into the new house, which will cost $550,000.

In the process of completing a financial plan, Jeffrey and Walter realized that they have two critical concerns. First, they want sufficient funds to pay off the $350,000 mortgage if either one of them dies. Second, they want to maintain their current lifestyle when they retire. Since Walter earns less than Jeffrey, $150,000 in capital is also needed to provide an additional $1,000 per month of survivor income for Walter in the event of Jeffrey's death.

Jeffrey is contributing the maximum to his 401(k) retirement plan at work. His employer makes a 50 percent matching contribution (e.g., if Jeffrey saves $10,000 per year his employer will contribute $5,000). Walter's firm has no retirement plan.

Walter has a $75,000 whole life insurance policy that he thinks will provide him with disability income and a retirement income. To help with the move from Boston, he used the cash in the policy. He doesn't really understand how his insurance policy works.

Jeffrey and Walter can meet their financial goals with a retirement income strategy called **retirement income from life insurance (RILI)**. It will allow them to build another retirement source with tax-deferred dollars and then receive tax-free income to supplement their retirement income from work. It will also provide death benefit protection.

INTRODUCTION

Life insurance is one of the best ways to achieve your family's goals. In some situations it may be the only way. You can use life insurance to create instant wealth or to transfer wealth without complications or publicity.

You need to consider two sets of issues when buying life insurance. The first set centers on the death benefit: how much insurance you should buy, how to obtain it, who should be the beneficiary, and who should own it.

The second set of issues involves how best to invest the cash value accumulation inside the policy. We will consider all these issues in addressing Jeffrey and Walter's needs. As you read on, you will discover tax benefits that many people can't believe are still available.

LIFE INSURANCE:
THE BASIC PRINCIPLES

Life insurance is a way to create wealth where there was none before. It is also a way to transfer wealth with favorable tax treatment. It is a contract between three parties: the insurer, the applicant or owner, and the insured. In exchange for the payment of a premium, the insurance company agrees to pay the death benefit when the insured dies.

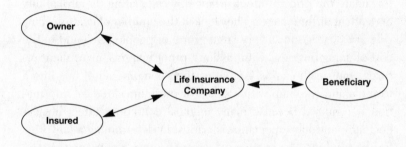

Because the owner, insured, and beneficiary can be separate people, different combinations are possible: the owner and the insured can be the same person; the owner and the beneficiary can be the same person; the beneficiary and/or the owner can be a person, organization, or trust. Realizing that these combinations are possible and understanding a little tax law enables you to purchase a life insurance policy in a way that solves your needs.

Questions, questions . . . and always the same questions! The following answers to the six questions asked most frequently by lesbian and gay couples will help you deal with sticky problems you may have had in the past in obtaining life insurance.

FREQUENTLY ASKED QUESTIONS

1. How do we buy life insurance?
No one type of life insurance is for everyone. Because there are so many options available, doing an analysis of your entire situation

can be very helpful in determining what type to buy and how much to buy. Life insurance is not one of those things you order from television. Buying insurance is serious business. We'll look at some of the options later in this chapter, and appendixes D and E will provide more detail. If you feel you need to know more about insurance companies and their products, a good resource is *The New Life Insurance Investment Advisor*, by Ben G. Baldwin.

Once you've made your decision, the next step is to complete the application and answer medical questions. Insurance companies formulate the price of life insurance by calculating the probability of death at different ages. They look at the number of deaths occurring at every age for a very large group of people, then add in the cost of doing business, commissions, profit margins, investment returns, and death claims. Actuaries then combine all of this into a formula and come up with a price, or premium. Medical information is required because many medical conditions affect life expectancy, and life expectancy is critical in determining a fair price for the product. The company does not want to lose money on you.

In addition to including medical history questions on the application, the insurance company may require a medical exam, depending on your age and the amount of insurance applied for. (Appendix F provides a list of steps you can take to improve the results on your medical exam.) The bigger the risk the company is taking, the more careful it is. If the amount of life insurance is substantial, you may have to submit a copy of your federal income tax return as well. The insurance company's decision-making process is called **underwriting**.

2. Who can be the beneficiary?

All life insurance policies and some types of investments (including annuities, IRAs, 401(k)s, and other retirement plans) require a beneficiary designation. For lesbian and gay couples, beneficiary transfers can be the easiest and least costly way to transfer money.

If you are the owner, you name the beneficiary. Whoever you name will inherit the death benefit when you die, superseding your will and any other prior designations. If you wish, you can split the proceeds among several beneficiaries. You can also name a contingent beneficiary to receive the proceeds if your primary beneficiary dies before you. You don't need the beneficiaries' approval to name them or to remove them. (This may differ for people who are legally married.)

When you name the beneficiary of a life insurance policy, you should consider who would suffer an economic or emotional loss if you died. That could be your lover, children, business partner, parents, or a favorite charity. Because circumstances and needs change, it's a good idea to review your beneficiary designations every few years.

3. What should we do if I can't name my partner as beneficiary?

Lesbian and gay couples often encounter difficulties when they name each other as life insurance beneficiaries. In many states, the law requires that a beneficiary must have an "insurable interest" on the life of the insured. An insurable interest arises from the relationship of the person buying insurance to the insured, provided that there is a reasonable expectation of benefit on the continuance of the insured's life, such as insuring your own life. The benefit may be economic (as between business partners, debtor and lender, or employer and a key employee) or love and affection (as between legally married spouses or parent and minor child). A person can always insure his or her own life. Insurable interest serves a social purpose because it prevents speculation, as in the case of a murderer insuring his victim. Some states, like California, allow anyone to be your beneficiary.

More astute companies will not question your beneficiary arrangements. Other companies may say, "Not married? Too bad, no insurable interest unless you are a blood relative or a business partner." Or they may discriminate against same-sex partners. But know that in most states insurable interest must exist *only when the policy is first issued*—therein lies the relief.

There are two ways to get around the problem. One is to name your estate as beneficiary on the application and then name your partner as heir in your will. When the policy is issued, you can change the beneficiary to your partner. The problem with this approach is that you might forget to change the beneficiary. If you do forget, this method has a major drawback: because your life insurance proceeds must go through probate if left in your estate, payment delays due to the probate process can occur and may last for years, and may trigger unnecessary taxes, expenses, and publicity. You can avoid probate by naming your mother, father, or sibling as beneficiary. But if you want your partner to receive the death proceeds, don't forget to change the beneficiary after the policy is issued.

The best solution if your state requires your beneficiary to have an insurable interest is to establish a **revocable living trust** and name the trust as beneficiary of the insurance and your partner as beneficiary of the trust. The trust then distributes the proceeds directly to your partner. This method avoids probate, delays, and unnecessary taxes and should not be questioned.

One great feature of a living trust is that it is confidential. Probate, on the other hand, is a matter of public record. If you want to keep your affairs private, then a revocable trust makes sense. See an attorney well-versed in lesbian and gay legal issues who specializes in estate planning.

4. How is life insurance taxed?

The way in which life insurance is taxed offers a unique opportunity for lesbian and gay couples. First, we will see what the tax treatment is. Then we will see how you can utilize life insurance to accomplish your financial planning objectives, especially in the area of estate planning.

Five tax benefits with every life insurance policy:

1. Death benefit proceeds are generally income-tax-free.
2. You can build up dollars called **cash value** within the policy on a tax-deferred basis for whole life, universal life, variable life, and variable universal life policies.

3. The proceeds are free from estate taxes if
   - they are not used to pay estate taxes
   - they are paid to a beneficiary other than your estate
   - the insured does not own the policy at the time of death or the policy was not transferred within three years of the date of death to someone else
4. Premiums that are used to buy a life insurance policy as part of a retirement plan or for a charitable gift are tax-deductible.
5. Dividends are tax-free for policies that have them.

So what does all this really mean?

It means that you can create a tax-free income from dollars that have been accumulating on a tax-deferred basis. It also means that in the event of your death, you can transfer wealth to your partner without estate taxes, just like a legally married spouse.

5. When should we use an insurance trust?

When two people are purchasing life insurance to protect each other, there are basically three ways to own each policy: each partner can own his or her own policy, each partner can own the other partner's policy, or a trust can own the policy. When the estate plan calls for the life insurance to be owned by a trust, it is called an **irrevocable life insurance trust (ILIT).**

In general, an ILIT is created by an individual known as a **grantor**. One party, called a **trustee**, holds property (usually life insurance) for the benefit of someone else. Unlike a revocable trust where you can change your mind and get your property back, with an ILIT you must give up all incidences of ownership to the property in the trust. If you use this trust, it's permanent. Again, unlike a revocable trust, you cannot be the trustee. Your partner or child can be a trustee, but the grantor cannot be the trustee. An ILIT is used to keep property out of the estate of the person who dies. Life insurance is an excellent vehicle for this type of trust.

6. How can we avoid estate taxes without a trust?

When an individual dies, everything she or he owns or controls is considered part of the estate and is taxed accordingly. When the surviving partner owns the life insurance, it stays out of the estate.

So, to keep life insurance out of an estate, each partner can own the other's insurance policy. The disadvantage to this is that, in the event of a breakup, the original partner may want back the money accumulated in the insurance. This is one reason domestic partnership agreements are so important.

The advantage of a cross-ownership strategy, where each partner owns the other partner's life insurance, is twofold: it keeps the life insurance proceeds out of the estate of the person who dies first, and unlike an ILIT, it allows access to the cash value during lifetime. If it is more important for you to be able to use the money accumulated in the policy to supplement retirement income or to help pay for college expenses than to have a tax-free transfer at death, then each partner should consider owning the other partner's life insurance, even if you have a large estate. If the estate is smaller than the unified credit equivalent exemption and there will be no estate tax, then the insured can be the owner. We will look at some numbers with Jeffrey's situation. Since this area can get very confusing, a qualified financial advisor, insurance broker, or tax advisor who understands estate planning for unmarried couples can help you with your specifics.

Now that you are an expert on life insurance, you are probably wondering how Jeffrey and Walter should set up their insurance program. First, let's examine Walter's old policy.

WALTER'S OLD POLICY

As you recall, Walter has a $75,000 whole life insurance policy; he bought it when he was 28 years old. He thinks it has a disability income benefit and that he will also receive a retirement income from it.

There are basically only two types of insurance policies—term and whole life. Term insurance provides insurance for a limited period of time, and the premium increases as one gets older. While term insurance can provide a lot of protection for a lower cost, it builds no cash value and has no permanent value. It can be tailored to fit almost any type of temporary insurance need—increasing, decreasing, or level. Permanent insurance, on the other hand, has often been called "whole life" because it provides for the "whole of life."

Walter's whole life policy is a form of permanent insurance. Its price is level as it's based on his whole lifetime and it provides for a tax-deferred accumulation of cash value over the life of the contract. His policy defines whole life as 100 years. Should he live longer, the death benefit will be the cash value at the time of his death. Walter's policy also has a disability premium waiver feature which will pay the premium should he become disabled.

The problem is that Walter withdrew all of his cash value as a loan to help pay for his move. Unless he repays the loan, he will not have any cash value as a retirement income source. He also thinks he has disability income with this policy—not true, unless he has actually purchased a disability insurance policy that will replace earned income if he becomes disabled. The disability premium waiver pays only the premium should he become disabled and unable to pay it. It does not give him any income.

Most policies issued before 1977 that were not term insurance were some form of whole life. Types differed by payment period: 20-pay life, life paid-up at 65, endowment, and others. These policies were and still are based on the underlying bond portfolio of the insurance company and are as strong as that company's portfolio, which varies from company to company. Whole life policies are distinguished by *fixed premiums* and by the fact that the insurance company selects the investments.

You may wonder if whole life policies provide a viable investment vehicle for Jeffrey and Walter. Not really. Let's look at the reasons:

- Whole life is based on the general mortgage portfolio of the insurance company and average 5 to 5.5 percent.[1]
- Bond mortgages provide insufficient investment diversification.
- The policy holder has no choice as to investments in the policy.
- Policies are inflexible—the premium or face amount cannot be changed.

Walter would want to keep this policy if he were uninsurable and not able to change to an investment-type policy. However, Walter is healthy and wants to be able to shelter more money in an investment-type policy.

Walter can consider doing a tax-free exchange (also called a Section 1035 exchange) of his old policy for a new investment-type policy, such as a variable whole life or variable universal life. Even though he has been paying the same premium rate since he was 28 years old, it may still be advantageous for him to switch to an investment-type policy. Since whole life premiums are generally higher than those of variable or universal life, he may be able to continue paying approximately the same premium even though he is older.

A FINANCIAL STRATEGY
FOR JEFFREY AND WALTER

A **variable universal life** (VUL) is the policy that solves Jeffrey and Walter's needs best. It has been called the "Swiss Army knife of financial products" by the American Society of Life Underwriters and it provides the following benefits:

- Supplemental income during your retirement years
- Survivor income should one partner die

1. Ben G. Baldwin, *The New Insurance Investment Advisor,* Irwin, Chicago, 1994, page 53.

- Accumulation of assets in mutual fund–type investments
- Flexibility in changing investments, premium, and face amount
- Tax-deferred growth with tax-free withdrawals while you are alive

Since Jeffrey and Walter want a supplemental income for retirement, their financial advisor recommends an insurance policy that gives them the greatest growth in cash value. A variable universal or variable whole life insurance policy enables them to invest the cash value in mutual fund–type investments that they choose. Hopefully, the investment value will grow. If not, they can switch investments within the policy. With this type of policy, they are using the same premium dollar twice: they are buying death benefit protection and accumulating cash value as another source for retirement income. (Appendix E describes the different types of policies that accumulate cash on a tax-deferred basis.)

Walter applies for a $500,000 VUL policy on Jeffrey's life and Jeffrey applies for a $350,000 VUL on Walter's life. The cross-ownership strategy will enable them to avoid estate taxes on the life insurance when the first partner dies. The value of Jeffrey's estate, with insurance, exceeds $1,000,000.

House less the unpaid mortgage balance	$150,000
Investments, 401(k), art, car, furnishings	450,000
Life insurance	500,000
Total estate	$1,100,000

Anything over the unified credit exemption equivalent will be subject to estate taxes. (Legally married couples, in contrast, have an unlimited marital deduction.)

The insurance is the easiest property to keep out of the estate. If Walter owns the policy on Jeffrey, it will not be included in Jeffrey's estate. An insurance trust is not recommended in this case because each partner wants to be able to access the cash accumulation as another source of retirement income.

When buying a variable type of insurance, it is important to remember that this is a security and that the broker or agent must give you a prospectus. The premium is so flexible that Jeffrey can stop paying premiums when he retires, or at age 65.

Sounds complicated? It is. This is why you want to use an advisor who is familiar with estate planning for unmarried couples.

Let's see how Jeffrey and Walter would set this up. The insurance premium is withdrawn monthly directly from their bank accounts. This way it is easy to track the money and there is a paper trail of who paid for what, for future reference.

Jeffrey and Walter plan to take as much taxable income from their 401(k)s, IRAs, and Social Security as they can in the early years of their retirement. They will start drawing supplemental retirement income from the life insurance when Jeffrey is 70 and Walter is 65. This way, the tax-free money from the insurance will be paid in the later years of their retirement when they think taxes will increase.

Jeffrey and Walter's financial advisor, who is also their insurance broker, provides a computer-generated insurance illustration which shows that they will have enough accumulation in their policies to supplement their monthly retirement income by $3,700 for Jeffrey and $2,500 for Walter. The advisor projects a rate of return of 10.25 percent after the cost of insurance is deducted. (You might ask how realistic it is to expect a 10.25 percent investment return rate. Remember that the stock market grew at an average rate of 10.2 percent from 1926 to 1994.)

You will need to do an annual review of your policy's performance to see if it is living up to expectations. If not, change the investments or rethink your goals. If you don't do an annual review, you won't know there's a problem until it's too late.

Many insurance brokers tend to use the maximum rate of 12 percent which the law allows when making cash accumulation projections. Be sure to ask your broker the cost of insurance and what projected fixed rate less the cost of insurance is being used. Don't be deceived—no one knows what the future will hold, so ask for a conservative projection as well.

Earnings rates for this type of insurance are estimates. They are never guaranteed. This is why you must receive the prospectus and do annual reviews. Be sure to ask about the performance history of the investments in this vehicle.

TABLE 6.1
LIFE INSURANCE ILLUSTRATION:
JEFFREY'S LIFE INSURANCE

Life insurance vehicle	VUL
Face amount	$500,000
Monthly deposit	800
Monthly income at retirement	3,700°

°Reflects 12% projected rate, or 10.25% after expenses; performance must be checked annually.

The monthly deposit of $800 comprises investment dollars and an expense factor for the cost of insurance for Jeffrey. These figures are based on the assumption that Jeffrey pays his premium for twenty years until he retires at age 65, then lets it grow until he is 70 years old, when he starts withdrawing an income for twenty years. If he can wait until he is 75 or 80 to take the income, the income stream will be larger. If he takes the income over a shorter period, say fifteen years instead of twenty, it will be also larger. This is where financial planning can prove really helpful.

Walter's situation is similar.

TABLE 6.2
LIFE INSURANCE ILLUSTRATION:
WALTER'S LIFE INSURANCE

Life insurance vehicle	VUL
Face amount	$350,000
Monthly deposit	400
Monthly income at retirement	2,500°

Reflects 12% projected rate, or 10.25% after expenses; performance must be checked annually.

Step-by-Step Instructions for Jeffrey and Walter

1. Walter applies for $500,000 of variable universal life insurance on Jeffrey. He is the applicant, owner, and beneficiary.
2. Jeffrey applies for $350,000 of variable universal life insurance on Walter's life. He is the applicant, owner, and beneficiary. They do not use trusts because they want to access the accumulation as a retirement income source.
3. At the insurance company's expense both will have a physical examination. The exam may consist of a blood test, EKG, and medical history.
4. Several days prior to the exam, Jeffrey and Walter take steps to improve the results on their medical exams: they stop drinking alcohol and using salt; they also avoid rich, high-fat foods and those with large amounts of sugar.
5. They stop drinking coffee with caffeine twenty-four hours before their exams and they drink plenty of water. (Appendix F provides additional steps you can take to improve your results.)
6. Jeffrey and Walter authorize the insurance company to write to their doctors for medical records. (Insurance companies call this process getting an APS [attending physician's statement].)
7. They also authorize the insurance company to do a credit bureau check on both applicants if required and to contact the

Medical Information Bureau (MIB) to determine if there is any negative medical history on either applicant that was discovered by previous insurance applications.

8. Jeffrey and Walter sign a domestic partnership agreement because they are mixing their assets and want to be able to recover their investments if the relationship doesn't work out.

9. At retirement, Jeffrey and Walter have a supplemental retirement income source which they use for monthly withdrawals from the cash value.

10. When one of them dies, the survivor receives the death benefit (less any withdrawals) both income- and estate-tax-free.

A VUL is not necessarily the solution for everyone. Each situation is different, and it is essential to get expert help.

ASSUME NOTHING

Life insurance is part of the financial planning process. A comprehensive plan can help you determine the right amount and type of insurance that will help you achieve your goals.

Life insurance, like a will, should be reviewed every few years to make certain your program is current with your situation and goals. If you purchase an investment-type policy, assume nothing. Monitor investment performance within the policy on a consistent basis at least annually.

CHAPTER 7

Buying Life Insurance When You Have a Serious Medical Problem

We will either find the way, or we will make one.
                    —Hannibal

Lydia, 42, has been having a tough time. A year ago she had radiation and chemotherapy for breast cancer. Although her lymph nodes have not been invaded by cancer cells and the breast tumor marker results have not been significant, she is worried. She knows there is a chance the cancer will return and she has heard that radiation doesn't prolong life. The chemotherapy has brought on early menopause, her libido is dissipated, and life has been a struggle.

The only saving grace in Lydia's life is her relationship with Paula, her caregiver, soul mate, and business partner, who has been totally supportive. Paula, a recovering alcoholic, is an artist whose canvases are in galleries all over the country, as well as in three museums. She has an art inventory worth $50,000 and a house worth $250,000. Lydia manages the sales and accounting end of Paula's art business. The two women live in Sugar House, a popular gay community in Salt Lake City.

Paula's brother Saul helps out in the business by selling her artwork and renting a small apartment at the back of the house. Saul is HIV-positive. So far, his medication has been working well, but he isn't sure what the future will hold. Even so, he is hopeful. He really wants to help provide for his sister should he die before her.

Lydia also wants to find some way to provide for Paula. She is concerned that because Paula is more talented in art than in business, she won't be able to manage the business or sell her work. Lydia has enough money to buy insurance but doesn't think she can get it because of her medical condition.

Both Lydia and Saul want to provide Paula with financial protection, but don't know how to do so.

A NEW VIEW OF LIFE INSURANCE

In chapter 6, the concern was how to purchase life insurance and still get good investment value. In this chapter, we'll look at how Lydia and Saul, and other people in their situation, can obtain life insurance. We'll also discover viable substitutes when it is not possible to purchase traditional life insurance.

The life insurance business is changing. People with medical conditions that were once thought to make applicants uninsurable may now be insurable. Insurance companies have liberalized their views somewhat, and some now offer a range of premium options for people with a serious illness or medical history. Some companies offer products that require few or no medical questions.

The focus of this chapter is on the life insurance options for people with HIV and breast cancer. However, these options apply to any form of life-threatening illness, including America's single largest killer, heart disease. Alcohol and drug recovery is also addressed in the chapter because of its relevance to many people.

WHAT YOU NEED TO KNOW
ABOUT LIFE INSURANCE RATES

The most important thing the insurance company wants to know about you is the state of your health. If you have a serious medical condition, you are likely to die sooner than a member of the general population. Therefore, if the insurance company charges standard rates, it will lose money—something it can't afford to do. Hence, the reason for medical questions and the medical exam.

When an individual is eligible for insurance but his or her medical condition is not standard, insurance companies call this an **impaired risk** or **substandard risk**. Every insurance company has rates for substandard medical histories. Rates are what the insurance company charges over and above the premium (what you pay for the insurance) when there is a medical condition that presents a probability of an early death. Your personal physician may disagree with the insurance company's determination. Remember, your physician looks at your condition from the standpoint of what will cause you a problem now, while insurance companies try to predict if you will die sooner than expected for someone of your age and sex. Each company has different rates and different ways of evaluating the medical history.

All companies use a flat percentage increase, called a table, to raise rate levels for a medical condition that affects life expectancy. For example, table A will be one level of increase in the probability of dying earlier than expected; table B, two levels; and so forth. Usually each table represents a 25 percent increase in the cost of pure insurance. Table D, for example, would be an increase of 100 percent. The total cost of insurance would be 200 percent of the initial or standard cost. If the pure protection cost is $10 per $1,000, then, at table D, the rate would be $20 ($10 plus 25 percent for each table, table D being four tables of 25 percent each). Other companies will use numbers instead of letters; table 4 is the same as table D.

If the medical condition is recent, the insurance company might also charge a flat extra amount per thousand dollars of insurance coverage for the first three to five years or until more time has passed and the condition can be better evaluated or has been cured. For example, if I had cancer two years ago, I might pay table B plus $5 per $1,000 for three years. If my premium were $10 per $1,000, table B would increase the premium 150 percent, from $10 to $15, plus $5 per $1,000 extra for three years. If I were buying $50,000 worth, I would pay $1,000 per year ($20 × 50) for three years and then $750 per year ($15 × 50) thereafter.

Had I been smart and listened to my insurance broker, I would have bought the insurance when I was healthy and it would have cost me $500 per year or less. This is why it is so important to buy insurance when you are healthy and you have choices.

Insurance policies have a two-year period after the policy is issued in which the insurance company can contest the validity of the risk, cancel the insurance, and refund the premium if it finds evidence of an illness or medical condition that was not revealed on the application. Even if there was fraud the period cannot be extended—two years is the limit.

Many insurance companies belong to an organization called the Medical Information Bureau. When an insurance company uncovers an adverse medical condition in the underwriting process, it reports it to the MIB. All member companies then have access to this information. The insurance company does not report its underwriting decision; nor does it report whether it provided the insurance, your medical history, or your insurance claims.

If you are a smoker, life insurance will be more expensive because smoking shortens your expected life span. If you buy a policy with smoking rates and subsequently stop smoking, many companies will reconsider and remove the extra charge one year after you have quit.

When looking for life insurance for the medically impaired, the key is to work with a broker who understands the substandard market.

LIFE INSURANCE AND HIV

If, like Saul, you are HIV-positive, there are a few options open to you. You can purchase an **immediate death benefit** policy. Another strategy is to purchase a delayed death benefit policy called **graded death benefit** life insurance. Let's start by looking at the immediate death benefit life insurance policy.

Immediate Death Benefit Life Insurance

Traditional life insurance has an **immediate death benefit**. You apply for the insurance, the insurance company makes an underwriting decision, and if you get the insurance, it pays the face amount to your beneficiary upon your death. Because the face amount is paid without a waiting period, it is an immediate death benefit policy.

As of this writing, I know of only one company that offers an immediate death benefit insurance policy for people who are HIV-positive. The company will issue a policy if you qualify and meet their criteria. Policies that are issued can be as low as $10,000 or as high as $250,000 for people ages 21 to 49. Criteria for this insurance can be quite stringent.

The applicant must be working at least thirty hours per week or be self-employed, never have received a diagnosis of AIDS, have been under medical treatment with antiviral drugs for at least nine months, not have become infected with HIV through intravenous drugs or blood transfusion, and never have had a CD4 test below 400 or a single viral burden over 20,000. You can expect the premium to be increased at least three tables plus a flat rate. As you can see, this policy is both expensive and restrictive.

If you meet the criteria and have no other options, this type of policy could be for you. Let's look at another option that is easier to obtain.

Graded Death Benefit Life Insurance

People do have another option even if they have an illness or a medical history such as HIV. It is called **graded death benefit** life insurance, also known as no-questions-asked life insurance. This insurance is guaranteed and it will be paid, but there are a few catches.

The application process for graded death benefit life insurance does not include medical questions, though some companies may ask if you are capable of working. These policies are issued by a very small number of insurance companies. Brokers, however, are prohibited from knowingly selling this insurance to people who are terminally ill or in a hospice, or who are expected to die in the near future.

Your most important question is whether you will live long enough for the full death benefit to be paid. Some of these policies pay the full amount after a two- to four-year waiting period, while others pay a reduced or graded amount if death occurs during the first two to four years. Companies that do not pay any death benefit during the first two to four years will return the premium plus interest if death occurs during the waiting period. Because of the advances in medical research and treatments like protease inhibitors, these policies are becoming more viable. Unlike immediate death benefit life insurance, these policies do not have conditional requirements. If you live the required period of time and pay the premium, the death benefit will be paid to your beneficiary at your death with no questions asked.

Graded death benefit policies, however, generally pay the full death benefit immediately only if death is accidental.

Graded death benefit life insurance was originally designed for older people with a serious medical condition, so most of these policies start at age 45 or 50. A few companies start them at age 30 or 40. This means that if you are younger than 30 and are HIV-positive, your options are limited. You may need to buy the immediate death benefit policy until you are old enough to qualify for a graded death benefit life insurance policy.

Some policies will use your current age and others will use the age you are at the nearest birthday within six months. The price increases as you get older, so the longer you wait to obtain coverage, the more expensive the policy will be.

The face amount of these policies is generally small. If you want more insurance than the policy provides, then you must "stack," or purchase additional policies. Saul can legitimately buy as many graded death benefit policies as he can afford.

This type of insurance is generally whole life and is expensive. Expense, however, is relative. When it is the only game in town, the amount you can afford rather than price becomes the issue. If you want to buy insurance and are uninsurable, then buy as much graded death benefit life insurance as you can afford, wait until you are healthy, and then check again for traditional policy coverage availability.

Since these policies tend to be whole life, they do accumulate cash value. If you qualify for traditional insurance and are interested in accumulating cash in a tax-sheltered environment, see chapter 6.

All graded benefit death life insurers use a **simplified underwriting process**. Simplified underwriting is based on an applicant's response to a minimum number of questions. Unlike traditional underwriting, the process involves no medical questions, physicians' statements, hospital and medical records, blood and/or urine tests. In California, for example, insurance law prohibits insurance companies from asking if you are HIV-positive. They can, however, ask if you have been diagnosed with or been treated for AIDS.

While preparing this chapter I had a client, Amy, who had survived leukemia. However, the chemotherapy she received when she was under treatment weakened the lining of her heart. Ten years after Amy recovered from the leukemia, she had a heart failure. Now, six months later, she works, plays, and plans for the future. Yet as far as most insurance companies are concerned, she has a very short life expectancy. They won't even accept an application. But there is hope—she can use the same strategy as Saul.

Step-by-Step Instructions for Saul

1. Saul contacts his insurance broker, who has never heard of graded death benefit life insurance. (This is not uncommon, since the larger insurance companies don't volunteer this information.)
2. Saul finds another broker who specializes in impaired risks. The broker tells Saul the good news: he can buy substantial amounts of life insurance. He must buy a number of small policies from different companies totaling the amount he wants.
3. Saul applies to ten different insurance companies for graded death benefit life insurance. One of the companies asks if he is capable of working, but there are no medical questions on any of the applications.
4. Saul stacks the ten small policies to achieve a cumulative death benefit of $200,000.

LIFE INSURANCE AND BREAST CANCER

While people who are HIV-positive usually cannot consider traditional life insurance an option, people with a history of breast cancer may qualify.

The insurance company will want to know how long the applicant has been healthy, the type of cancer, and the staging. Many companies will not consider an application until more than two years have passed since treatment was completed. There will be a table rating and possibly a flat extra charge for a number of years.

If a woman's breast cancer is treated in the early stages and is well differentiated, and if chemotherapy has not been prescribed, she may be insurable after one year. In this situation, life insurance can be purchased without the need to use graded death benefit life insurance. The applicant should anticipate a rating of approximately $7 per $1,000 as well as a flat extra charge.

Breast cancer cases that have metastasized and are moderately or poorly defined may be insurable three or four years after treatment. The approximate rating would be a table 4 or D plus $10 flat extra per $1,000 of life insurance coverage.

In cases where traditional life insurance is unavailable, a graded death benefit policy may be an effective temporary solution until the applicant qualifies for less expensive insurance.

Lydia does not want to wait three or four more years to buy life insurance. She wants to be able to protect Paula now. The best strategy for her may be to stack a number of graded benefit life insurance policies for the amount she wants or can afford and keep them until she qualifies for less expensive insurance. After three or four years, she should apply for traditional life insurance or have her broker do an "informal inquiry" by having an insurance company review her medical records to see if she can get a cash-accumulating or investment-type policy. This way, her partner will have some financial protection until Lydia finds less expensive insurance.

LIFE INSURANCE AND ALCOHOLISM OR DRUG ABUSE

Unless the applicant is in a recovery program leading to total abstinence from alcohol dependency or drug abuse, graded death benefit life insurance is the only option. The rules for drug history are generally the same as for alcohol. Let's look at Paula's situation and see what she would qualify for as a recovering alcoholic.

Most traditional insurance carriers would postpone considering an application until there have been one to two years of sobriety. Graded death benefit life would then be the only option. If the applicant has been sober for two years, the insurance company would apply table 4; for three years, table 2; and for four or more years, standard rates. Since Paula has been sober for over five years, she should qualify for a traditional policy with a standard rate. In fact, she may qualify for a policy similar to the one discussed in chapter 6 if she desires a tax-deferred investment for her accumulation dollars.

Step-by-Step Instructions
for Lydia and Paula

1. Lydia and Paula decide that they should each have life insurance to protect the other.
2. They consult their financial advisor, who recommends a variable life policy for Paula and refers Lydia to an insurance agency that specializes in impaired risk coverage.
3. Paula applies for her life insurance and takes a physical examination, and her medical records are checked. She gets the insurance coverage.
4. Lydia applies for graded death benefit life insurance, knowing that when she is healthier she will be able to apply for less expensive insurance on a traditional basis.
5. Lydia buys as much graded death benefit life insurance from a number of insurance carriers as she and Paula can afford. Paula helps pay for the insurance.
6. Four years after the conclusion of treatment, Lydia applies for variable universal life insurance.

OTHER STRATEGIES FOR PEOPLE WITH SERIOUS ILLNESSES

There are several other strategies to consider when traditional life insurance is not an option: **credit life**, **open enrollment**, **annuities**, and **mutual funds**.

Credit Life

Credit life is insurance issued by banks to make sure a mortgage, debt, or credit card balance is paid off at the borrower's death.

Obviously if there is a mortgage you must have collateral for this type of coverage to be available. Paula could apply for a mortgage on her house, or refinance if her house was already mortgaged. She purchases the credit life policy offered by the lender with the lender named as the beneficiary. Paula invests the proceeds from the mortgage and uses the income that the investment may generate to pay off the mortgage. At her death, the house transfers to her heir through her will since she owns the house individually, free of the mortgage. The funds that are invested take on a resemblance to insurance proceeds and pass to her heir, as per her beneficiary designation for the funds.

A careful reading of the loan application and the life insurance application may reveal no medical questions or disqualifying questions. If this form of insurance is available, consider taking it.

Open Enrollment

Open enrollment is the period of time (usually once per year) when you can join your employer's health plan or life insurance plan without medical questions. People with a terminal illness should look for companies that have an open enrollment policy period and obtain all the coverage they can get.

Annuities

This area provides a whole different strategy. Annuities, also discussed in chapter 5, are a life insurance product used in managing money payouts over long periods of time. Payments from you to the insurance company are generally made by one of three methods: a single large payment (called single-premium annuity); a series of fixed periodic payments (called fixed-premium annuity); or a periodic payment that can vary (called flexible-premium annuity). Payments from the annuity to the annuitant will either start immediately (immediate annuity) or will be deferred to start at some point in the future (deferred annuity).

When an annuity is purchased to start paying immediately, payments will generally be made for the life of the annuitant or for the life of the annuitant and for some period of time defined in the contract for a second person. The second person can receive the payments for life on a reduced basis if the annuitant elects the payments on a joint and survivor basis or for the balance of time known as the *certain* period. Certain means that the payments will be made for the life of the annuitant but at least the certain period that can be five, ten, or twenty years.

Let's assume that Saul has $100,000 to invest from the proceeds of his partner's life insurance. His partner, Jerry, died from AIDS. Saul wants to create an income for his sister that is guaranteed and that will not fluctuate with changes in the stock market.

Since there are no medical questions in conjunction with the purchase of an annuity, Saul learns that he can create an income for himself and for his sister with an annuity that exceeds the amount he will be investing. Since it will be fixed and guaranteed, she won't have to worry. Saul considers purchasing an annuity with a joint and survivor benefit, since he really doesn't know how long either one will live. Any gain will be taxed as ordinary income.

An additional financial planning strategy for Saul to consider might be to use the income from the annuity to buy the graded benefit life insurance discussed earlier. If Saul dies first, Lydia will continue to receive the income from the annuity and, in addition, the death benefit from the life insurance. If Lydia dies first, he can cash out of the life insurance or change the beneficiary and continue to receive the income from the annuity during his life.

Mutual Funds

Let's say Saul likes the idea of a lifetime income but he doesn't like the low yields or the tax treatment accompanying an annuity. His accountant told him that if he buys a mutual fund and liquidates a fixed portion every month, he will only pay capital gains taxes of 20 percent on any gains rather than his normal income tax rate of 28 percent.

Saul invests his $100,000 in a balanced mutual fund that has a good history of growth since its inception. He has heard that the stock market has averaged 10 percent growth per year over the last seventy years. Saul takes out $650 per month from the mutual fund, and purchases several graded death benefit life insurance policies. When he dies, the principal remaining in his mutual fund will pass to his heirs tax-free, as will the proceeds from the graded death benefit life insurance policies.

The mutual fund strategy, unlike the annuity strategy, must be monitored, as the value of the fund will fluctuate with changes in the stock market. If Saul's monthly withdrawals from the mutual fund exceed the average growth rate, then he may begin to exhaust the value of the mutual fund. This is not the case with the annuity because the payments are fixed per the terms of the annuity contract and are guaranteed for the life of the annuitant.

Which strategy is best for you? This is situation specific and is a question you and your advisors must determine based on your unique circumstances.

WHEN YOU CAN'T FIND AN INSURANCE COMPANY

In the case of any of these strategies, where you live is important, since life insurance is regulated by state law. Not all insurance companies operate in every state. If your insurance broker does not know whether a particular company does business in your state, have him or her check *Who Writes What in Life & Health Insurance*, published by the National Underwriter.

There you have it—some creative ideas on how to buy life insurance to obtain protection under extreme medical conditions.

CHAPTER 8

Buying Disability Insurance

A feast is made for laughter, and wine maketh merry: but money answereth all things.   —Ecclesiastes 10:19

Nick and Paul live in a two-bedroom apartment in Minneapolis. Paul is the leading salesman for a small computer company that specializes in corporate and institutional customers. He receives a small salary plus commissions and a large yearly bonus.

Nick, an assistant vice president for a bank in town near Loring Park, earns $48,000. Another VP at the bank, Gary, had a heart attack a year ago. When Gary's wife lost her job and the couple could not make ends meet, Gary went back to work too soon. While shoveling snow, he slipped on the ice, had another heart attack, and died at the age of 32. Gary's death scared Nick enough for him to start asking questions about his disability insurance and wondering if he could get more. Paul, on the other hand, being in excellent physical shape and a health nut to boot, didn't see the need for another expense.

They thought they had enough insurance until they started to list all of their expenses and identify the coverage they actually had. Nick discovered that his group disability insurance would replace two thirds of his monthly income. He also discovered that his plan deducted for Social Security and that he would have to pay income taxes on the benefit since the plan was paid entirely by his employer.

Paul discovered that two thirds of his base pay of $30,000 was covered but that there was no protection based on his bonus and commissions. He figured out that his group insurance actually covered 28 percent of his total compensation. No way could he and Nick live on that! But even so, he thought he was adequately covered with workmen's compensation. He also thought that since so many of his friends were collecting Social Security Disability Income because of AIDS, collecting Social Security benefits would be easy.

PREVIEW

The disability insurance industry and its products are changing, as are people's needs. Increasingly stressful environments, uncertain careers, changing social values, and advances in medical technology—including early treatment and life and disability-sustaining care—are driving the demand for increased disability income protection.

In this chapter, we'll find out what questions Nick and Paul asked themselves to identify their disability insurance needs and what alternatives are available to them and to you. By the end of the chapter you will be in a better position to protect yourself, your lover, and your children.

DISABILITY: THE HARD FACTS

Paul, like Gary, doesn't realize that the risk of serious illness or disabling injury is greater than he thinks. He thinks that because he practices safe sex, is in a committed relationship, and takes care of himself, there is little chance of a disability occurring.

Table 8.1 shows the probability, at various ages, that an individual will become disabled for at least 90 days by the time they reach age 65.

BUYING DISABILITY INSURANCE

TABLE 8.1
PROBABILITY OF LONG-TERM
DISABILITY PRIOR TO AGE 65*

Age	Probability
25	52%
30	51%
35	48%
40	45%
45	40%
50	34%
55	27%
60	16%

*Source: Based on Commissioners' Individual Disability, Pictorial; Disability Income Concepts, 2nd Edition, January, 1998.

Paul also thinks that injuries don't occur very often. Table 8.2 addresses that myth.

TABLE 8.2
TIME STATISTICS*

Every second:	33 people visit a physician
	$10,220 is spent on medical care
	Insurance companies spend $18 on disability claims
Every 4 seconds:	Someone is injured in an accident
Every 10 seconds:	Someone is injured in an accident at home
Every 17 seconds:	Someone is injured at work
Every 19 seconds:	Someone is injured in an auto accident

*Source: National Underwriter Co., National Safety Council, American Council of Life Insurance.

As a banker, Nick has seen statistics that support Paul's discoveries about the frequency of disability. He used to think that the chance of foreclosure because of financial loss due to death was greater than that due to disability. History says otherwise.

TABLE 8.3 FORECLOSURE COMPARISON*

Cause of Foreclosure	FHA Mortgages	VA Mortgages	Conventional Mortgages
DEATH	4%	3%	2%
DISABILITY	48%	49%	46%

*Source: Federal Housing Administration, Pictorial; Disability Income Concepts, 2nd Edition, January, 1998.

Paul and Nick's disability income protection needs are no different from anyone else's. The couple need to be assured of income continuity since expenses do not stop when one stops working.

Should disability occur, your living expenses can increase dramatically while your income decreases:

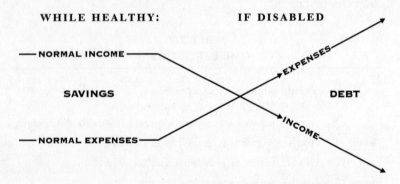

There are several ways to compensate for this loss of income:

- You can liquidate your savings. But if you normally save 5 percent of your income each year, one year of disability would use up twenty years' worth of savings.
- Your partner can increase his or her workload. But can one

person be a lover, parent, private nurse, and employee—all at the same time?

• You can borrow money. It would, however, be difficult to convince a bank to give you a loan once you became disabled.

None of these alternatives is very attractive. Here are some questions to use in determining whether you need more income protection.

QUESTIONS TO HELP YOU GET STARTED

• **Where do you stand today?**
What is your budget? How much do you spend on food, clothing, transportation, shelter, saving for retirement, bills, credit card debt, school loans? Make up a list of everything you regularly spend money on. Ask yourself which expenses would stop if you were sick for an extended period of time. Which would increase?

• **What resources do you have?**
Think of disability as long-term unemployment without an unemployment check. How much group disability insurance do you have at work, how long will it last, and is it taxable? How long do you have to wait to collect it? Under what circumstances will your disability insurance *not* pay? Does your state offer a sick-pay benefit and, if so, how long will it last?

How much individual disability insurance do you have and how long will that last? Under what circumstances will your disability insurance *not* pay?

Does your partner earn enough to pay for *your* cost of living? What if he or she gets sick—do *you* earn enough for both of you? What impact would this have on your relationship? What if both of you were to become disabled? The time to talk about these possibilities is now, while you're healthy.

> • **Where do you hope to be in the future?**
> What would you like your life to be like in twenty years? In
> ten years? In five years? How would you afford to retire if
> your partner's income were going into supporting both of
> you now?
> • **What if you break up?**
> How will you support yourself during a disability if you do
> not have a partner?

REPLACING INCOME: PAUL

Group Disability Insurance

Paul's first task was to learn about his group disability benefits. He
discovered that if he changes jobs his disability insurance does not go
with him. Very few companies offer conversion options. Paul must
continue to work for the same employer to collect this benefit. Then
he found out that the plan would pay only if he could not work at all.
If he returned to work part time after a period of not working full
time, he would not collect his disability benefit. The other shocker he
discovered was that his group disability benefits stop at age 65. He
had thought that he would be able to collect for the rest of his life.

Paul's biggest surprise, however, was to learn that his group insurance only protected up to 66⅔ percent of his base pay. His bonus
and commissions were not part of the formula. Since his employer
paid for this insurance, the benefit would be taxable, further reducing the amount he would receive. (If you pay for your group disability insurance, the benefit is tax-free.) He also learned that he
would have to wait seven months to collect his first check—six
months for the **elimination period**, or waiting period, plus one more
month. Payments are always after the month and not at the beginning. The box on the next page summarizes the characteristics of most
group long-term disability insurance. Your plan may be different—
check with your human resources department or benefits manager.

**CHARACTERISTICS OF
GROUP LONG-TERM DISABILITY (LTD)**

- Pays 60% or 66⅔% of salary
- Covers salary or base pay only (some richer plans will cover bonus and commissions)
- Pays benefits to age 65 (can be earlier if the employer requires early retirement)
- Has strict definitions of disability
- Pays maximum of $10,000 per month (sometimes more but usually less)
- Reduces benefits for Social Security
- May deduct for state sick pay
- Benefits are taxable to employee if plan paid by employer
- There is no cost-of-living increase on benefits
- Has six-month waiting period (some plans will have a shorter waiting period)
- Ceases when employee leaves employer
- Almost always restricts benefits for alcohol, drug, or stress to two years
- Cost of premiums to the employer may increase with age (which could be passed to you if an employee pay plan)
- Can be canceled by the insurance carrier after the rate guarantee expires, with a thirty-day required notice (which means you may lose your insurance)

Paul thought that Social Security would pay him an income if he became disabled because so many of his friends with AIDS were collecting SSDI. He discovered how difficult it really is to collect SSDI. The definition of disability required to collect Social Security benefits is very restrictive—the disability must be permanent, have lasted at least five months, and lead to death. That's pretty severe. He also discovered that Social Security benefits are generally reduced at age 65. Once Paul understood the shortcomings in his present group disability plan, he applied for individual disability insurance to supplement his group long-term disability insurance.

State Sickness Plans

Paul next tried to find out if his state had a sickness plan since his friends in California told him they had one. State sickness plans are designed to provide short-term disability protection until Social Security Disability Income begins to pay benefits. He discovered that only five states and Puerto Rico had such a plan: New York, New Jersey, California, Hawaii, and Rhode Island. Had he lived in one of those states, his employer would have been required to provide such a plan. He also learned that these plans generally have either a one-week or no waiting period and pay the benefit for a maximum of six months or one year.

If you are in a new business that has no income history, or if you work from home and are having a tough time buying individual disability insurance, consider buying your state's sick-pay plan (if it has one) until you can get more coverage.

Individual Disability Insurance

Because Paul decided to purchase individual disability insurance, he gathered a lot of information on the subject. He found out that the most comprehensive disability insurance is called **noncancelable, guaranteed renewable (NCGR)** disability insurance. It is difficult to qualify for and obtain, but once you own it, it's your best protection. The insurance company cannot cancel the policy as long as you pay the premiums and they cannot raise the premium unless you obtain more insurance. If you do not qualify for an NCGR policy, other plans may be available, such as renewable contracts, contracts with shorter benefit periods, or a disability plan from an association you belong to.

To qualify for individual disability insurance and especially NCGR insurance, you must be in good health and meet certain income and occupational requirements. Some insurance companies require a minimum level of earnings, other companies have a maximum level of earnings. Many companies will not sell you an individual disability policy if you are a government employee.

Government employees are in a difficult position because of the nature of their retirement plan. U.S. government employees and employees of some municipalities have a retirement plan that is also their disability plan. Once a government employee is permanently disabled, she or he must retire in order to collect. The problem is you may have to wait six months to a year to determine if you are permanently disabled. What do you do for income during that time? Some insurance companies sell a short-term disability plan for one or two years that can fill the gap while you are waiting to see if you will come back to work or take early retirement. To supplement the government retirement plan, you might be able to purchase disability insurance from an association to which you belong.

Paul learned that the single most important feature of any insurance policy is the definition of disability. The best type of insurance will have a liberal definition of disability and will pay you under most circumstances. A liberal definition of disability will say you cannot work in your occupation doing what you normally do, or words to that effect. For example, under a liberal definition, a surgeon who must now teach because of arthritis in her fingers would still be able to collect even though she has had an occupational change. Group insurance, on the other hand, stipulates it will be paid only if you cannot work at all. The definition for Social Security is the most restrictive—total disability leading to death. Liberal definitions are becoming difficult to find.

Individual disability insurance can be tailored to your needs. The longer the elimination period, the cheaper the premium. Many contracts today have a 90-day elimination period, meaning that you must be out of work for 90 days before you can collect your first check. You must, however, plan for 120 days since the first check does not arrive until one month after satisfying the elimination period. If you can find a 30-day plan, you will collect after 60 days.

The box on the next page summarizes the features most commonly found in individual disability insurance.

CHARACTERISTICS OF
INDIVIDUAL LONG-TERM DISABILITY INSURANCE

- Pays 60% or 66⅔% of salary, commissions, bonuses
- Maximum payout of $15,000 per month
- Typically will pay benefits to age 65, or less, if desired
- Liberal definition of disability
- Does not deduct for Social Security or state sick-pay plans
- Cost-of-living provisions available
- Waiting period determined by policyholder—30, 60, 90, 180, 365 days
- Policy stays in force no matter where you work in the world
- Plan continues if you change jobs, do more hazardous work, or become unemployed as long as you pay the premiums
- Rates can't change if policy is noncancelable, guaranteed renewable
- No restrictions for alcohol, drugs, or stress (most carriers going to two years)

When Paul applied for disability insurance, he found out that there were several areas that insurance companies were very concerned about. Since he went to a chiropractor for health maintenance, the insurance company wrote to his chiropractor to determine if he had a back ailment. Although Paul was in fact seeing the chiropractor for nutritional guidance, if he had been treated for a back problem, the insurance company would have "waived," or refused coverage on, any claims related to his back or lumbar region.

Paul also found that if he were currently seeing a psychiatrist, psychologist, or psychotherapist, many companies would have declined coverage automatically. Since he had been out of therapy for a number of years, therapy was not a consideration. And as a nonsmoker, he was able to get better rates than a smoker.

OTHER IMPORTANT FEATURES IN
INDIVIDUAL DISABILITY INSURANCE

Other features, called options or benefits, can be purchased for additional premium dollars. Some of these are essential for your financial security. While different companies will have different names for these features, they are basically the same.

Future purchase option (FPO) or **guaranteed insurability option (GIO):** With this option, base plan benefits may be increased up to specific amounts without additional medical underwriting. This feature allows you to adjust your disability benefits to keep pace with inflation and earned income growth and guarantees that you can purchase more insurance even if your health is worse. Increases to the base plan may be elected each year or through an automatic increase feature. Premiums are adjusted to reflect your age when you exercise this option and the increase in the benefit.

Cost-of-living adjustment (COLA) rider: This rider enables you to retain a level of income during a disability without losing purchasing power to inflation. After you become disabled, this option increases your base plan monthly benefit amount starting after one year of disability. The amount of the increase is determined by changes in the consumer price index or another inflation factor used to calculate the change in the cost of living.

Waiver of premium: Premiums are waived after you are either totally or partially disabled following the elimination period. Premiums that are due during the elimination period may be refunded once the waiver of premium is in effect, depending on the company. Your basic benefit premium usually includes the cost for this benefit.

Rehabilitation benefit: This benefit will pay for the cost of education, equipment, and/or training to assist you in returning to work with a disability. Some companies will pay a specific dollar amount while others will pay a multiplier of your monthly benefit. The benefit paid for rehabilitation is in addition to the monthly disability benefit and is usually included as part of the contract.

Social insurance substitute (SIS): This option provides an added benefit when you are disabled but are receiving no benefits, or limited benefits, from Social Security. The SIS benefit is offset dollar for dollar for Social Security benefits received. Some companies pay certain legal fees if you need to appeal a denial of Social Security benefits.

Recurrent disability: If you suffer a disability from the same or a related cause within six months of your return to work, the elimination period may be waived for disability. The cause is assumed to be related to the previous period of disability. If you have a five-year benefit, and were disabled for three years from the first disability, the recurrent benefit would only be applicable for two years of benefits. The recurrent disability benefit is usually included in the contract.

REPLACING INCOME: NICK

Nick's situation is somewhat different from Paul's situation because his group insurance is at the maximum level for his earnings and he suspects he cannot buy more disability insurance. He asks his broker to make sure. The broker checks his company's "Income and Participation Table," which shows how much insurance an applicant is eligible for at each level of income. The broker determines that he can supplement his group plan with additional insurance and, in fact, bring his total protection up to 75 to 80 percent of his compensation for his occupation class.

The broker informs him that his company would be willing to offer him an additional $732 per month with a 90-day waiting period before benefits start. This would bring his coverage up to 78 percent of his compensation and would give him additional insurance he could keep should he change jobs.

GROUP ASSOCIATION INSURANCE

There is another form of insurance available for people who do not have access to individual coverage or are not part of an employer group. Self-employed individuals, for example, with less than a year of business experience on their own will generally have a difficult time obtaining individual disability insurance because insurance companies want to see one to two years of work history in the current occupation. Group association plans provide an alternative but require membership in the association.

Since this type of insurance can be valuable protection when there is no other option, the list below provides its key features.

**CHARACTERISTICS OF
GROUP ASSOCIATION DISABILITY INSURANCE**

- Maximum payment of $2,500 per month (depending on the association)
- Usually will pay benefits up to five years
- Coverage stops when membership is terminated
- Insurer can increase premiums
- Elimination period is usually one or two choices between 30 and 365 days.
- No cost-of-living benefit

The biggest risk with this type of coverage is if the insurance carrier drops the association or the association decides to change insurance carriers while you are on claim and collecting benefits. If this happens to you when you are receiving benefits, then when you come off of the claim, you will have a preexisting condition that may prevent you from getting coverage with a new carrier.

If you are a professional and you have a choice between an expensive quality individual disability policy and an inexpensive group association plan, it is always wiser to buy the individual policy first. Once you have the individual policy, you can supplement that plan with an association plan. You will get better benefits and have better protection. This area should be discussed with your insurance broker.

DISABILITY INSURANCE AND TAXES

Except in the case of government employees, the tax treatment of disability insurance is very straightforward. If you pay the premium with after-tax dollars, then the disability income benefit you receive is tax-free. If your boss includes the premium as a bonus and you pay a tax on that bonus, then here, too, the disability benefit is tax-free. If you are self-employed and you pay the premium with after-tax dollars, the benefit is tax-free. If, on the other hand, your employer pays the premium as a business expense and you do not contribute to the cost or take the premium as taxable income, then the benefit will be taxable to you. The benefit is also taxable if you are self-employed or have a business and deduct the premium as a business expense.

If you are a U.S. government employee, your disability insurance is probably your retirement annuity if there is no insurance plan in place. Your retirement annuity is generally taxable even if it is a substitute for disability insurance. If you are a state, city, or county employee, you must discuss this with your tax advisor because your benefits are complicated and may include retirement benefits.

**Step-by-Step Instructions
for Paul and Nick**

1. Paul and Nick prepare an analysis of their present financial position and discover that both have a shortfall in their disability protection. Paul earns $72,000 including bonuses and commissions, but his company plan will only pay 66⅔ percent of his $30,000 base pay, or $1,667 per month. Paul learns that he can purchase an individual disability to supplement his group benefits.

2. Paul applies for $2,500 per month more disability insurance from an A+ rated insurance company that sells noncancelable, guaranteed, renewable (NCGR) insurance and Nick applies for an additional $732 per month.

3. Paul and Nick take a physical exam that includes a blood test and urine sample. They authorize the insurance company to obtain their medical records from their physicians and to do a credit check.
4. Paul and Nick provide proof of earnings for the prior year (a copy of each U.S. form 1040) and a recent pay stub with their applications.
5. Both men elect to pay for their new insurance by automatic transfer from their bank account.
6. Paul and Nick accept policies which include a 90-day elimination period, a cost-of-living rider, and a future purchase option.

SUMMARY

As you may guess, the best disability insurance is the most expensive. Price is based on a number of factors: age, income, type of plan, elimination period, length of benefit paying period, and features selected. The less the insurance company has to pay, the lower the premium. Longer elimination periods reduce the price. Shorter payment periods reduce the premium. There are many different choices, but the best kind of disability insurance you can have is the most liberal one you can afford, already in place when you need it. Your insurance broker can custom design the plan for your needs and budget.

Even a great investment portfolio without adequate disability income protection will disappear quickly. A financial planner who understands your needs can help you be prepared with the right kind of disability insurance. Together, you should create a comprehensive financial plan that takes into account all your sources of income (including your partner's income, investments, and other insurance you already have) to determine the gaps and overlaps in the event of a disability. Once again, planning ahead is your most powerful insurance.

CHAPTER 9

Surviving the High Cost of Health Care

*Live all you can; it's a mistake not to. It doesn't so much matter
what you do in particular, so long as you have your life. If you
haven't had that, what have you had?* —Henry James

When Roger was turning 50, he heard that the period between
50 and 55 were key years, medically speaking, for many
men. He didn't believe it. Now, at 55, he sees things differently. Those five years were something else. Who would have known?

About three years ago, Roger went to the doctor for a routine
exam. He had been procrastinating, but his partner, Jerry, insisted.
A digital rectal exam revealed hardness in his prostate. "No big
deal," his doctor said. "But to be on the safe side, I want you to get
a PSA [prostate-specific antigen] blood test." The readings were
higher than normal. "Roger, this is not good," said the doctor. "I
want you to have a biopsy."

Not long after Roger had the biopsy, he found out that he had
prostate cancer.

Roger learned that there was no real agreement on the best
treatment for prostate cancer. He decided to have a radical prostec-
tomy rather than radiation. The oncology urologist he saw said that
a cure was possible with surgery, and Roger wanted to be rid of the
problem since he was young and the cancer hadn't metastasized.

It's been almost three years now, and much to Roger and Jerry's
happiness, his PSA readings have been 0.0. If the tests continue at

that level for a full three years, his surgeon told him, he is likely cured of prostate cancer.

After this very difficult experience, life has been going well for Roger. He has been an accountant for a number of years with a large corporation and has started a small practice on the side. Even though he earns only 10 percent of his income from the practice, he gets 100 percent of his satisfaction from running his own business. He is ready to move on and become an independent accountant. Jerry has assured him that he doesn't need to worry about money at the start, since Jerry earns enough for the two of them.

Shortly after giving notice at work Roger found out that he needs a cataract operation. Because Roger has glaucoma, the doctor told him to prepare for a six- to eight-week recovery period. All of Roger's friends have told him it's nothing to worry about, but his biggest fear is not his health—it's that when he becomes an independent accountant he won't be able to obtain the kind of health insurance coverage he currently has. Almost all of his health expenses have been paid by his employer's health plan until now. Since Jerry works for a small computer-consulting firm, he earns good money but doesn't have domestic partner benefits that could help Roger.

Jerry's concern is different. Health problems run through his family: his father had a stroke when he was 60; his uncle has a heart condition. At 44, Jerry is concerned about the high cost of health care after he retires. In fact, his biggest worry is that if he needs nursing care like his father, he and Roger won't be able to afford it. He wouldn't want Roger to become his nurse as well as his provider and lover. He remembers his father saying that he outlived his own assets, and he doesn't want to find Roger and himself in the same boat.

THE GOOD NEWS

When Roger went to his internist, he asked, "Am I the only one with such a long medical history?" The doctor replied, "Anyone who takes care of himself has a medical history."

The good news is that taking care of yourself and using the medical resources available today enable you to live a long, full life. The bad news is that it may leave you with a medical history that insurance companies look at negatively. Fortunately, there are ways to solve that problem. As we follow Roger's story, the first part of this chapter will show you how to obtain the insurance protection you need.

In the second part of the chapter, we will take a look at Jerry's situation and identify the "gay penalty" on long-term care. We will examine how long-term care insurance works and see what it can do for you.

HEALTH INSURANCE

People who have *no* medical history should not have a problem getting health insurance. If you have a *good* health history, all you really need is the money to buy the protection you want. The best plan for you will be determined by your health and work circumstances, what your employer provides, what you can afford, and what state you live in. This portion of the chapter will focus on how to obtain health insurance benefits when you do have a *significant* medical history.

If, like Roger, you have had serious medical problems, you have seven options:

1. COBRA/OBRA
2. Group conversion
3. HIPAA conversion
4. High-risk pools
5. Small-group
6. Large-group
7. Affinity group association plans

COBRA/OBRA

The **Consolidated Omnibus Budget Reconciliation Act (COBRA)** of 1985 is a federal budget law that contains a section requiring employers of twenty or more employees to allow their workers the right to continue health insurance benefits for eighteen months after their employment terminates. Termination can be for any reason except gross misconduct. If the employer stops providing coverage to everyone, such as in a bankruptcy or a cutback of benefits, or stops paying premiums, then COBRA would not be available. (If you live in California, you can check with a health insurance broker or your health insurance carrier to determine if you are eligible under CAL-COBRA.)

In some instances, coverage under COBRA can extend beyond eighteen months. If you have reached the maximum age in the plan, then benefits will continue for thirty-six months. But if your benefits were ended because you no longer work enough hours to be considered a full-time employee, the limit is eighteen months.

Be aware that if you or your partner has domestic partner benefits on a health plan, spousal benefits under COBRA do *not* apply. Generally the partner who is covered under the domestic partner benefits would not be protected in the same way that a spouse in a legal marriage would be protected when the covered employee terminates for any reason (except gross misconduct). Some large plans do continue benefits if the partner who is employed dies, but they do not continue benefits in the case of "divorce" or separation. If you qualify to go under your partner's domestic benefits plan you might want to explore private insurance as an alternative and compare it to the domestic partner benefits. The partner having the plan that offers domestic partner benefits should contact his or her benefits department and ask about COBRA and limitations in the plan.

A terminated employee has 60 days from the date of termination or notification of COBRA rights, whichever is later, to elect COBRA coverage and 45 days to begin paying premiums. If you want "seamless" coverage, then begin to pay the premium as soon as you can after the offer is made. If you wait the full 105 days, you will have to pay the entire back premium from when you terminated plus the new month's premium. Also, by waiting until the last minute, you risk losing your right to benefits by going over the time limit.

The former employee pays the premium to the employer, who

then pays the premium to the insurance carrier or HMO. The employer can charge 102 percent of the premium to the former employee. In California, it can be 110 percent for CAL-COBRA eligible groups. It is generally a good idea for you to verify with the carrier that your premiums have been paid by your former employer; not all employers are honest.

Roger has a more difficult situation. Currently, the company he left subsidized the cost of his insurance by paying 50 percent of the premium. This means that Roger's cost will increase significantly since he must now pay the full premium plus 2 percent. The coverage, however, will be exactly the same as it was before he terminated.

The **Omnibus Budget Reconciliation Act (OBRA)** of 1989 is a federal budget law that includes a section allowing former employees who are disabled to continue health benefits for an additional eleven months. To obtain the OBRA extension, you must get the Social Security Administration (SSA) to certify that your disability occurred before the COBRA qualifying event or within 60 days of the qualifying event when electing COBRA. You must submit a copy of the SSA award letter to the COBRA administrator. The combination of COBRA and OBRA totals twenty-nine months of benefits. The employee is responsible for 150 percent of the premium under OBRA, including the portion that the employer was paying for the eleven-month extension.

OBRA requires that former employees receive the same health insurance benefits as current employees of the employer. As under COBRA, if the employer stops providing coverage to everyone, then OBRA is not available. Most health insurance policies terminate when an individual becomes eligible for Medicare. (Medicare begins in the thirtieth month after a Social Security–approved disability.)

Roger is not a candidate for OBRA since he does not have a disability which qualifies under Social Security rules. (He doesn't have a disability but he does have a medical history that is making it very difficult for him to obtain health insurance.)

GROUP CONVERSION

If COBRA is not available to you because of the size of the company or because the employer is exempt (as in the case of the federal government), then you may be able to convert to an individual health insurance policy within 31 days of termination or reduction of hours of employment.

Benefits are not guaranteed to be the same in a converted health plan as under the group health plan. There might be no prescription, vision, or dental benefits; the maximum may be considerably less; the deductible may be higher, or the premium may be higher. Roger could pay a substantially higher price for a lesser health plan if he had to go this route.

HIPAA CONVERSION

The Health Insurance Portability and Accountability Act (HIPAA) of 1996, also known as the Kennedy-Kassenbaum Bill, changed the way health care coverage is handled on a nationwide basis.

HIPAA was designed for the individual who exhausts his or her COBRA benefits and cannot get individual coverage. HIPAA can also apply to nongroup health insurance. HIPAA requires insurers to accept for individual policies people who are moving off group coverage. It states that the person may not be denied coverage or be subject to preexisting condition limitations under that individual plan. In order to have access to a group-to-individual policy on a guaranteed basis, you must meet the following requirements:

1. You must have at least eighteen months of aggregate creditable coverage.
2. You must have been covered under a group, church, or government employer health plan during the most recent period of creditable coverage.
3. You must have elected and exhausted coverage under COBRA.
4. You must not be eligible for other coverage, including COBRA, Medicaid/Medi-Cal, Medicare, or any other group coverage.
5. You must not have other health insurance coverage.

6. You must not have lost prior coverage due to fraud or nonpayment of premium.

The purpose of the **creditable coverage** is to give you credit for previous health coverage against application of a preexisting condition exclusion period when you move from one group health plan to another, from a group health plan to an individual plan, or from an individual policy to a group health plan. You will receive credit for your previous coverage as long as you have not had a break of 63 days or more in your coverage. Most health coverage is creditable coverage.

Insurers must offer their two most popular individual plans to eligible individuals. Since most people taking this coverage will be those who have a preexisting condition, the premium could be very expensive.

On March 18, 1998, the Chronicle News Service reported that government investigators found that insurance carriers were charging 140 percent to 600 percent of standard premium to people who were trying to use the law to convert group insurance to individual policies. In some cases, high-risk pools could prove less expensive. You can obtain additional information on HIPAA by calling the U.S. Health Care Financing Administration regional office for your state.

HIGH-RISK POOLS

Some states have established insurance plans to cover state residents who are unable to buy insurance from private carriers due to the state of their health. States usually contract with private insurers to provide this coverage. The provisions in these plans can be very similar to those in plans available in the open market. Upper benefit limits tend to be lower. These plans, however, do have requirements which must be met:

1. Eligibility is limited to state residents.
2. Applicants must document that they are ineligible for private

insurance or that they have a condition that makes them auto-matically eligible for the state plan.

3. Enrollment may be limited by the availability of funds to pay the premium. If that is the case, there is generally a waiting period from which applicants are admitted on a first-come, first-served basis.

4. There is a waiting period before preexisting conditions will be covered.

5. Benefits may be more limited than in private insurance plans and premiums will usually be higher.

6. The insured must pay premiums on time or coverage will be canceled.

If you have a preexisting condition and have been turned down, or if you have a letter from the insurance carrier saying that if you applied for health insurance you would be turned down, or if you are coming off COBRA with no coverage, you may have to consider your state's high-risk pool. If no phone number for your state is listed in Appendix J, contact your state's insurance commissioner or board of insurance, or an insurance broker who specializes in health insurance.

SMALL-GROUP: A SOLUTION FOR ROGER

The best strategy for Roger is to go into another group health plan or HMO on a guaranteed basis. When he forms his company, he can hire an employee and have a group plan for as few as two employees. Roger had planned to have a part-time employee for tax season and then a larger staff after twelve or eighteen months when the business was financially solvent, but he's not able to afford to do this yet.

What should Roger do, since he cannot afford a small-group plan at this time? A good strategy for him is to go on COBRA and then, when he can afford it but before the eighteen months are over, estab-lish a small-group plan for his business after hiring an employee. If he cannot afford to do this, after he exhausts COBRA he will have to choose between an HIPAA conversion and his state's high-risk pool.

Alternatively, Roger could affiliate with a professional employer organization (PEO). The National Association of Professional Employer Organizations defines a PEO as an organization that provides an integrated and cost-effective approach to the management and the administration of human resources. By contracting with a PEO, Roger's personnel management duties will be relieved, which will allow him to concentrate on making more money. The PEO can manage Roger's personnel, health benefits, worker's compensation claims, payroll and payroll tax, and unemployment claims. It can even do his hiring and firing of employees, but Roger must ultimately make the decision on whom to hire.

If the PEO has a cafeteria plan, Roger can join that. Cafeteria plans, also called "flexible spending" or "flexible benefit plans," allow participating employees to choose between a number of nontaxable benefits. These plans offer a "cafeteria menu" of benefits that can include group term life insurance, medical expense insurance, dependent group term life insurance, child care, dental expenses coverage, and disability insurance.

The benefit for Roger in contracting with a PEO is threefold: he gets the health coverage he needs, he avoids all of the compliance issues required in managing employees, and he can have access to a flexible spending plan that he would not be able to do as a self-employed individual.

If you are interested in this concept, contact the National Association of Professional Employer Organizations (they can be reached at 703-836-0466 or www.napeo.org).

LARGE-GROUP

If Roger's business does not work out, he can go back to work for another large employer and join that company's health plan. If he does this, he will have a probationary period before he is eligible for the company's plan. Employer-imposed probationary periods do not count toward the HIPAA 63-day period. So the problem is that he will have no insurance while he is waiting out his probationary period. If Roger decides to go this route he must get his new job before his COBRA runs out, or he must get other insurance (high-risk pool or HIPAA plan).

Obviously, this is a complex and confusing area. Talk to a health insurance specialist or a benefits counselor before giving up benefits.

AFFINITY GROUP ASSOCIATION PLANS

Some professional associations provide health insurance plans for their membership. Some of these plans have open enrollments. If you can join an association that has a health plan, this is an area that could be worth looking into.

Step-by-Step Instructions for Roger

1. Roger notifies his employer that he is leaving.
2. The company notifies him of his COBRA benefits. Roger elects COBRA benefits within sixty days of the notice and pays the premium as soon as he can to avoid a gap in his coverage.
3. Roger pays the former employer the premium for his health benefits and the employer in turn pays the insurance carrier.
4. Roger calls the insurance carrier regularly to confirm that his former employer is paying his premiums.
5. Roger builds his new business.
6. A year after starting his accounting practice, he hires an employee and promises health insurance.
7. Roger contacts an insurance broker who specializes in health plans for small businesses.
8. Roger adopts a small-group health plan providing a choice between a PPO and an HMO for himself and the employee. Since this is group insurance, he is able to go into the plan on a guaranteed basis without preexisting requirements.
9. Three months after hiring his first employee, he has a traumatic time firing her because she has been stealing checks, forging his signature, and dipping into his checking account.
10. Roger contracts with a professional employer organization

which hires his new employee based on his criteria and manages payroll for both himself and his employee.

11. Roger joins the PEO's group health plan and focuses on managing his business.

AVOIDING THE "GAY PENALTY" ON LONG-TERM CARE

Jerry is right to be concerned about the cost of care for the elderly because 43 percent of individuals turning age 65 have a chance of spending some time in a nursing home. Once in the nursing home, 21 percent will stay in the nursing home at least five years. Two thirds of single people and one third of married people exhaust their funds after just 13 weeks in a nursing home, and 90 percent will be bankrupt within two years.[1] What he doesn't realize is that the need for long-term care protection applies to younger adults also, and is even more acute for lesbian and gay couples because of the "gay penalty" on long-term care.

Lesbian and gay couples, much more than straight couples, have to consider the cost of long-term health care as part of their financial security needs. The gay penalty on long-term care comprises three factors.

First, Medicaid rules treat unmarried couples differently than married couples. When an ill spouse in a legally recognized marriage requires nursing care that is covered by Medicaid and the couple owns a home, the healthy spouse can remain in the home. In a lesbian or gay partnership, however, the unmarried partner cannot stay in joint property unless that person buys out the interest of the ill partner who requires Medicaid. If you don't have the money to pay for long-term care, how will you be able to buy out your part-

---

1. Donald F. Cady, *1998 Field Guide to Estate Planning, Business Planning, and Employee Benefits,* The National Underwriter Company, 1998, page 221.

ner's half of the home? If you can't afford to buy out your partner's half, where will you live? Medicaid rules treat the house as the property of the ill person even if it is jointly owned. The law presumes that your partner owns it all with joint ownership. This means that Medicaid will go after the property of the deceased to be reimbursed for its expenses. Medicaid was designed for people who do not have assets or income to pay for long-term care needs.

The second factor is family dynamics. Can you or your partner depend on your siblings or relatives to help out if either of you needs help to take care of the other?

The third factor is the absence of children in many gay and lesbian unions. Again, who will be there for you when your partner can't help you? Who will change your bedpan if your partner is too frail to care for you and you don't have money to hire help? Will you be able to help your partner with the essentials of daily living? If you do have children, there is another side to the problem. If you have elderly parents and you are taking care of children, who will take care of you if you need help? Once you have children, you become part of the "squeeze" generation.

As disturbing as these questions may be, fear not. There is a solution.

What You Need to Know about
Long-Term Care Insurance

Long-term care (LTC) insurance is as important as life insurance or disability insurance in easing the economic consequences of premature death or disability. An LTC insurance policy can be customized to meet your unique needs. You can choose the elimination or waiting period, the daily benefit, length of coverage, and how much inflation protection you want.

"Long-term care" refers to the services provided over an extensive period of time to persons with chronic illnesses who need assistance with everyday activities such as eating, dressing, transferring, and toileting. Long-term care is typically "custodial" rather than "skilled" and has traditionally been provided by family members until the burden of caregiving requires outside intervention. *Custodial care* is personal assistance with the activities of daily living while *skilled care* is medically necessary care by a licensed medical professional on a constant day-in and day-out basis working under the supervision of a physician. Custodial care is *not* paid for by major medical insurance, HMOs, disability insurance, Medicare, or by Medicaid/Medi-Cal unless you are destitute.

Long-term care can be provided in the home (if there are sufficient funds to pay for companion services or visiting nurses), in the community (adult day care), or in a facility (assisted-living residence or nursing home). Without adequate resources or long-term care insurance, the cost can wipe out your life savings and impoverish you. Even worse, the appropriate professional care may not be affordable. Jerry does not have family other than Roger to help out; nor does he have the money to hire a caregiver.

LTC insurance can be purchased by people as young as their early twenties. Since few people have the financial resources of Christopher Reeve, LTC insurance is imperative.

The best time to buy this type of insurance is when you are young, before age, disease, or illness limits your ability to pass underwriting requirements. An inflation factor can be included in the policy that increases the benefit every year while maintaining the original premium.

The federal government is changing the rules to reduce the anticipated growth in long-term care funding requirements for Medicare and Medicaid. (States can already deny benefits for years when assets have been given away within the previous three to five years to qualify for Medicaid and can recover Medicaid costs from the estate of the deceased. It is illegal to transfer assets to help individuals qualify for Medicaid.)

To encourage the purchase of LTC insurance, Congress passed legislation effective January 1, 1997, that

- Makes reimbursement for long-term care expenses nontaxable for policies that qualify under the law. Payments under $175 per day are tax-free for qualified plans.
- Treats employer-based LTC insurance policies the same as ac-

cident and health insurance policies. Employers can deduct 100 percent of employees' LTC premiums without reporting the payments as employee taxable income.

- Allows self-employed individuals to deduct a portion of the premium. The percentage started at 40 percent in 1997 and will grow to 80 percent in 2006. The balance of the premium can be deducted as unreimbursed medical expense.
- Allows everyone else to deduct LTC insurance premiums as unreimbursed medical expenses when medical expenses exceed 7.5 percent of adjusted gross income. This deduction is subject to the following limitations:

Under age 40	$ 200
Age 41–50	375
Age 51–60	750
Age 61–70	2,000
Over age 71	2,500

- Grandfathered all LTC policies issued prior to January 1, 1997. LTC insurance policies issued after that date must meet strict federal eligibility standards, which require certification by a licensed health practitioner that the insured is impaired for a minimum of ninety days in at least two of six **activities of daily living (ADLs)** or that the insured needs substantial supervision due to severe cognitive impairment.

With a tax-qualified plan, medical necessity does not trigger benefits. This means that if your doctor says that you cannot function independently due to injury or sickness or a stable medical condition, you will not receive benefits. But if he or she certifies that for a minimum of ninety days you cannot do at least two of six ADLs or that you need substantial supervision due to cognitive impairment, then benefits will start. (Cognitive impairment is confusion or disorientation resulting from loss or deterioration of intellectual capacity that is not related to or a result of mental illness, but can result from Alzheimer's disease, senility, or irreversible dementia.)[2] Appendix I describes the ADLs required by qualified LTC insurance plans.

Jerry learned through his father's experience that Medicare does not pay for custodial care on an ongoing basis. Medicare may pay for limited home care or the first twenty days of nursing home care, and for an additional eighty days of nursing home care in excess of $97 per day.

The purpose of LTC insurance is not just to pay for the nursing home—this insurance may be the only thing that keeps you *out* of a nursing home. For every person in a nursing home, six others are being cared for at home or in a community setting such as an adult day care facility.[3]

Jerry and Roger decide that buying LTC insurance is really a priority for both of them. Jerry knows that caregiving help can make life considerably more tolerable for both of them should they need long-term care, and he wants to be sure it will be available as soon as possible when they need it.

They each purchase a "comprehensive" policy that provides for nursing care both in the home and in a facility. They also purchase a feature that will increase their daily benefit by 5 percent compounded every year. This will help protect them against increases in health care costs due to inflation. Since nursing care currently costs approximately $150 a day in the area where they live, they purchase plans that provide $150 a day for long-term care. The inflation protection feature in the policies will increase the daily payment to $398 in twenty years. Their premium will be constant from the first day and will remain the same even with the increasing daily benefit.

Because they are young and the premium is low, the LTC insurance policies they purchase have a number of other features they

2. With permission, Sandi Kruise Insurance Training, California Long-Term Care CTQ Program, 1997, page 6.

3. *Overcoming Common Objections to Long-Term Care Insurance,* Life Insurance Selling, December 1997, Jesse R. Slome, CLU, ChFC.

consider important. There is a short elimination period, twenty days, which is the period Medicare pays in full but no waiting period for care in their home or a residential care facility. They also have a bed reservation benefit that pays to keep their bed available should they go to a hospital from the nursing home; an assisted-living benefit in a licensed residential care facility; restoration of benefit should they not need benefits for six continuous months; and money to provide training and respite for an unpaid caregiver. Since they want to stay out of a nursing home as long as possible, they also have a feature that pays for home modification. Should one of them have a stroke, for example, this feature would pay for the installation of a ramp and special bars for support.

Step-by-Step Instructions for Jerry

1. Jerry contacts his insurance broker and requests proposals from several financially sound long-term care insurance carriers. Jerry wants LTC coverage for both of them.
2. They ask their insurance broker to find a company that discounts the premium when two people in the same household purchase LTC insurance at the same time.
3. Jerry and Roger apply for the most they can afford in a comprehensive LTC policy. Since they are both young, they lock in the benefit at $150 per day with a twenty-day waiting period and a lifetime payment. Their daily benefit will increase but their premium remains constant.
4. They complete a medical questionnaire as part of the application, and authorize the insurance company to send an APS (attending physician statement) request to their doctors.
5. Once their policies are issued, they pay the premium by direct deposit from their checking account.

SUMMARY

In this chapter, we have seen that it is possible to obtain health insurance even if you have a medical history. Here are two other strategies using a professional employer organization. If you have a hobby that can be turned into a business, then talk to your accountant. Many a hobby has become a successful business. The IRS actually rewards you when you turn a hobby into a business—you can have a loss in three out of five years. What if you and your partner worked at your part-time hobby business together? If this is your case and you are having a tough time getting health insurance, consider contracting with a PEO to be your human resources department and joining their health plan.

Here's how Roger can deduct his COBRA premium. When he starts his business, Roger can contract with a PEO even while he is still on COBRA. He can then be reimbursed for his COBRA premium through the PEO's cafeteria plan. If he does that then his COBRA premium will be fully deductible as part of his business expense when he pays the PEO. He can join the PEO's health plan after he exhausts his COBRA benefits or at the beginning of the next new year.

If you have not considered LTC because it's too costly or you think that you are too young, think of it as an investment. What other investment will give you enough money to pay for assistance when you can no longer manage on your own and increase in value without increasing your cost? Think of long-term care insurance as part of your disability insurance program. Remember, LTC will pay when Medicare, disability insurance, or your health benefits won't. It will help you avoid the gay penalty on health care.

CHAPTER 10

Documents That Protect You When Marriage Laws Don't

The only certainty is that nothing is certain. —Pliny the Elder

After living together for seven years, Sharon and Pauline thought they had it all. Sharon loved Pauline's children and they loved her. The two women had a joint checking account and were quite comfortable sharing expenses. They also shared a bank money market account that was in Pauline's name, depositing extra funds whenever they could. The title to the house was held so the survivor would get it if one of them died. Since Pauline earned considerably more than Sharon, the car and the mortgage were in her name. When they redecorated last year, Pauline bought Sharon a new bedroom set as an anniversary gift. Life was good. Pauline and Sharon dreamed of retiring together and enjoying each other's company for many years.

Then disaster struck. One night as Pauline was driving home from work in Boulder, a drunk driver slammed into her car and she was seriously injured. The hospital wouldn't let Sharon visit. "Not family," they told her. When Pauline died, members of Pauline's family who had seemed supportive revealed their true feelings. Sharon's right to the house was challenged because there was no will confirming her intentions for the house. Since Pauline hadn't changed the beneficiary on her retirement plan, Sharon lost access to those funds. Sharon learned that it doesn't matter what everyone takes for granted.

Both women had wanted to be buried in their community so their friends could come to the funerals, but no arrangements had been made. Pauline's parents took her remains back East for a family funeral that excluded Sharon and their friends.

Sharon never saw the children again. She was left financially and emotionally destitute—no home, no furniture, no car, no retirement funds, and no children.

This kind of tragedy happens all too frequently in the lesbian and gay community. It is particularly poignant because it is usually avoidable. With proper financial and estate planning, Sharon would have been at Pauline's bedside in her last moments, and her future could have been secure. Many lesbian and gay couples either don't see the possibility of a future problem or don't know that help is readily available to avoid it.

INTRODUCTION

Sharon and Pauline probably sound familiar. You may know of situations just like theirs. In this chapter, you will learn about important documents that can be used to avoid a similar tragedy. This is one of the most important areas in which you should be proactive.

As a lesbian or gay couple, you cannot take anything for granted when it comes to families, medical emergencies, employment benefits, and death. It doesn't matter how long you have been together, how favorable you think the area where you live is, or how supportive your relatives are—people become weird around death, and opposition can arise where you least expect it. If you have not read *Why Can't Sharon Kowalski Come Home*, by Karen Thompson and Julie Andrzejewski, now would be a good time.

In this chapter, we examine protective documents from several angles: first, how you can ensure that your partner can be present and make decisions for you in a medical emergency or when you are not available; second, what you should have in place to protect yourself, your partner, and your children if you break up; and finally, what you should do to protect yourself, your partner, or your children in the event of death.

Since rules, family definitions, and/or local treatment will vary by state or jurisdiction, I strongly advise that you work with a gay or lesbian attorney or a gay-friendly attorney in your area who does estate planning or family law. This chapter has been written to encourage a discussion between you, your partner, and your advisors, including your attorney. If you do nothing else after reading this chapter, get an attorney and put in place medical and health powers of attorney that are valid in your jurisdiction and in any area to which you travel frequently. I will define these for you in greater detail shortly.

While writing this chapter, I heard of a couple in Colorado who had been together for over thirty-five years. One partner had Alzheimer's disease. The healthy partner was appointed guardian and conservator at considerable expense that could have been avoided with proper estate planning. The couple's business was sold and the proceeds from the sale were unavailable to the well partner. Don't let their tragedy be yours.

POWER OF ATTORNEY

A **power of attorney (POA)** is a written document that allows another person to act on your behalf during your lifetime. The other person is called the **attorney-in-fact** or **agent** and you are called the **principal**.

There are many situations in which you would want someone to act on your behalf. If you are out of town and you want your partner to cash your bonus check, can she or he do that? Or let's say that your partner is not listed on the deed to the house and you're in Paris on a business trip. The bank calls with a question about your last mortgage check. Can your partner handle the problem? Without the right paperwork in place, she or he may not be able to settle what would otherwise be a "no big deal" problem.

Without a POA, your partner cannot act on your behalf and you cannot act on his or her behalf. You each should have a POA signed by the other partner. However, if you are using a form found in a book or even one drafted by your attorney, it might not be acceptable when you need it. Since banks, financial institutions, and hospitals may have their own POA form, you should make sure you have the proper power of attorney in place at the institution you plan to deal with. This is a cumbersome process, but if you want the protection, you should do it.

Typically, the POA is valid only for acts performed on behalf of the principal when he or she has legal capacity, that is, when *not* disabled, mentally incompetent, under some other incapacity, or dead. If you want the POA to continue in the event you become ill or incapacitated, it must be written as a **durable power of attorney (DPA)**. Under the Uniform Probate Code, the power of attorney is "durable" if it contains the following or similar words: "This Power of Attorney shall not be affected by subsequent disability or incapacity of the principal or lapse of time." All states have some form of the durable power of attorney.

There is a risk of abuse when using a general POA. If you do not put time limitations or activity restrictions into this document, then your partner or whomever you name as your attorney-in-fact could clean you out. Yes, this has been known to happen. Robert Frost's saying, "Good fences make good neighbors," applies here. Without limitations or restrictions built into this document, you are giving your agent full legal power to make decisions on your behalf. One strategy is to draft the DPA so that it only "springs" into effect when you are disabled and states what powers the attorney-in-fact has.

PROTECTION DURING A MEDICAL EMERGENCY

Every person—gay, lesbian, and straight—should ask themselves the following three questions:

1. Who do I want to make life-and-death medical decisions for me if I am incapacitated?
2. Who do I want at my bedside?
3. How long do I want to stay on life support if my condition is hopeless?

If you don't ask yourself these questions, you will have no say when a medical emergency arises. Protect yourself by being proactive while you are healthy. Sure these issues are uncomfortable and procrastinating is easier, but the alternative is far worse. Why risk it? There are two documents that give you the power of choice in these situations: the durable power of attorney for medical care and the living will.

Durable Power of Attorney for Medical Care

With a **durable power of attorney for medical care (DPAMC)**, you designate a person to be your attorney-in-fact, to make medical decisions for you when you can't. This document is also known as a **durable power of attorney for health care (DPAHC)**. You may put restrictions into the document to limit what the attorney-in-fact can do. For example, you may wish to specify that you do not want to have artificial life support.

In some states, life support decisions are in the DPA or the DPAMC; in other states, they are in a separate document called a **directive to physicians**, **health care proxy**, or **living will**. The name of these documents can vary by state and may *not* be accepted where you live. It is essential that you work with an attorney who is familiar with these documents and the issues in your area. The living will is a different type of document from the other two; it will be discussed in greater detail in a few pages.

You should always name a backup person or alternate in case your first choice is unable to serve—your attorney-in-fact may be out of town, sick, or not your lover or friend anymore. You may also name two people to serve together as joint attorneys-in-fact. This, however, is not advised, as it can be cumbersome when important decisions need to be made swiftly. What if one or both can't be found or they don't agree?

Your DPAMC document should be reviewed every few years, since hospitals and medical practitioners may be reluctant to accept an old document. One good strategy is to review all your POAs annually, on an anniversary date. Also, make sure you discuss the POA with the person you have appointed as your attorney-in-fact and that she or he knows what your wishes are. This is much better than your agent trying to figure out what you want from the document during a medical emergency.

In his book *Cancer as a Turning Point*, Lawrence LeShan emphasizes that one of the most important ways to survive the hospital is to have a personal advocate there with you. If your partner is to be your advocate, then you must have your health care powers in place prior to your hospital stay.

Durable Power of Attorney for Financial Management

In a medical emergency, you may not be able to manage your money, pay your bills, request insurance and company benefits, or file taxes. The list goes on and on. Exhaustion, dementia, and long periods in the hospital take their toll. With a **durable power of attorney for financial management (DPAFM)** you can name someone to manage your affairs. Again, be sure you name a backup person because the attorney-in-fact or agent may not be able to serve.

If you are concerned about giving away too much power over your legal affairs, you can put restrictions into your document or you can make it task-specific. The document, for example, can be limited to paying utility bills and depositing your paycheck, or it can be quite broad, such as covering all your legal powers. It is your decision how narrow or broad your DPA should be as long as you discuss the implications with your attorney.

The DPAFM or DPAMC can become effective when the document is written or it can spring into effect when you are incapacitated. Four fifths of all states recognize the "springing" DPA. There are several disadvantages to the springing power. First, it introduces a possible argument about whether you are actually incapable of making your own decisions. It also requires, in most instances, a court's determination of capacity so the agent can act. This can be time-consuming and expensive. Finally, it is a public process—you may not want your affairs discussed in court where you run the risk of encountering a homophobic judge with a bias against giving your partner this power.

If you trust your agent enough to give him or her these powers, consider making the DPA immediately effective, with limitations, to avoid courthouse questions. The purpose of the DPA is to avoid litigation. If the DPA is limited to when the individual becomes incapacitated or disabled, then litigation tends to be created, since the issue becomes, "Was Pat incapacitated when Lee used the DPA?" An immediate DPA with medical certification, properly drafted by a knowledgeable, community-friendly attorney, can avoid the problem.

Living Will

My mother was very depressed and wanted to die. She had had it with hospitals, surgeries, and life. My father wouldn't hear of it and couldn't accept it. My brother and I had written instructions from my mother stating that she did not want to continue medical treatment under those very circumstances. Dad, my brother, and I argued. What we really needed was more communication between us before those final terrible moments. My mother ultimately made her own decision, in her own way.

Having gone through that experience with my mother, I can tell you that a living will is absolutely essential when continuing treatment is the issue. A **living will** allows you to decide ahead of time what treatment you want when you are terminally ill and faced with end-of-life decisions. You may decide that you don't want to be on life support or you may just want "palliative care" (making the dying person comfortable). It's your choice—if you make it while you are healthy. If you wait to make these decisions when you are not healthy, you may not be physically capable of doing so, or your family may not honor your wishes. When you make no plans, you waive your right to self-determination.

The living will should be used in conjunction with the DPAMC. Think of it as detailed instructions to your physician or agent. Always be sure the two documents are consistent. Also, make sure your primary care provider has an original or certified copy in your medical records and that you take a copy to the hospital with each admission. If you travel frequently or spend a lot of time in your car, it's a good idea to have an original or certified copy of both documents in the glove compartment.

Every state has its own laws concerning these documents. In states that do not have living wills, like Michigan and Massachusetts, instructions for life support decisions can be written into the DPAMC or, as it is called in Massachusetts, the health care proxy. Utah has living wills. In Colorado, the DPAMC can prioritize whether the doctor is to follow the instructions of the agent or those contained in a living will in the event of a conflict in directions.

I cannot emphasize strongly enough the importance of a DPAMC properly prepared for your situation and goals under the laws of the jurisdiction in which you live. Because this is *not* an area for practicing do-it-yourself law, no forms have been included in this book. You will be best protected if you work with a community-friendly attorney, one who is knowledgeable in this field of law in the state where you live or spend most of your time.

PROTECTION WITH REGARD TO RELATIONSHIPS

Let's look at another real-life problem: separation or gay divorce.

How do you protect yourself if your partner falls in love with someone else? How do you divide your property when there are no marital laws to protect you? What are your expectations if your partner has more income or assets than you? What are the issues? What are the challenges? What can you do if you are co-mingling your income and assets?

Tough questions? You bet.

Avoiding a Horrible Gay Divorce

The best way to protect your relationship is through clear communication. When one partner in a relationship earns substantially more money or has substantially more assets than the other, tension and uncertainty can exist. This tension should be dealt with openly and incorporated into a partnership agreement. For example, an agreement can recognize the value of monetary contribution by one partner and intangible contribution by the other partner.

We all bring our own "stuff" with us when we enter a relationship, including our family's attitude toward money. If we don't talk about it in the beginning of our relationship, money issues are sure to erupt later. Different attitudes about money are one of the biggest reasons for straight divorces—why would it be different for lesbian or gay couples?

The exercises found in the book *Money Harmony: Resolving Money Conflicts in Your Life and Relationships*, by Olivia Mellan, are a good resource to help you open a channel of communication.

Domestic Partnership/ Living-Together Agreements

Under state marital laws, a nuptial or prenuptial agreement changes the marital rules for property division in the case of death or divorce. A **domestic partnership agreement**, or a "living-together" agreement, sets forth the agreement you and your partner have should you separate or divorce in the future. This agreement serves in place of the divorce laws available to heterosexual couples. In essence, it is the use of contract law in place of state marital law. As not all courts may honor such a document, it is important that you review this area with your attorney.

A domestic partnership agreement is similar to a prenuptial or nuptial agreement in that it opens a channel of communication between the partners and helps bring clarity early in the relationship. By revealing each partner's assumptions, you can discover expectations that may differ, or that are unacceptable to each other. Would you rather find out in the beginning of the relationship or ten years later?

The difficult part of doing a domestic partnership agreement is deciding how the relationship should end and who gets what. The best time to do this is when you are in love and you really want to get to know each other, not when you are angry and hate each other.

As a financial planner for over twenty years, one of the things that I have discovered is that couples really don't talk to each other about finances. The fact that there are no marital laws to protect you in the event of separation is a major advantage you have over straight couples. You are, in effect, forced to tackle issues that straight couples tend to procrastinate about. If you don't tackle the issues, you give up the advantage.

WHAT TO ASK YOURSELF AND EACH OTHER

The process of drafting a domestic partnership agreement includes revealing all of your assets, liabilities, expenses, and income. All financial sources must be disclosed. Whether your estate is large or small, consider using separate attorneys. This avoids a later claim by one party that he or she was intimidated or didn't understand the agreement. It helps make the agreement a legally enforceable contract.

A good domestic partnership agreement often includes a clause stating that if the parties break up or disagree about their finances, they will resolve their differences through **mediation**, a process in which a trained neutral person helps disputing parties to resolve their differences without going to court. Even if the partners do not have a domestic partnership agreement, a community-friendly mediator can do wonders to resolve problems.

Creating a domestic partnership agreement can be difficult because there are no rules to guide you in the event of death or separation. Let's look at some questions that Sharon and Pauline didn't address, but you can.

If you contribute more to your relationship financially or came in with more assets than your partner, how would you want your money, investments, and possessions distributed if you die or break up after being together five years? Ten years? Twenty years? If you contribute less to your relationship financially or came in with less assets than your partner, how would you expect the money, investments, and possessions that the two of you have shared be distributed if either one of you dies, becomes incapacitated, or if you break up after being together five years? Ten years? Twenty years?

How would you expect your partner to provide for you if you were sick for two, five, or ten years? What would you do for your partner? Would you pay his or her debts when you had no legal obligation to do so? What are your partner's answers to the same questions? Relationships are about communication, support, caring, and, yes, money.

The tax code says that you can give anyone up to $10,000 per year gift-tax-free. If one partner supports the other, then you are making gifts. Have you been filing gift tax returns? Most couples don't, creating a ticking time bomb. If you are audited, this bomb could explode. What financial planning have you done to make sure you or your partner is not surprised in an audit and required to pay extra taxes?

Get the picture?

This process is not easy. Think of the process as an opportunity to reach new levels of communication in your relationship. And have fun doing it.

PROTECTION FOR PARENTS AND CHILDREN

Second-Parent Adoptions

The National Center for Lesbian Rights (NCLR) originated the concept of second-parent adoptions in the 1980s as a means of protecting the children in lesbian-headed families. In the years since NCLR originated the concept, second-parent adoptions (also called co-parent adoptions) have been granted in a steadily growing number of state and county jurisdictions.

A **second-parent adoption** is a legal procedure that allows a same-sex co-parent to adopt his or her partner's child. It is similar to a traditional adoption in that it establishes the legal relationship between an adult and a child without requiring the biological or other legal parent to relinquish his or her parental status.

Second-parent adoptions protect children in lesbian and gay families by giving the child the security of having two legal parents. It also protects the rights of the nonbiological or nonlegal parent by ensuring that she or he will continue to have a legally recognized parental relationship with the child if the couple separates, or if the biological or the original adoptive parent dies or becomes incapacitated.

The laws concerning second-parent adoptions vary by state and even by jurisdiction and are beyond the scope of this book. If you are in a family with children or are considering having children, consult an attorney in your community who specializes in this area or contact NCLR for a referral: 415-392-6257. This is not a matter that should be postponed as your family's survival could depend on it.

Alternatives When Adoption Is Not Possible

If second-parent adoption is not possible, then it is essential that you have the following documents or their equivalent in your state. While these documents are powerful and effective statements of intention, there is a chance they may not be enforceable if challenged.

- **Will** nominating a guardian for the minor child in the event of your death. Wills must be current and spell out why the non-biological parent has been nominated as guardian
- **Nomination of guardianship** in case you are incapacitated and cannot care for the child
- **Durable power of attorney for medical care** for your child in case you are not available. Everyone who has legal responsibility for your child(ren)—day care and child care providers, gymnastic coaches, dance instructors—should have original or certified copies of the DPAMC. In some states, like Texas, you need to have a separate power of attorney for health care and a durable power of attorney for everything else.

With all of these documents, it is recommended that you also tell your friends and family, if appropriate, about your intentions and desires, so that they can serve as witnesses in the event of a legal challenge to your nominations. When only one parent is a legal parent and there are no written instructions, there are basically no legal rights available to the nonbiological parent or the couple's children. At times like this, homophobia can have a disastrous effect on your life and the life of your child.

PROTECTION IN THE EVENT OF DEATH

Last Will and Testament

A **will** is a formal expression of your wishes with respect to who gets what after your death. It only "speaks" at the time of your death, and it has no significance during your lifetime other than the fact you know it exists and you have your final wishes in writing. You can change your will at any time while you are alive and are competent to do so, but the changes must be formally made, just as when the will was drafted. The person whom you have named as your **executor** (the one who implements the provisions of your will) has authority to act only after your death; he or she has no authority if you become disabled or incapacitated.

If you die without a will, you are said to have died **intestate**. Every state has specific laws that determine distribution of property in estates that are intestate. Intestacy laws treat you and your partner as strangers, no matter how long or committed your relationship. This is exactly why Pauline's parents could get away with leaving Sharon destitute. A will would have prevented Pauline's estate from falling under the intestacy laws in their state.

Even though the will is a set of instructions for the disposition of your property, the process is not automatic. While wills are instructions for your executor, that person's authority to act as your executor comes from the probate court, which must approve your nomination. The probate court will be the one in the jurisdiction where you lived at the time of your death.

The main advantage of using a will and the probate process is simplicity. Writing a will is easy. Your instructions will usually be carried out, and once the probate process is complete, the document has the authority of the court and cannot easily be disputed. If you don't have a will, then your property will be equally divided among your family in a specific order—children, then parents, and then siblings—but *not* your partner. Your partner has no legal right to any portion of your estate without a will or other testamentory instructions.

The disadvantages of a will are the time the probate process takes, the fact that the will becomes public information, and the expense of having an attorney shepherd your executor through the proceedings. It is important to check with your attorney when preparing a will, since small estates in some states, such as California and Texas, may not have to be probated. Other states, like Utah, have expedited probate procedures for small estates and simple estates. Under the Uniform Probate Code the process is simpler but it can still take six to twelve months for average-size estates.

Wills and Real Estate

If you own real estate jointly with your partner, a will confirms your intentions. On occasion, family members have argued, and courts have accepted, that the decision to hold title to property as joint tenants with right of survivorship was actually a casual decision made because the real estate agent or the accountant recommended it, or because "everybody does it." This is exactly what happened to Sharon and Pauline.

If your property is titled "joint tenants with right of survivorship" and the will also says that the property is to go to your partner, then obviously you thought this out beforehand and it was not a casual decision. Under these conditions, your wishes are more likely to be upheld. If your will leaves your non–real estate property to someone other than your partner and you want the real estate to go to your partner, you need to include a clause like this:

> *All of my property to _____, with the exception of my property at _____ to go to my partner, _____.*

Some states, like Texas, do not recognize the holding of property as "joint tenants with right of survivorship." You can, however, create survivorship interests with a separate filing consistent with the Texas probate code. Such nuances underscore the necessity of selecting an attorney familiar with legal issues and state requirements that affect the lesbian and gay community.

Alternatives to a Will

Not all property requires a will. Life insurance, annuities, and qualified retirement plans such as IRAs and 401(k)s have beneficiary designations that can take the place of a will. It is important that beneficiary designations be reviewed from time to time and be kept current. If the beneficiary is not living and there is no contingent beneficiary, the property will go to the estate and the estate will incur unnecessary expense and delays. Any beneficiary designation changes should be photocopied and sent by certified mail. This is your only proof if the notification is lost in the mail or ignored.

Accounts and investments with payable-on-death or transfer-on-death designations pass directly to the named beneficiary with proof of death and avoid the probate process. If Pauline had a payable-on-death designation on her savings account, Sharon would have collected the account without question and outside the probate process.

In some states TOD designations may be used for other assets. For example, in California, you can register your car at the Department of Motor Vehicles with a TOD. If you share your car and your will isn't current, check this out with your DMV.

Totten trusts, generally found on bank accounts, will pass directly to the named person at death. Not all states use the Totten trust designation. If you have a bank account, for example, that you want to share but don't because your partner is subject to liability risks or credit risks, you can keep it in your name as a Totten trust or POD account and give him or her a POA for that account. The Totten trust or POD designation and the POA would be established using forms provided by your bank.

If you are afraid of a challenge by unhappy relatives, it is prudent to also have a will confirming your intentions even though the POD transfer occurs outside the will. Why risk the aggravation when trouble can be avoided by the small step of having a will confirming your intentions?

Final Expenses

A will can help the executor minimize estate settlement costs. It can also specify where the money comes from to pay your final expenses, which generally include medical bills, funeral or cremation costs, and taxes.

Probate can be costly. In some states, probate fees can be as high as 5 percent of the assets that pass through probate. And, unlike the federal estate laws where debt is deducted from the estate, some states calculate the probate fee based on all assets passing through probate, while ignoring debt. This is cash paid out of the estate that is gone forever. There could be other costs: legal fees, preparation of tax returns, litigating will contests, filing fees, and so on.

These costs can be reduced if your partner or a family member is the executor or personal representative as it is called in some states. She or he may charge fees but does not have to. Ethical attorneys will tell you in advance what their fees will be for certain services or will charge by the hour and document their time. In states where probate is expensive and time-consuming, a living trust can help avoid a large part of the cost.

In some states, you can designate an agent to control the disposition of your remains. In this manner, you ensure that your wishes concerning burial or cremation instructions are met. You also ensure your partner's inclusion in the memorial service.

Revocable Living Trust

Once you have a will in place, you can get more sophisticated. A living (inter vivos) trust is one way for you to avoid probate and its associated costs and delays. A living trust can be used to give your property to whomever you want. Because this trust is revocable during your lifetime, you can think of this as a change-your-mind-trust. Once you die, the trust becomes irrevocable, or permanent; your property passes to your beneficiaries under the trust without a court proceeding (probate).

Unlike a will, trusts are private and are not part of the public record. They avoid delays and reduce administration fees and costs. You can use a living trust when purchasing life insurance (see chapter 6). A will is still important because it covers property you acquired after you established the trust and property you haven't put in it or may have forgotten about. Had Sharon and Pauline's house been in a trust, or had there been a will confirming transfer intentions, Sharon could have kept the house and might still be living there.

One strategy is to hold title to the house as tenants in common, a form of ownership in which each partner owns half and has a will. A separate living trust for each partner where the trust is the owner of that partner's half of the house might also be appropriate, depending upon the size of the estate. At death everything passes to the beneficiary. Should the relationship or distribution change, the living trust can be changed. Is it expensive? Ask your attorney. It's certainly cheaper and less problematic than doing nothing and hoping for the best!

The problem with the revocable living trust is twofold: you must keep it current by putting all newly acquired property into it, and it does not reduce federal estate taxes. When you use a revocable living trust, all of your property must be retitled into the trust's name, even if you appoint yourself as trustee. Also, trusts cost more to prepare than wills do.

If both of you have a large estate or significant assets—investments, businesses, furniture, cars—a good strategy is for each of you to have your own living trust. This way, there is less chance of the deceased's relatives (or anyone else) stepping in and challenging the trust.

Large Estates

A revocable living trust will *not* reduce federal estate taxes. Since you can buy, sell, or transfer property in the trust during your lifetime, assets in a living trust are considered to be in your estate and are subject to all federal estate taxes. Estates exceeding the unified credit exemption equivalent will require more sophisticated estate planning, such as the use of the irrevocable life insurance trust discussed in chapter 6, charitable trusts discussed in chapters 11 and 12, or family limited partnerships or other sophisticated estate planning strategies. In this area you will want to seek out an estate attorney experienced in advanced estate planning and with a background in tax law.

Business Interests

If you or your partner owns an interest in a business, you will probably have large estate issues. Your community-friendly financial advisor, insurance agent, or attorney can help you here.

A key issue to consider is whether or not you want the business to continue after your death. If the answer is yes, then you will need a "buy/sell agreement" or "practice continuation agreement" with the person or persons who will continue the business. Life insurance is usually the means to fund a buy/sell agreement because cash will be needed to buy out the deceased's interest in the business.

In many states, when a partner dies the business ceases to exist unless there is a written plan for the business to continue.

Step-by-Step Instructions
for Pauline and Sharon

1. Sharon and Pauline call the local gay and lesbian resources center in their town for a reference to a family-law attorney familiar with the needs of lesbian and gay couples.

2. They prepare a list of all of their assets, liabilities, sources of income, and expenses prior to meeting the attorney.

3. They request that the attorney prepare documents that will enable them to make medical decisions for the other one should there be a medical emergency. The attorney prepares a durable power of attorney for medical care and a living will for both of them and for Pauline's children.

4. At their request, the attorney prepares wills for them.

5. At their request, the attorney prepares a living-together agreement (Colorado's name for a domestic partnership agreement).

6. Sharon tells the attorney that she would like to adopt Pauline's children and learns that Colorado does not allow co-parent adoptions. They ask their attorney what they can do to protect themselves and the children in the event of death or divorce. The attorney recommends that they have a joint custody agreement (although the nonbiological parent will not be recognized as a legal parent).

7. Pauline changes the beneficiary designation on her retirement plans to Sharon.

8. Sharon and Pauline review the beneficiary designations on their personal and group life insurance policies and name each other as the beneficiary.

9. Pauline goes to her bank and adds a payable-on-death designation to her accounts with Sharon as the beneficiary.

10. Having taken care of their legal documents, Pauline and Sharon contact a financial planner to review their life insurance and investment portfolio, as their attorney feels there might be financial and estate planning needs beyond the scope of her practice.

11. Pauline and Sharon decide that if they want adoption rights they'd better get politically active and campaign for it rather than hope for the best.

A FINAL NOTE OF CAUTION

Preparing your legal documents is a state-specific activity. What is valid in one state may not be true in your state. Document names may differ from state to state. A court decision could change the ground rules in your jurisdiction or state overnight.

While the temptation might be there to prepare your own legal documents to save a few dollars in legal fees, just remember the cost, if tragedy strikes, will be far greater than any amount you could possibly save in dollars. Educate yourself and read NOLO Press's books, but don't practice law yourself. The books don't have the latest nuances for your situation in your jurisdiction.

This is the one area where you must work with a community-friendly attorney who understands the legal issues of lesbian and gay couples and their children. *This is not a do-it-yourself area!*

STEP 3:

THINK COMMUNITY

Step 3 shows you ways to overcome estate laws that do not allow you to transfer unlimited amounts of property to your partner without the government taking a portion of it in the form of estate taxes.

Chapter 11 shows you how to avoid capital gains taxes on property that you want to sell while creating a source of income for your surviving partner.

Chapter 12 deals with two critical issues concerning retirement plans for lesbian and gay couples. The first part of chapter 12 shows how to transfer assets in a retirement plan to a surviving partner who cannot do an IRA rollover. The second part of the chapter shows how to protect a surviving partner when the assets in his or her lover's retirement plan revert back to the employer's retirement plan.

CHAPTER 11

Avoiding
Capital Gains Taxes

*In necessary things, unity; in disputed things, liberty; in all
things, charity.*   —Motto used by 17th-century English
clergyman Richard Baxter

Jimmy and Ryan live in Ryan's big old Victorian house in San
Francisco. Jimmy, six-foot-two, with pearl-blue eyes and gray
temples, and bronzed from too much sun, looks much younger
than his 60 years of age. Ryan, on the other hand, never works out,
loves to sit and draw at his computer, is a little wide in the middle,
and has wrinkles from laughing a lot.

Their other house is a rental property that Jimmy owns. Jimmy
bought it in 1965 for $62,000 and put enough improvements into it
that his cost for tax purposes is now $100,000. One tenant argues all
the time with his partner resulting in complaints from the neighbors, and the other tenant always pays his rent late.

The house has a $12,000 mortgage and a rental income of
$18,000 after operating expenses. Jimmy thought he had an 18 per-
cent return, until he divided the house's current value into the net
rent and discovered that it is yielding only 3.4 percent before taxes.
He also knows that his income is barely keeping up with inflation.
He wants more income and he's tired of dealing with tenant problems. He desperately wants out of the real estate rental business.

Several people have indicated that they would like to buy the rental property from Jimmy. He estimates that he would receive $535,000 after selling expenses if he sold the property based on a recent appraisal. If Jimmy were to sell his rental property, he would lose a substantial portion of its value to taxes. Because he hates the idea of paying taxes even more than the grief he suffers from owning the building, he hasn't put it on the market yet.

Ryan, a graphic artist, has not been concerned about finances. His stock "portfolio," currently worth $250,000, is composed entirely of stock in one company—which he bought on a hot tip from a New York cab driver thirty years ago. At the time, Ryan had $1,500 in the bank. He invested it all in a little hamburger company with golden arches. He just forgot about the stock, which had cost him 30 cents per share. What did he know about stocks? Now that he is older and wiser, a vegetarian, and in a relationship with a man he loves, he wants to diversify his portfolio and live on his investment income when he retires in ten years at age 65.

Ryan has the same problem as Jimmy. If Ryan sells to get more diversification, he too will lose a significant portion to taxes. He is not crazy about this idea.

Both Jimmy and Ryan are committed to helping the gay community. Jimmy is an active member of his church, which has a gay outreach ministry. Ryan's last lover died from AIDS and he would like to make a difference in the community by helping the local AIDS foundation. He currently volunteers a lot of his spare time to various AIDS programs. Jimmy and Ryan think they have enough assets to create a secure retirement income, but they don't know how to put it all together.

LOOKING AHEAD

Jimmy and Ryan are faced with a dilemma. On one hand, they want to sell their property and reposition the proceeds. On the other hand, they don't want to give the government one fourth of their gain. In this chapter we are going to see how they can have their cake and eat it too.

Let's begin by looking at the portion of income and property you think is yours. If you add federal income tax (between 15 percent and 39.6 percent as of this writing) to state income tax, capital gains tax, gift tax, sales tax, and Social Security and Medicare taxes, you really only get to keep approximately half of your income. And, when you die, what's left may be subject to estate tax. Between federal estate taxes and state estate inheritance taxes, your heirs may receive half or less of what you had before you died.

What happens to the half that is taken in taxes? It belongs to society. The traditional way it goes back to society is by government spending. How do you feel about the way the government distributes your money? What if there was a way to control the amount that goes to society? What if you could say how society should use it, instead of letting the government decide?

Well, the good news is that you can. In 1969, Congress passed some wonderful laws establishing clear rules for charitable giving. It is now possible to establish a trust that lets you give your property away, reduce your income tax, not pay capital gains tax, and increase your income. Hard to believe, but true.

Jimmy and Ryan want to convert low-cost, low-yield property to higher-yielding income property. They want to retire without getting killed on taxes. Essentially, they want more money.

They are also concerned about the community and would like to help in some larger way, but feel they can't afford it. They want to protect each other if one of them dies, and they want to keep investment-management control of their assets.

In this chapter, we look at the use of charitable trusts to solve Jimmy and Ryan's problem and help them achieve all of their goals.

THE CHARITABLE REMAINDER TRUST

A Way to Give Yet Keep—
and Increase Your Income

A charitable remainder trust enables you to make a gift to charity today with delivery deferred until the future. This way, you, or you and another person (called an income beneficiary or beneficiaries) can receive income before the assets are actually delivered.

The **charitable remainder trust (CRT)** takes on the tax-free characteristics of a charity when it is established. When you give an asset to the trust and that asset is then sold by the trust, it pays no tax on the sale and you keep the income, which can increase. The trust can invest the proceeds and change investments, even realizing gains without being obliged to pay taxes. In this respect, it is like an IRA.

You have two options when determining what the payment to the income beneficiary or beneficiaries will be. The trust can pay out a percentage of the fair market value of its assets as re-valued each year (but not less than 5 percent), or it can pay out a fixed dollar amount. The payments are called distributions. The first strategy is called a **charitable remainder unitrust (CRUT)**. The second one is called a **charitable remainder annuity trust (CRAT)**.

A Way to Give Your Partner More Income

The distributions paid by the trust go to the income beneficiary or beneficiaries for life, or for a term of years. If there is more than one income beneficiary, the distribution is paid for the life of the beneficiary and then the successor beneficiary. At the end of the life of all the income beneficiaries—or the end of the term if the trust has a set number of years (not to exceed twenty)—the trust assets go to one or more charities that the donor designated in the trust document.

If you are wondering why a charitable remainder trust works so well for Jimmy and Ryan, it is because Jimmy will get an estate tax deduction that effectively makes up for part of the lost marital deduction. When a husband or wife dies, the deceased spouse can pass any amount of assets to the surviving spouse without federal estate taxes. As you will recall from chapter 3, you cannot do this. You can only pass an amount equal to the unified credit exemption equivalent ($650,000 in 1999) to your partner without federal estate tax. The property that Jimmy puts into a charitable remainder trust can continue to give Ryan income without being taxed in Jimmy's estate. The rest of the chapter explains how this works.

The donated property is usually sold by the trust and converted to income investments so that the trust can make its required distributions. Many times people will put appreciated stocks or mutual funds into the trust. Jimmy's rental property is in the Castro district, a highly desirable gay neighborhood in San Francisco, so he is confident that the trust can sell it easily, especially since he has received several informal offers. As long as they have not signed an agreement or received a binding offer, they can use the charitable trust.

The percentage of fair market value of trust assets that is used to determine the percentage payout from the CRUT, or the fixed dollar amount from the CRAT, is set when the trust is established; it does not have to be the same as the earnings of the investments held in the trust.

Income Hedged Against Inflation

CRUTs can help you inflation-hedge your income. The payment based on a percentage of annual asset value will also grow, if the value of the assets in the trust grows. Income, then, will be hedged against inflation. Of course, if trust investments drop in value, income will be lower.

Let's summarize the benefits and see how this strategy would work, using Jimmy's rental property as the example:

- No capital gains tax on appreciated assets sold by the trust
- Income for life or for a term of years
- Income can be higher than that available from current investments
- Increasing income in an "up" stock market
- Tax-deferred growth
- Tax deductions

If Jimmy and Ryan establish a two-life charitable remainder unitrust with an 8 percent payout rate, their situation will improve

138 percent over keeping the rental property and 27 percent over an outright sale. The following summarizes their income alternatives:

Establish a charitable remainder unitrust $42,800/year
Sell outright, pay taxes, invest the proceeds $33,600/year
Keep the rental income $18,000/year

If we assume that the house nets $535,000 after selling costs and that the trust is paying 8 percent, then $42,800 per year is the distribution from the charitable remainder unitrust. If the house is sold outright, but without the CRUT, then the net remaining after taxes is closer to $420,000. At 8 percent, the income would be a fixed $33,600, compared to Jimmy's current net rental income of $18,000.

FREQUENTLY ASKED QUESTIONS

Let's review twelve frequently asked questions. Then, we'll learn the specific actions Jimmy and Ryan must complete to achieve their goals: to make more money, pay less in taxes, and help the community.

1. What can I put into the charitable trust?
Anything that you can legitimately give to charity can go into the trust. For example, if you have art that has increased in value since you purchased it, and you know there is a market for it, you can put it into the trust. You can put an "interest" in a property, such as a 25 percent or 50 percent ownership interest in a shopping center, stocks, bonds, mutual funds—almost anything. If, however, you are contributing property that is not publicly traded, then you will have to provide an appraisal by a qualified appraiser to justify the value of the asset contributed to avoid a disqualification by the IRS.

You can donate your home as long as you are not living in it at the time of the donation. If, for example, you want to sell your home that has considerably more gains in it than your $250,000 exemption because you are moving into your lover's home and you would like to use the proceeds to generate income. Consider the following: a split interest gift where you keep the $250,000 exemption and that portion of the cost basis that exceeds any unpaid mortgage. The portion that exceeds the $250,000 plus the cost basis goes to the charitable remainder trust.

You can also donate life insurance that you own. You must, however, be careful with the cash value. If the cost basis that is the total premium paid is less than the accumulated cash value in the policy, then you will have a taxable profit that will require taxes to be paid prior to the contribution. The law does not allow you to give away taxable income without paying taxes.

2. What about debt?

You also cannot give property that is encumbered with debt to a charitable trust. If the debt is forgiven, the IRS will say that you have just received a windfall. Windfalls are taxable. The debt must either be paid off or transferred to another property before the gift is made. This can be tricky with mortgages and unmarried couples.

There may be other solutions as well. An attorney who specializes in advanced estate planning can help you.

3. What are the tax benefits?

First, there is avoidance or deferral of capital gains tax. No capital gains tax is due on property sold by the trust. If you put property into the trust that cost you peanuts many years ago, when the trust sells it for a higher figure, it pays no capital gains tax. The full market value can be invested to generate income.

Second, investments in the trust can grow in a tax-deferred environment, similar to an IRA.

Third, what you put into the trust is partially tax-deductible in the year of donation. The amount that cannot be deducted in the year of donation can be carried forward, for up to five more years.

Fourth, the value of the asset or property that goes into the trust is deducted from your estate when you die. If you are using a single-life trust, it is fully deductible from the estate at the time of death.

If you are using a two-life trust and your partner will continue to receive income from the trust after your death, the deduction from the estate is calculated differently. In a two-life trust the property is included in the estate and the estate tax charitable deduction is based on the life expectancy of the second beneficiary. Obviously, this calls for a knowledgeable estate planning attorney.

4. What is the income tax charitable deduction?
The amount of the income tax deduction is based on the payout rate (which cannot be less than 5 percent for a charitable remainder unitrust), the length of time the trust is assumed to last, a Treasury Department discount rate that changes each month and the type of charity (personal foundations and social organizations have lower deduction limits). In financial planning jargon, the deduction is the present value of the future gift. In our example, since the trust will not pay the principal to the charity until after Jimmy and Ryan have both died, the deduction will be relatively small.

The table below shows the effect on the deduction as income increases. The most a CRUT can pay out for a two-life trust based on Jimmy's and Ryan's ages (60 and 55) is 9.235 percent. People who are older can receive a larger payout.

TABLE 11.1
TWO-LIFE CRT TAX REDUCTION AND INCOME COMPARISON

	6%	8%	9.235%
Tax Deduction	$113,554	$70,764	$53,511
Annual Income	$ 32,100	$42,800	$49,407

Source: WealthNet® Charitable Trust Services © 1998.

5. How much can I deduct on my tax return every year?
If the donated property has appreciated in value since you acquired it, the most you can deduct in the year of donation is 30 percent of

your adjusted gross income. Any excess can be carried forward for up to five years.

If the property that is going into the trust is not appreciated property, you can deduct up to 50 percent of your adjusted gross income and carry forward any excess for up to five years.

"I can give this stuff directly to the charity and get a full deduction," you might think. You are partially correct. If you give the property directly to the charity, its total value is deductible. You still have the deduction limitations—30 percent for appreciated property and 50 percent for nonappreciated property—with a carryover for any excess.

Let us not forget that the purpose of the trust, however, is to provide an income, not just give the stuff away. When you retain the right to derive an income from property that is eventually going to charity, you don't get a deduction for its full value. You get a deduction for the "present value" of the future gift to the charity.

In Jimmy's case, the most he can deduct is 30 percent of his AGI in the first year, because he is giving appreciated property, and he can carry forward the excess.

Let's say Jimmy's AGI prior to establishing the trust was $50,000. Now that he is retired, it's $75,000 because of the payments from the trust, his pension, and Social Security. Jimmy can deduct $22,500 (30 percent of $75,000) and carry forward the excess for up to five years, or until the deduction is used up. (Jimmy will use the last of his deduction in the fourth year). If he takes income out at 6 percent, instead of 8 percent, his deduction will increase from $70,764 to $113,554, and he will use up the last of his deduction in the sixth year, assuming his income remains level.

6. How are distributions taxed?

Income that comes out of a trust as distributions generally retains the character of the income earned by the trust and is taxed on a complicated basis that separates ordinary income, capital gains income, tax-exempt income, and tax-free distributions of principal.

If you put cash into the trust, for example, and the trust invests it in tax-free municipal bonds, the income comes out as tax-exempt income. If you put capital gains assets into the trust, then the income that comes out will be subject to capital gains tax. Income, therefore, retains the character of the asset that went into the trust.

This area is so complicated that you must use either an administrator or an accountant who specializes in charitable trusts. The person who does your tax return every year may not be the right choice if she or he doesn't specialize in this area of tax law.

7. Can I control the assets?

This question is really about who can be the trustee. Some people want to retain control of their property and continue to manage it after the trust is established. Other people want to move on and not worry about it. Either approach can work. The trust can be written so that the donor continues to control the property as trustee, or the charity may serve as trustee, or an outside source such as a bank, attorney, or professional administrator can be the trustee. Unless you already have expertise in investing, the investments in the trust should be managed separately by professional money managers.

If you are going to put ownership of your business into the trust, you cannot continue to operate it. You can, however, continue to manage it to maintain value while the trust is selling it. You can do this only for a few months and then you must be able to prove to the IRS that the trust is selling it and that you are really not operating it as your business.

8. How is my partner protected?

You can protect your partner by also making him or her a successor beneficiary. This way, the income from the trust is paid to you and then, after your death, to your partner for the rest of his or her life.

If you are healthy and want an even bigger tax deduction, you can establish a single-life charitable trust and purchase life insurance payable to your partner to replace the assets that will go to the charity at your death. If your estate exceeds the unified credit exemption equivalent, consider using a life insurance trust as discussed in chapters 3 and 6.

9. What if my partner and I break up?

Establishing a charitable remainder trust is a reflection of your commitment to accomplishing your charitable goals and your commitment to your partner. Charitable remainder trusts are irrevocable. If you are going to use a two-life trust, you should be very sure this is what you want to do.

There are, however, two ways to partially protect against the problem of breaking up. One strategy is to use a single-life trust with a life insurance policy to protect your partner. If you are the owner of the insurance, you retain the right to change the beneficiary. However, the law says that if you retain this right, you have not given up all incidents of ownership, and therefore the policy *will* be included in your estate.

If you will be using an irrevocable life insurance trust (as discussed in chapter 6) to keep the life insurance out of your estate because you have a large estate, then you will definitely have a problem if you break up and you are the trustee on the life insurance trust. ILITs are irrevocable—they cannot be changed by the grantor. If you are going to use this type of planning strategy, you should be secure in your relationship and someone else should be the trustee.

The simplest strategy that can be used when you are using a two-life trust and not using an ILIT is to keep the right to change or revoke the successor beneficiary. By doing so, you will be protected in the event of a breakup.

10. When does the sale take place?

If Jimmy is going to sell the property that will go into the trust, then the sale must occur after the property has been transferred to the trust. You must be extremely careful in this area. If you have gotten a commitment on property to be sold, and you realize that the capital gains tax is going to be huge, it may be too late. Because the trust rules are very complicated and have many potential legal pit-falls, you must get an attorney well versed in advanced estate planning to help you.

11. Can I get my money back?

The answer to that question depends upon what you mean by "get my money back." If you hope to get back the exact amount that you put into the trust in the form that you put it in, the answer is no. If you want to receive an income that over the years will exceed what you put in, avoid capital gains tax, get tax deductions, and control where your money goes in society, the answer is yes.

12. How can a CRT substitute for a marital deduction?

As you may recall from chapter 3, the loss of the unlimited marital deduction is an area where gay and lesbian couples really lose, big time. A combination charitable reminder trust and life insurance can effectively replace the effect of the marital deduction. Here's how it works.

If your estate exceeds the unified credit exemption equivalent and you have property you want to pass to your partner, then consider putting it into a charitable remainder trust. If it is income-producing property, then the income can continue to go to you and your partner via the trust. If it is low-yielding but highly appreciated property, you can either let the trust sell it and replace it with income-producing property or put additional liquid property into the trust until you are ready to sell it.

At the same time or before you make the transfer, you purchase life insurance to replace the property that is going into the trust. Since the trust will ultimately go to a charity, the life insurance replaces the property that would have gone to your partner and the taxman. If you have a large estate, you will want an irrevocable life insurance trust to own the life insurance. Some advisors call such an ILIT a **wealth replacement trust (WRT)**. A wealth replacement trust is an irrevocable trust with life insurance in it used to replace the asset going to the charity.

What have you accomplished? You have continued the income from the asset to you and your partner. When you die, your partner will receive the equivalent value of the property she or he would have received had there been an unlimited marital deduction.

If you are uninsurable, you may want to review chapter 7 and ask your attorney about other strategies, such as the use of a charitable lead income trust or a family limited partnership.

Let's see how Jimmy and Ryan would put their plan together.

Step-by-Step Instructions
for Jimmy and Ryan

1. Jimmy and Ryan go to a financial advisor, who does a comprehensive financial and estate plan.
2. Jimmy, Ryan, and their financial advisor go to an attorney who is well versed in charitable estate tax law.
3. Jimmy establishes a two-life, 8 percent CRUT.
4. Jimmy uses personal funds to pay off the $12,000 mortgage.
5. He has the house appraised by a qualified appraiser.
6. Jimmy transfers ownership of the house to the CRUT.
7. Jimmy gets a $70,764 charitable income tax deduction and is able to take $22,500 of that on his federal form 1040 in the year of the transfer and carries forward the excess deduction to following years until used up.
8. Jimmy sells the house as trustee. No capital gains tax is paid.
9. Jimmy as trustee invests the proceeds from the house sale into mutual funds in the name of the trust.
10. As trustee, Jimmy distributes $3,567 per month to himself as income beneficiary.

The CRUT will pay Jimmy $3,567 per month. In the years that the investments in the trust are increasing at a rate greater than 8 percent, his income will increase. The trust will continue to pay the income to Ryan, as successor beneficiary should Jimmy die first, since this is a two-life trust. After Jimmy and Ryan have both died, the trust will be liquidated. The principal and any appreciation remaining in the trust will be paid to the charities that Jimmy designated when he established the trust.

Okay, what about Ryan? Ryan's situation is just a little different. He wants to do the right thing for the community, maintain investment-management control of his assets, and retire in ten years, when he will be 65. How can he sell his property, get an income tax deduction, avoid capital gains tax, retain investment-management control, and receive a higher retirement income? To resolve Ryan's situation, we are going to use a variation on the trust that Jimmy used.

ANOTHER KIND OF CRUT

Let's look at the facts. Ryan has stock that has gone up in value significantly since he bought it that he now wants to sell without getting wiped out by taxes. What to do?

Ryan can use a charitable remainder trust that pays out the *lesser* of the income it earns or the required percentage payout. The strategy here is to have the trust sell the stock and then invest in a low-yield investment—or better yet, no yield—for the accumulation period. At retirement or when Ryan wants income, the trustee then switches from the low-yield or no-yield investment to income-producing assets. This form of trust is called a "net-income with make-up charitable remainder unitrust" or, to use the jargon, a **NIMCRUT**.

Since a NIMCRUT is really just another form of charitable remainder trust, it qualifies for the income-tax deduction that applies to the distribution rate set at the time the trust was established.

During the accumulation period, a good investment vehicle that distributes no income is a variable annuity (as discussed in chapter 5). It is a tax-deferred investment that pays no dividends or interest. Since a NIMCRUT must pay out income, if it has any, a variable annuity is an ideal vehicle. The investments within the variable annuity can be a portfolio of mutual funds that adds diversification and risk management to Ryan's overall portfolio. At retirement, the trustee (Ryan) could either liquidate the variable annuity and reposition the proceeds in income-paying assets or start withdrawing income from the variable annuity. If he liquidated and repositioned the proceeds, he could use a bond fund. If he takes income from the variable annuity, he would have to follow the parameters of the variable annuity.

The trust then pays Ryan the percentage payout rate he used when he established the trust. The payment is based on the appreciated value of the assets in the trust less the portion that wasn't paid out during the accumulation periods. The portion that was not paid out during the accumulation period is available as either a lump sum or as income, if there are earnings that exceed the principal.

The easiest way to think of the assets accumulating within the NIMCRUT is as if they were in two portions of the same account. One portion pays out income and the other is a deferred or an IOU portion. The deferred portion can distribute income or a lump sum after the normal payout and if there are excess earnings in the account. The distribution from the deferred portion can be made on demand by the trustee. If Ryan wants to buy a car at retirement, for example, he could take the money out of the deferred portion. Whatever comes out of the NIMCRUT—income or lump sum—is taxable income.

Since this is really complicated, let's see how a NIMCRUT would work for Ryan assuming he uses a 7 percent single-life NIMCRUT. As trustee, he invests $250,000 from the sale of his stock into a variable annuity comprised of a number of mutual funds. If the variable annuity grows at 10 percent, in ten years he would have enough in the trust's assets to give himself an income starting at $30,188. If the principal within the trust continues to grow at 10 percent, his income would grow. If it declines, his income would decline. Table 11.2 compares a 7 percent trust to a 5 percent trust. The lower the payout rate, the larger the deduction. The higher the payout rate, the larger the deferred portion and, of course, the higher the income. (The table shows income at five-year increments for summary purposes, but it is really increasing annually as value increases.)

TABLE 11.2
CHARITABLE TRUST COMPARISON
(5% VS. 7% NIMCRUT)*

	5%	7%
Payout Rate	5%	7%
Return (Growth Rate)	10%	10%
Income Tax Deduction	$ 88,880	$ 62,937
Deferred Amount	$166,250	$217,181
INCOME		
11th Year	$24,109	$30,108
15th Year	$30,530	$40,337
20th Year	$45,567	$54,833
25th Year	$64,026	$71,633

*Source: Wealth Net ® Charitable Trust Services © 1998.

Since the asset going into Ryan's trust is a publicly listed stock, a professional appraisal is not necessary. Also, the trustee does not have to worry about a ready market, because the stock is publicly traded.

Step-by-Step Instructions for Ryan

1. Jimmy and Ryan go to a financial advisor, who does a comprehensive financial and estate plan. Their advisor then works with an estate-planning attorney.
2. Ryan has his attorney establish a single life, net-income with make-up charitable remainder trust (NIMCRUT) with a 7 percent distribution rate.
3. Ryan signs an agreement with a charitable trust administra-

tion firm to provide the accounting and reporting services to the IRS for the trust (as it is a tax-exempt trust).

4. Ryan retains his financial advisor as his investment advisor to guide him on the investments within the trust.

5. To protect Jimmy if he dies first, Ryan buys a universal life insurance policy for $250,000, to replace the assets he puts into the trust.

6. Ryan transfers the golden arches stock to his trust.

7. Ryan reports the portion of his $62,937 charitable income tax deduction that he can on his federal and state income tax returns and carries forward the unused portion up to five years or until it is used up.

8. Ryan as the trustee sells the stock and pays no capital gains.

9. Ryan as trustee invests the proceeds from the stock in a variable annuity with a diversified portfolio of growth mutual funds. He has his financial advisor do an asset allocation analysis to determine the best mix of mutual funds to put in the variable annuity (discussed in chapter 5).

10. When Ryan retires at age 65, the trustee (Ryan) instructs the variable annuity to pay out 7 percent of the fair market value of the trust less the deferred portion (the IOU account).

11. After retiring, Ryan and Jimmy decide to buy a new car. Ryan, as trustee, withdraws enough from the variable annuity to pay for the car in full. Ryan reports the withdrawal on his federal and state income tax returns in addition to the income he receives from the trust.

THE FLIP TRUST

In this chapter we have seen how a CRT can help you avoid capital gains tax on highly appreciated property you may want to sell and how you can use it to reduce estate taxes while increasing your income. What can you do, however, if you have to sell property that you want to convert to as much income as possible as soon as possible? A NIMCRUT may not be the best solution for you if it doesn't meet your objectives.

There is a new form of trust called a *flip* unitrust. A flip trust provides for the use of a net income with a make-up provision and then, when the property is sold, provides a fixed percentage payout. A flip trust, in effect, starts as a NIMCRUT and then becomes a CRUT. The real question, however, is what's the right trust for you?

A qualified financial advisor can help you develop alternative strategies first. If you are the trustee, you do not have to give up control of the management of your assets under most situations as long as the trust is properly established. Charitable estate planning is an advanced form of estate planning. Work with an attorney who specializes in this area and who is familiar with lesbian and gay issues.

CHAPTER 12

Avoiding the "Gay Penalty" on Retirement Plans

The legal right of a taxpayer to decrease the amount of what would otherwise be his taxes, or altogether avoid them, by means which the law permits, cannot be doubted.
   —Justice George Sutherland, United States Supreme Court

Louise is a professor at Texas Woman's University. She and her partner, Betty, an engineer with the city of Dallas, live in the suburb of Coppell. Betty's 22-year-old son, Reuben, has just graduated from college.

Louise is worried. She wants to find a way that Betty can receive her retirement plan assets without paying additional taxes if Louise dies before retiring. She doesn't want Betty to have the same surprise she had when her first partner, Ruthie, died.

When Ruthie passed away in 1992, she left Louise $80,000 in her 401(k). Louise thought she could transfer the proceeds from the account into an IRA in her own name, let the money grow, and start taking out an income when she retired. No big deal. Certainly made sense to her and her friends. Was she ever wrong!

To say that Louise was surprised when she had to fork over $24,800 out of her own pocket to the IRS for taxes on Ruthie's 401(k) would be an understatement. When she learned later that her sister did not have to pay any extra taxes on her husband's retirement plan when he died, she was outraged.

Now Louise has accumulated $350,000 in her own retirement

plan, a 403(b) tax-sheltered annuity. She also has $150,000 in a self-employed retirement plan (also known as a SERP or Keogh Plan) invested in mutual funds. The stock market has treated her very nicely, as she only invested $66,000 during her previous career as a writer. She hasn't added any money to the plan in ten years.

Betty has a different problem, but one that could also result in a substantial loss to Louise. Betty's retirement plan is fully funded by her employer. But what will happen to the money in the plan if she dies before retiring? She has heard that because it is an employer-funded plan, Louise will get nothing. Betty is also a little fuzzy about what would happen to her retirement assets if she retired and died before Louise.

Both Louise's and Betty's problems stem from their status as unmarried partners.

WHAT IS THE GAY PENALTY?

Lesbian and gay couples face two major problems that married couples do not have when it comes to retirement plans:

- The inability to roll over funds tax-free into an IRA when a partner dies
- The loss of retirement plan assets when a partner with an employer-funded plan dies

The first part of this chapter shows you how to avoid paying the extra taxes that are generated when you cannot roll over your partner's retirement plan without tax. (Taxes are always due on retirement plans, but lesbian and gay partners have to pay more tax and sooner than married couples.) In the second part of the chapter, we will address the employer-funded retirement plan problem.

When a person dies, the government wants its due. Income that has not yet been taxed in the year of death is called **income in respect of a decedent (IRD)**. This is a term that you should get to know. Use of this term will definitely impress your accountant and attorney. It probably won't impress your mother (unless she is an accountant or attorney). Money in a retirement plan belonging to the decedent is considered IRD and can become a taxable burden for unmarried couples. Let's take another look at Louise and Ruthie.

When Ruthie died, her estate included a $200,000 condo, jewelry, her car, furnishings, a life insurance policy that was used to pay off the mortgage, and a 401(k) worth $80,000. All of Ruthie's savings were in her 401(k). Her total estate, including the retirement plan, came to $342,000. Since the size of the estate meant that there were no federal *estate* taxes to pay, there was no reason for Louise to think that *she* was going to have to pay taxes.

However, the $80,000 in the 401(k) was never taxed; it is IRD and is subject to income tax. Because there was no cash in the estate since the life insurance was paid directly to the mortgage lender, Louise, as the only beneficiary, had to pay the shortfall in taxes to the IRS. Table 13.1 compares Louise and Ruthie's situation to that of a married couple in the same predicament.

TABLE 13.1
ESTATE COMPARISON

	Lesbian Couple	Married Couple
Condo—net	$200,000	$200,000
Personal property	62,000	62,000
401(k)	80,000	80,000
TOTAL	**$342,000**	**$342,000**
Income tax on IRD°	24,800	deferred

°*Assumes 31% federal income tax rate on the IRD.*

How is this possible? In addition to the marital deduction that allows husbands and wives to give each other any amount of money with no current tax liability, legally married couples are granted an exception to the rule on IRD for retirement plan distributions. The surviving partner in a legal marriage can do a tax-free IRA rollover and pay the tax later when he or she receives the income from the IRA at retirement. But an unmarried partner is not allowed the same privilege. Bad news, yes, but solvable, as we shall see.

Louise's estate situation will be somewhat different because of the **Taxpayer Relief Act of 1997 (TRA '97)**. Under TRA '97, the **estate tax threshold** will gradually increase to $1 million by the year 2006. Any amount in an estate that exceeds the unified credit equivalent exemption in the year of death is subject to estate tax. The limits are shown in Table 13.2.

TABLE 13.2
ESTATE TAX THRESHOLD

Year	Unified Credit Exemption Equivalent
1999	$ 650,000
2000–01	675,000
2002–03	700,000
2004	850,000
2005	950,000
2006 & after	1,000,000

Let's assume that Louise dies in 1999 and her estate totals $1,150,000 after estate closing costs. What would be the impact of additional taxes because she was in an unmarried relationship? The gay penalty would be additional taxes of $199,393, or 72 percent more taxes. Here's how it's calculated.

TABLE 13.3
ESTATE COMPARISON: FIRST PERSON'S DEATH

	Lesbian Couple	Married Couple
Retirement plans	$ 500,000	$ 500,000
Other assets	650,000	650,000
TOTAL ASSETS	$1,150,000	$1,150,000
Income & estate taxes on IRD°	$ 331,600	0
TAX AT 1ST PERSON'S DEATH	$ 331,600	N.A.

ESTATE COMPARISON: SECOND PERSON'S DEATH

	Lesbian Couple	Married Couple
Inheritance	$761,650	$1,150,000
Own assets	200,000	200,000
TOTAL ASSETS	$961,650	$1,350,000
Estate tax	$138,043	$277,000
Tax on first person's death	331,600	0
TOTAL TAXES	$ 469,643	$277,000
GAY PENALTY	$192,643	0

°*Generally, IRD must be included in gross income of the recipient; however, a deduction is normally permitted for estate taxes on the income. The $331,600 included $137,600 in federal income taxes and $194,000 in federal estate taxes. If you or your partner may be in this situation, see an estate-planning attorney.*

The gay penalty, in reality, can be a double hit. First, it is the extra tax lesbian and gay couples must pay on the excess over the unified credit exemption equivalent ($650,000 in 1999) because there is no marital deduction. Married couples can use a special form of trust that allows them to double the unified credit exemption equivalent (to $1,300,000 in 1999) when doing estate planning. (This form of trust has been referred to as a bypass, unified credit, credit shelter, or credit equivalent bypass trust and is *only* for married couples.)

Although the estate tax credit exemption equivalent increases from $650,000 in 1999 to $1 million in 2006, there probably will still be an estate tax because it's likely that Louise's and Betty's estate will increase in value from additional investments, retirement plan contributions, the effect of inflation on their assets, investment in retirement plan assets, and investment performance.

If Louise's estate grows at a net-after-tax rate of 7 percent, for example, in ten years her estate will be worth approximately $2.2 million. Subtracting the $1 million unified credit exemption equivalent still leaves a taxable estate of $1.2 million. Even though the unified credit exemption equivalent increases with the Taxpayer Relief Act of 1997, the problem does not go away—it just gets worse.

The second problem is the tax on IRD, which married couples do not have to deal with, as the surviving spouse can do an IRA rollover. The combined gay penalty in Table 13.3 is additional taxes of $192,643.

SOLVING THE ROLLOVER PROBLEM

There are three ways to reduce the effect of the gay penalty on retirement plans:

- Spread the problem out
- Convert to the "Roth estate"
- Use a charitable remainder trust

Spreading the Problem Out

In 1996, an IRS Letter Ruling said that a nonspouse beneficiary could direct the IRA trustee to transfer the IRA funds to another trustee with the nonspouse as beneficiary after the participant's death and take the distribution out up to five years.[1] Had this ruling

---

1. IRS Letter Ruling 9623037. A private letter ruling is a statement issued by the IRS National Office to a taxpayer that interprets and applies tax laws to the taxpayer's specific set of facts.

existed in 1992, it would have helped Louise by allowing her to spread the IRD out over five years.

The ruling does not eliminate the problem—it only buys time, because a beneficiary has up to five years to take the funds out. Once it comes out, however, it is fully taxable to the beneficiary. Obviously, a qualified tax advisor is essential for proper planning.

The "Roth Estate"

The **Roth IRA**, first available in 1998, lets you put up to $2,000 per year of after-tax dollars into a tax-free retirement account if your adjusted gross income is under $160,000. Withdrawals from a Roth IRA aren't taxed as income, and there are no required distributions. People who have enough money can convert an existing IRA to a Roth IRA by paying the taxes currently. Such a conversion can mean a larger estate for heirs.

The tax-free nature of the Roth IRA in combination with the conversion can make the Roth ideal for passing wealth to a surviving partner or to children. Louise can transfer her old Keogh to a traditional IRA, which she can then convert to a Roth IRA. Louise would have to pay the income tax on the $150,000 in the Roth IRA. When she dies, the Roth IRA would go to Betty tax-free. There would be no IRD problem.

There are a few drawbacks with this strategy. Louise's tax bracket would probably increase in the year she converts. And she would have to be willing to pay the tax to convert. If her tax bracket increased to 39.6 percent, she would have to pay $59,400 to convert her regular IRA to a tax-free Roth IRA. Not everyone wants to do that or has the funds available. Also, if Louise's AGI exceeds $100,000 she cannot do a Roth conversion, as that is the maximum adjusted gross income for a Roth conversion.

The $350,000 that Louise has accumulated in her 403(b) tax-sheltered retirement annuity could not be converted to a Roth IRA because it is an active retirement plan in which she is participating at work. At her death, Betty would have an IRD problem with these funds unless Louise uses the third strategy.

The Charitable Trust Strategy

In the previous chapter, we learned how to put appreciated property into a charitable remainder unitrust (CRUT) to defer capital
gains tax on property to be sold during your lifetime. Why not put
an IRD asset at death into a CRUT to avoid getting slammed on the
lump sum distribution? Wouldn't it be better to spread income over
the beneficiary's lifetime and factor in tax-deferred growth? Or better yet, defer it until it is actually needed by the beneficiary. If there
is a child, wouldn't it be great if you could spread the income over
the course of the partner's and the child's life?

If you plan to make a charitable bequest, the gift should be made
from IRD rather than capital. Conventional wisdom advocates
making a charitable gift from the estate while giving to the heirs
from outside the estate. This strategy worked very well for Jimmy
and Ryan in chapter 11 because that was a situation in which both
partners were alive. As you may recall, Jimmy put his rental property into a CRUT while Ryan put his highly appreciated stock into a
NIMCRUT and provided life insurance for his partner.

Even though Louise is not charitably inclined, she should consider making a charitable bequest of her retirement plans because
of the high taxes imposed on IRD assets. The combination of estate and income taxes on the deceased person's income can trigger
an effective marginal tax bracket of 75 percent or higher on a large
estate.

The charitable trust strategy offers relief to both income and
estate taxes on IRD, accomplishes charitable goals, and provides
for the partner in the same way an IRA rollover does for a married
couple. If the couple breaks up, Louise would simply change the
beneficiary on her plan and do another CRUT with a new income
beneficiary or give the proceeds directly to charity at her death, if
there were no other heirs.

Many times people will ask me if it's possible to take the money
from their IRA or their retirement plan at work and put it into a
CRUT or pay it directly to a charity and avoid income taxes. Of
course it would be a great idea. It's just not legal. You are able to do

it at death because the estate is getting a charitable deduction for the CRUT or charitable gift.

Louise's use of a charitable remainder trust will enable Betty to avoid paying $331,600 in estate taxes, as seen in Table 13.4, when Louise dies. This strategy will also keep a major portion of the growth out of the taxable estate over the years and hence lower the tax when Betty dies. Betty will receive more income with this strategy than without it, as seen by the comparison in Table 13.4. Charity can really begin at home with sophisticated estate planning.

TABLE 13.4
ESTATE COMPARISON

	Conventional Estate Planning	Charitable Estate Planning
Gross estate from Table 13.3	$1,150,000	$1,150,000
Less exemption in 1999	650,000	650,000
Net estate	500,000	500,000
Less charitable deduction	0	500,000
TAXABLE	**$ 500,000**	**0**
Income and estate tax on IRD	$ 331,600	0
INCOME (at 7%)	**$ 11,788**	**$ 35,000**

Don't assume that taxes won't be paid because a charitable remainder trust is used. Taxes will be paid, but they will just be paid over Betty's life as she receives income from the trust. The gay penalty will be avoided because there will be no tax on IRD at Louise's death since the retirement plan will never pass through her estate. Income tax will be paid on small increments as they are paid by the CRUT rather than on lump sum distributions from the deceased partner's retirement plan. Yes, it is complicated, and, yes, you will need the help of a tax advisor who specializes in advanced estate planning.

As you can see, in this situation the CRUT is better than an IRA rollover because it is a different instrument with different rules.

Step-by-Step Instructions for Louise

1. Louise and Betty do a dual financial plan and identify their long-term goals. They discover that the use of a CRUT can help avoid the tax problem that Louise had when Ruthie died.

2. Louise has her attorney draft a standard single-life charitable remainder unitrust, using a 7 percent payout rate with Betty as the income beneficiary. No funds are put into the trust because it will be funded after Louise's death with the proceeds from her retirement plans.

3. Louise also asks her attorney to prepare wills for all of them. Louise's will must specify that all charitable gifts come from property that constitute "income in respect of a decedent," as defined in the Internal Revenue Code. If her will does not include this wording, the charitable gift can be deemed to come from principal. (It is essential that retirement plan assets never go into the probate estate or onto the income tax return to avoid being taxed as IRD.)

4. Louise asks her attorney to prepare documents that will protect her, Betty, and Reuben in a medical emergency. The attorney prepares durable powers of attorney for the three of them.

5. Louise changes the beneficiary designation on her retirement plans from Betty to the CRUT. If Betty dies before Louise or the relationship falls apart, Louise can change her plans.

6. Louise also buys a second-to-die life insurance policy with Reuben as beneficiary. (This type of policy will pay the proceeds to Reuben after both women have died.)

7. Louise avoids much of the gay penalty on retirement plan distributions.

SOLVING THE EMPLOYER-FUNDED RETIREMENT PLAN PROBLEM

Betty's planning problem is similar to Louise's because Louise will lose out if Betty dies before retirement. It is different because it is not an IRD problem. It's worse!

When a person with a retirement plan fully funded by the employer dies, the money in the plan goes back to the plan rather than to the partner. There is no IRD because there is no money to pass to the heir. This is also true when the employee is a parent and the beneficiary is a child, parent, or sibling. There is, however, an exception. If the person who dies is legally married, the money in the plan goes to the spouse. The problem is that the rules don't recognize partners as spouses. This is the second gay penalty on retirement plans.

Unfair, you say? You bet it is!

There is a way to address this problem, but first let's see what happens after retirement.

When people in an employer-funded plan retire, they receive a fixed amount every month, paid to them for life. The employee generally can have the income paid over his or her lifetime jointly with a spouse. Check with your benefits manager to determine if your plan will pay you on a joint and survivor basis for you and your partner. If not, your partner will *not* receive the income when you die. If the plan will pay for your partner, ask what will happen if you break up or change partners. If you cannot make a change after you have elected your distribution option, consider the following solution to solve this problem also.

The Solution

These problems are simpler to deal with than the IRD problem. A CRUT does not help in these situations. You can solve these problems with life insurance. Think of it as an additional investment into your retirement program, one that will protect your partner and accumulate more funds for you in a very tax-favorable way.

The best kind of insurance to use in these situations is a permanent policy—variable universal life, variable life, universal life, or whole life. Term insurance does not work as a permanent solution because it can get very expensive as the insured gets older. A permanent policy will level the cost over the insured's lifetime. It may also have a premium that gets less expensive if cash in the policy is used to pay the premium. (See appendixes D and E for more information about the different types of insurance policies available today.)

In Betty's case, she would buy a life insurance policy equal to the amount that she expects to receive from the retirement plan over her lifetime (her benefits department at work should provide this information). She would designate Louise as the primary beneficiary and Reuben as the alternate (the policy pays the benefit to Reuben if Louise dies before him). If Betty should predecease Louise, the face amount of the policy is paid to Louise, replacing her retirement plan.

If Betty can't afford to purchase full coverage as a permanent policy while she is working, a good strategy would be to buy a variable or universal life policy for the amount she has accumulated in her retirement plan and buy term insurance for the balance of what she expects. As she earns more money, she can convert the term insurance to a permanent policy. This protects her insurability. In the long run, however, it is cheaper to buy the full amount up front because she is getting the permanent insurance at a younger age, when it is less expensive. What you decide to do is a planning question.

There are several additional tax advantages to using life insurance. The life insurance proceeds pass income-tax-free. The face amount of the insurance can be paid out as either a lump sum, which is tax-free, or as income in the form of an annuity. If it is paid out as an annuity, only the interest will be taxable. If Betty's estate is substantial, the policy can be in an irrevocable life insurance trust or she can have the beneficiary own the policy. She can continue to pay the premium. Either strategy keeps it out of her estate and thereby avoids estate tax. (This area is discussed in greater depth in chapters 3 and 6.)

If Betty cannot get the insurance for health reasons, then she would need to consider graded death benefit life insurance as discussed in chapter 7. If she has a serious health problem that is not terminal, then she should have her insurance broker shop the market for the best rates.

Step-by-Step Instructions for Betty

1. Betty and Louise sit down with their advisor and ask how much income they will receive at retirement. They also ask what happens if one of them dies before retirement.
2. Betty asks her employer's benefits department for a present-value calculation of the expected retirement income from her retirement plan.
3. Betty has her financial advisor do a present-value calculation to check if this amount is reasonable.
4. Betty applies for life insurance. Since she is investment-minded, she buys a variable universal life policy.
5. Since Betty has had flack from her family about her relationship with Louise, she has her attorney prepare an irrevocable trust and makes the trust the owner and beneficiary of the life insurance. Louise and Reuben are the beneficiaries of the trust.

A STRATEGY FOR THE AGGRESSIVE INVESTOR

Louise's friend George enjoys taking risks and playing the stock market. He has built up a substantial portfolio in his IRA account by being an aggressive investor and would like to do a Roth conversion to protect his lover in the event of his death. George lives in the present moment and wants his tax benefits now, not when he dies. He would never do anything charitable.

There is yet another strategy for people whose AGI is too high to do a Roth conversion if they have the money to pay the tax on a Roth conversion, the money to do additional investments, and meet suitability tests imposed by the state where they reside. The purpose of a state's suitability requirements is to make sure the investor can afford the risks inherent in this type of investment.

George can invest some of his investment dollars in a natural gas and oil drilling program. These investments are partnership programs that do developmental drilling for natural gas and oil. The tax law allows an income tax deduction during the first year of the investment for costs incurred that have no salvage value, which are called *intangible drilling costs* (IDC). IDC are costs that are incidental to and necessary for the drilling of wells and for the production of oil and gas. They do not include the cost of equipment, facilities, and storage. IDC can equal 70 to 80 percent of total well cost. The amount of income tax deduction is based on the investment and can be substantial during the first year of the investment.

If the drilling is successful, these investments can provide income on an ongoing basis. Income from these programs is partially sheltered from taxes due to depletion, which is similar to depreciation in buildings. An investment in a natural gas and oil-drilling program can be used to reduce AGI so that George can qualify to do the Roth conversion. If he decides not to do the Roth conversion, the deductible portion will lower his AGI and he will save dollars that would have gone to taxes.

There are risks with these investments: the price of oil or natural gas could be low due to warm winters, the drilling partner might not be experienced, wells could be dry, or a new synthetic fuel could be developed. There are no guarantees. These investments are illiquid and should be regarded as long term. The reason the government allows tax benefits for this type of investment is to help move money into domestic drilling activity and to help encourage a strong domestic industry.

Is this program right for you? Talk to your investment advisor *and* your tax advisor. The answer will depend on your income, assets, net worth, and whether you meet your state's suitability requirements.

The other solution to avoiding the gay penalty on retirement plans is to become more politically active and work to change unfair laws that discriminate against gay and lesbian couples.

STEP 4:

USE UNCONVENTIONAL WISDOM AND TAKE ACTION

This step deals with the "Lazarus effect"—the phenomenon of people recovering from "terminal" illnesses only to have to face the reality of their financial situation. In chapter 13, you'll learn ways to recover from financial disaster due to illness, including filing for bankruptcy and rebuilding your credit history. Chapter 14 covers the pros and cons of viatication (selling your life insurance policy for cash) and takes you through the process. Chapter 15 will help you understand the issues you face if you are reentering the job market while you are receiving Social Security benefits. It also provides effective strategies for conducting your job search.

Chapter 16 takes you through the planning steps for someone who is terminally ill and has a very short life expectancy. The last chapter, chapter 17, is really the beginning. It's now up to you to take action by taking the first step.

CHAPTER 13

Getting a Fresh Start

The woods are lovely, dark and deep. But I have promises to keep. And miles to go before I sleep.   —Robert Frost

Larry and Owen, both diagnosed with AIDS years ago, never expected to be alive today. After spending all the money they had on a lover's holiday in Hawaii, doctors, and visiting family and friends, they have been pleasantly surprised to find themselves still alive. But now they also face a financial crisis.

Larry, who had his own consulting business before he got sick, owes almost $125,000 in unpaid medical bills, outstanding credit card charges, and back taxes. As he slowed down, he fell farther and farther behind on his estimated taxes. He used his credit cards to help balance the budget. When he was very sick and thought he had only six months to live, he cashed out of his life insurance for the surrender value. Using this money only slowed the outflow, it didn't make it go away. Now the money from the life insurance is gone, but at least Larry is working once again. He is trying to pay the minimum on his credit card debt, which is more than half his take-home pay.

Larry is in a very bad financial position: he owes money due to his illness; debt collectors are hounding him; and the IRS has put a lien on his salary. He thinks that if he files for bankruptcy, he can get a fresh start.

LAZARUS AND BANKRUPTCY

Larry and Owen are suffering from the Lazarus effect. Like Lazarus in the Bible, they thought they would be dead and now they have a second chance. They never expected to live this long, so they spent everything they had. Now that they not only are alive, but may live for many years, they are broke, in debt, and worried about the future. Larry and Owen don't know how they can afford to prepare for the future if they can't make ends meet today.

On the good side, they are alive, they have each other, and they do have options. In this chapter we will see how Larry can get a fresh start by filing for bankruptcy. In the next chapter we will address Owen's situation and see how he can use his life insurance to help move on in his life.

Two types of bankruptcy filings are generally available for individuals. One form of bankruptcy requires the debtor to liquidate assets before discharging unsecured debt. This form of bankruptcy is known as a **Chapter 7** bankruptcy. Unsecured debt is debt that does not have assets that have been used as collateral. Credit card debt are loans that are not collateralized. Auto loans and mortgages are examples of secured debt. (Taxes are very difficult to discharge. But after bankruptcy, Larry will be in a better position to work out a staged payment plan or installment agreement with the IRS.)

When there are assets that you don't want liquidated, a **Chapter 13** bankruptcy should be considered. A Chapter 13 is not a liquidation or discharge of debt but rather a plan where you pay off your debt over a period of time, generally at a reduced amount. Larry is a candidate for a Chapter 7 filing since he has no assets to protect.

The argument that filing for bankruptcy will damage your credit is rather specious. While a bankruptcy may remain on your credit report for a ten-year period, people who file generally already have a poor credit history. Obtaining credit after the bankruptcy will be difficult but not impossible. If you can show a means of repayment of your new debt, credit should be available.

CHAPTER 7 BANKRUPTCY

Once you have decided that your debt, rather than you, is running your life, there is a series of steps you take in filing for Chapter 7. Let's follow Larry as he goes through the process.

The Petition

First, Larry must see an attorney who practices in the field of bankruptcy law. While the bankruptcy laws are federal, the courts look to state law for the definition of which assets are exempt. Exemption statutes differ by state. For example, in California the debtor might lose her house in a Chapter 7, while in Texas she would keep it. And some states, such as California, are harsher than others when it comes to retirement plan assets.

Since Larry does not have an attorney or know any friends who have one, he calls the local bar association for a referral. The attorney advises Larry to improve his situation prior to filing by not using his credit cards for any further charges or cash advances, and to continue making minimum payments on cards with recent charges. The attorney prepares the Petition, Schedules, and Statement of Financial Affairs.

Schedules and Statement of Financial Affairs

These documents set forth the financial conditions as of the filing date and list all of Larry's assets and liabilities. Everything that Larry owns and owes, including his recent financial history and the address of each creditor, goes into the schedules. All of his credit card debt, loans, and overdue taxes to all taxing authorities are listed.

The documents are filed with the United States Bankruptcy Court in the jurisdiction where Larry lives. The court gives notice to all the creditors listed in the Schedules and tells them when the Meeting of the Creditors will take place.

The Meeting of the Creditors

Approximately sixty days after the petition is filed, there is an examination by the bankruptcy trustee who has been appointed by the court to oversee the Chapter 7 case. The creditors don't have to be there, but Larry, as the debtor, is required to show up. At this meeting, the trustee or the creditors can question the financial condition of the person filing the bankruptcy and challenge the debtor. If a creditor feels that there has been fraud, the creditor has sixty days to sue the debtor and block his or her discharge or to object to the discharge of a specific debt.

Here are some examples of actions that may be considered fraud:

1. An application for a credit line that far exceeds the debtor's earning ability
2. Charging luxury items or transferring assets outside of the reach of creditors in anticipation of bankruptcy; the period in question can range from sixty days to up to one year before filing
3. A pattern of spending or taking cash advances beyond the means of the debtor to repay them
4. Juggling or using one credit card to finance another

Larry is really an honest debtor—he has been using his credit cards to pay the rent and buy groceries after he ran out of money and continued to live. His attorney advises him that some creditors are getting aggressive and examining tax returns and personal records. Larry's attorney wants to make sure that creditors do not say that some of the debt should not be discharged because Larry has been taking cash advances on a regular basis.

Larry also owes his friend Bob $5,000. He had planned to pay Bob off prior to the bankruptcy out of his love for him. The attorney advises Larry to pay his moral obligations with new money, after the bankruptcy. Larry learns that the trustee would have the right to ask

Bob for the payment back, because Bob would have been given a preference over other creditors before the bankruptcy filing.

Liquidation

In a Chapter 7, assets are liquidated to pay off debt. This means that if Larry had a valuable stamp collection, a fine art collection, mutual funds, stocks, bonds, bank accounts, or other assets not exempt in the state where he lives, then the assets would be liquidated to pay off as much debt as possible before any debt could be discharged. In some states, had Larry owned a permanent type of life insurance policy with cash value, that policy might be treated as an asset to be liquidated. Larry's term insurance, on the other hand, is not an asset since it has no cash value. Larry can keep that insurance policy.

Discharge

Larry's legal obligation to pay his debts is relieved after his assets have been used to pay off debt. Since he has no assets, his debts are discharged and he is free to start his financial life again.

After the Discharge

If Larry wins the lottery, receives an inheritance, or receives a large payment within six months of his bankruptcy filing, the trustee has a claim on those funds for the benefit of creditors. Lottery winnings and inheritances may be in the public records. If you are in this situation, talk to your attorney.

Debt incurred after filing a bankruptcy is not discharged. You must pay it. If there is a mortgage and you live in a state where your house is exempt from the bankruptcy, then you must pay the mortgage. If not, the lender will be able to pursue its state law remedies and foreclose on the property.

Step-by-Step Instructions for Larry
1. Larry contacts the local bar association for a referral to an attorney in his area who specializes in bankruptcy.
2. At the request of the attorney, Larry provides a list of all of his assets, liabilities, income, and expenses. He also provides the addresses of all of his creditors. The attorney prepares the Petition, Schedules, and Statement of Financial Affairs using Larry's financial information.
3. On the recommendation of his attorney, Larry stops using his credit cards for his daily living expenses and starts paying a token amount against the outstanding debt.
4. Since Larry has no assets to protect, he has the attorney file a petition for a Chapter 7 bankruptcy for him.
5. Larry contacts one of his credit card carriers on which he has a low balance and asks to reaffirm that credit card so that he can use that credit card rather than give it up.
6. Sixty days after the petition is filed, Larry and his attorney attend a Meeting of the Creditors with the court-appointed trustee. None of the creditors nor the trustee challenges Larry's debts.
7. Larry's discharge goes through about sixty days later.

CHAPTER 13 BANKRUPTCY

When There Is Nonexempt Property

Larry's friend Michael is in a similar boat. He too is alive when he thought he would be dead. The difference is that Michael owns a house in San Francisco worth more than a half million dollars. He has fallen behind on his mortgage payments and is faced with foreclosure. He is living on his partner's income and his own disability income, but doesn't have enough income to get current on the mortgage. He is afraid of losing his house and the equity in it. The lender has accelerated the mortgage and asked for the full principal. For most people, a request for either the full principal or the amount in arrears plus legal fees is just too great a hardship—it's a virtual impossibility. This is true for Michael.

Although he owes for medical bills, credit card debt, and federal taxes, Michael has worked out a payment plan with most of his creditors. Some have been very reasonable in working with him, but even those payments he agreed on are getting to be too much of a burden. He would like to sell the house and move into his partner's home now that he is working again and has an income.

If Michael files a Chapter 7 in California, he will lose the house because the value of the home exceeds the debt to the lender and his homestead exemption. Under present law, a Chapter 13 is a viable alternative for Michael.

Chapter 13 was designed for individuals with a sufficient recurring source of income and is commonly called the "wage earner" plan. A Chapter 13 allows you to repay a portion of your debts—whether they are a mortgage in arrears, auto loans, personal loans, student loans, or credit card debt—over an extended period of time, usually between three years and five years. Debts to taxing authorities may even be paid over a six-year period, and you are given a "stay" or stop on penalties. If you have assets to protect and are in a state where the exemptions are very restrictive, then a Chapter 13 may be more appropriate for you than a Chapter 7. Your attorney can help you with this decision.

As a Chapter 13 debtor, you are obligated to turn over all of your disposable income to the Chapter 13 trustee on a monthly basis. These funds are distributed to your creditors on a pro rata basis. The amount that you contribute to your plan, the length of the plan, and the percentage of distribution to creditors are based on your particular financial situation. Again, an attorney who specializes in bankruptcy law in your state is essential.

Many people think that a Chapter 13 looks better than a Chapter 7 because it is a payback plan. It doesn't matter—it also goes on your record as a bankruptcy and can stay there for as long as ten years.

The Petition

The initial procedure for filing a Chapter 13 is very similar to that for a Chapter 7. Simply filing a bankruptcy petition in the United States Bankruptcy Court will automatically "stay" (stop) any foreclosure proceedings or forced sale, repossession of automobile or other property, auction sale, or lien on income.

Michael is faced with a pending foreclosure because he does not have enough income to pay the full mortgage or to catch up with the payments in arrears. A Chapter 13 will give Michael the time to sell his house at the fair market value rather than in a forced sale. By selling the house at market value, he will earn enough money to pay off the outstanding mortgage balance, keep the remainder of the equity, and formulate a repayment plan for his other creditors with a smaller monthly payment. In a forced sale, he would lose the equity and still struggle with his other payments.

When Michael prepares the petition, he should provide his attorney with his last two tax returns, current wage stubs indicating gross and net income, all bills whether defaulted or current, a list of all assets and their current value whether owned or transferred within the last year, and a list of all bank accounts and investments. He must also provide all of his creditors' current addresses. The information about his assets, liabilities, income, and expenses are used to calculate the payment plan.

The Meeting of the Creditors

As in a Chapter 7, Michael is required to attend a Meeting of the Creditors to be examined by the trustee. At this meeting, the trustee and the creditors have the right to question Michael. If there is fraud, the Chapter 13 can be disallowed.

Payment Plan

People who have enough disposable income to fund their Chapter 13 plan and repay their debts in full or in part will keep their assets. Arrearages on a defaulted mortgage can be reinstated and paid off under a payment plan; however, payments on the mortgage after the petition has been filed must be made directly to the lender. Unsecured debts can be paid over a period of time through the Chapter 13 plan.

Michael and his attorney submit a payment plan on the date the petition is filed. Payments must begin within thirty days of filing the petition and must be made monthly until the entire plan is completed. Payments are made by cash, money order, bank check, or certified check, but not a personal check. The attorney recommends a certified check so that Michael has the canceled check as proof of payment.

The Trustee

A trustee is appointed to administer Michael's case as soon as the petition is filed. The trustee's function is much more active in a Chapter 13 than a Chapter 7, as he or she will collect all payments from Michael and then distribute those funds to the creditors. The trustee's function is that of overseer—he or she protects the rights of the creditors.

If you are not qualified for a Chapter 13 because your secured or unsecured debts exceed statutory limits, the trustee or creditor(s) can move to have your case dismissed. If you fall behind in payments, your case can also be dismissed. You pay the trustee a set amount every month per the payment plan and the trustee pays the creditors after taking his or her fee.

Step-by-Step Instructions for Michael

1. After reading a do-it-yourself bankruptcy book, Michael realizes that he needs help and talks to a legal firm that refers him to an attorney specializing in bankruptcy in his state.
2. At the request of the attorney, Michael provides a list of all of his assets, liabilities, income, and expenses. He also provides the addresses of all of his creditors, including the ones he has a payment agreement with.
3. Michael files a Chapter 13 instead of a Chapter 7 per his

attorney's recommendation because his residence is not exempt property in the state where he lives. He also stops using his credit cards.

4. Michael provides the attorney with his financial information that the attorney then uses to prepare the Petition, Schedules, Statement of Financial Affairs, and Payment Plan. The Payment Plan is a sixty-month plan and is consistent with Michael's budget and ability to pay.

5. At Michael's request, the attorney files the Petition, which stops the pending foreclosure and freezes the actions of the IRS and other taxing authorities against Michael. Taxes due are included in the Payment Plan.

6. Within thirty days of filing the Petition and Payment Plan, Michael begins making payments to the trustee, who distributes the funds to the creditors, starting with the taxing authorities.

7. Sixty days after the Petition is filed, Michael and his attorney attend a Meeting of the Creditors with the court-appointed trustee. None of the creditors challenges Michael's debts or his Chapter 13 plan, nor does the trustee.

8. Sixty months after the filing of his Petition, Michael completes his plan. He receives an order of the court stating that his bankruptcy has been discharged.

REBUILDING YOUR CREDIT

Bankruptcy is not the end of the road—it can be your chance to get a fresh start. You can get credit cards and a car loan, and can even become a homeowner. If you apply for a loan or credit card and you are turned down, it is because the report will show your credit history as far back as ten years ago.

In her book *Bounce Back from Bankruptcy: A Step-by-Step Guide to Getting Back on Your Financial Feet*, Paula Langguth Ryan discusses steps you need to take to get back on your feet financially. The following are key steps from her book.

Clean Up Your Credit Report

The first step is to check your credit report. You have a right to know what is on your credit report, and you are entitled to a free one anytime you are denied credit. The three major credit bureaus are Equifax, Experian, and Trans Union; there are also many smaller regional and local ones. (Appendix J provides their addresses and phone numbers.) When you write to each credit bureau include your full name, present address, previous address(es) for the past five years, Social Security number, date of birth, and the fee for the report. Because the fee varies, you should call first.

When you receive your credit report make sure your personal information—name, address, Social Security number, and employment information—is correct in the report. Next, make sure all of the accounts listed are yours. Then check for out-of-date information. All information over seven years old, whether correct or not, must be removed, with the exception of bankruptcies and tax liens. Bankruptcies can remain on the report for ten years, and tax liens stay on for seven years from the time you paid them off. Last, check for other incorrect information.

If you know that any of the information is incorrect you can challenge it. You may have to go back to the original lender and then provide proof to the bureau. *Bounce Back from Bankruptcy* provides step-by-step instructions to help you clean up your credit report.

Your credit report should come with an investigation or dispute form. Fill it out indicating the wrong information and providing the correct information. If there is no form send a letter. Keep copies of everything you send. If nothing has happened after forty-five days, write again. If again nothing happens call the Federal Trade Commission (FTC) in Washington, D.C., at 202-326-2502 and file a complaint.

With your bankruptcy papers in hand, compare your discharged debts with the credit report. Each of those debts should say "discharged under bankruptcy protection," or "reorganized under Chapter 13 bankruptcy." If the report shows as delinquent accounts that were discharged or paid off, then you must send a copy of the bankruptcy papers to the credit bureau showing them that that is the case. Send them a letter with proof of the discharge and request that they update your records.

If the credit bureau does not respond or cooperate, you can go to the FTC as well as to your state attorney general's office or office of consumer protection. The sooner you start cleaning up your credit report the better—the process will take time.

The Fair Credit Reporting Act (FCRA) allows you to add a statement to your credit report explaining the factors that led to your bankruptcy. Larry's and Michael's bankruptcies were caused by illness and high medical expenses. A note in their files will show future creditors the nature of their problem and how they are better able to handle their credit responsibilities now.

It might seem that it's easier to hire a credit repair company to update your credit problems. Don't. Many of these companies are expensive and not legitimate. You can do it yourself. Bob Hammond has written a number of books that you may also find helpful, including *Life after Debt* and *Life without Debt*.

Start a Savings Program

Prior to bankruptcy, you were probably paying the minimum amounts on your credit cards and other loans. Michael even negotiated minimum payments on his medical bills. Now that the debts are gone, continue the payments but to a savings account or to a growth mutual fund. If the minimum amount you were paying is too much, save half or one third of that amount. With dollar-cost averaging (see chapter 5) you put a fixed amount every month into an investment that fluctuates. In the months when the stock market is down, you get more shares. In those months when the stock market is up, you have more value in your account. It really doesn't matter whether you use a bank or a mutual fund, as long as you invest consistently.

Obtain a Secured Credit Card

A secured credit card is one where you deposit funds into an account at the issuing bank and the funds are then used to back your card. Yes, you are using your own funds, but remember, the goal is to rebuild your credit history. Beware of great offers that come in the mail, especially if the promotion piece says you can't be turned down or it's a "guaranteed" offer. As we all know but sometimes forget, "there ain't no free lunch." Call the Better Business Bureau, the state attorney general's office, or your local consumer affairs office and find out the company's history.

Paula Langguth Ryan offers two guidelines to keep in mind when obtaining a secured credit card:

- Make sure the credit card helps you rebuild your credit history. Ask if the issuing bank reports your payment history to the major credit bureaus—Experian, Equifax, and Trans Union. If it doesn't, you are not really helping yourself get a fresh start.
- Ask if the issuing bank will keep your secured status confidential. Only you and the bank need know that your new credit card is secured, not the credit bureaus.

Bounce Back from Bankruptcy lists the best secured card companies and how to go about obtaining such a card.

Once you have a new credit card you must be very careful not to go overboard. Follow these guidelines from Ryan's book and you will be okay:

- Only charge what you can pay off this month—you are not buying out the store, you are rebuilding your credit history.
- Pay off the bill as soon as it arrives. If you make late payments, you'll be right back where you started. It's easy to misplace bills. Pay it off right away and then don't worry about it.
- Prepay your credit card bill. You will build up your account and stay out of debt.

Get a Gasoline Card

If you apply for a gasoline card directly, you probably won't get it. A smarter way to go, according to Ryan, is to become an investor. Contact the major gasoline companies that have stations in your area and ask if they have a "DRIP." **DRIP** stands for a **dividend reinvestment program** (not what happens at the pump when you take the nozzle out of the tank).

Once you find the gasoline company you want to invest in, call the company's 800 number and say that you want to invest at least $250 in their dividend reinvestment program. Do not say that you want to apply for a credit card—if you do, you will end up in the credit card division and they will see your recent bankruptcy. Since you are becoming an investor, Ryan recommends that you consider companies that are leaders in their industry, show consistent sales and profit increases, have less than 30 percent tied up in debt, and have had an annual return of at least 10 percent for five or more years. These are stringent requirements but you want your investment to grow.

Some gasoline companies allow your investment to go into an IRA account—just check off the "IRA" box when you fill out the application for the DRIP account.

Once you are an investor, Ryan says that all you need do is wait until the gasoline company sends you an application. They will send one with either a quarterly financial report or the annual report. The application will be coded that you are a shareholder (this means that your debt will be secured by your investment). Remember not to go to them, as you don't want the credit department involved at this point. Once you get your gasoline card, pay the bill as soon as it arrives.

SUMMARY

Whoever thought that Lazarus would be back in our lifetime? People who thought they would be dead are "reborn." Pre-death financial planning for some people meant spending to the last dollar. For others, medical bills, precious moments together, and caregiving have left them deeply in debt, faced with starting over, new cost-of-living expenses, and retirement planning.

Bankruptcy for some people can give them the opportunity to start fresh. Talk to your attorney about either a discharge or a repayment plan. You will not, however, be able to discharge loans for college expenses.

Whether you have filed bankruptcy or your credit history is a mess, take steps to correct it. Get copies of your credit report, correct the mistakes in your report, and clean them up. Start to rebuild your credit history, get a secured credit card, and start an investment program. It will take time but you can rebuild your financial history.

CHAPTER 14

Cash for Your Life Insurance

Money is like a sixth sense without which you cannot make a complete use of the other five. —W. Somerset Maugham

Gordon and Pat, partners for sixteen years, love to travel. For the past few years, they have been doing house exchanges with other couples in Europe. Last summer they went to Sitges, Spain. They dream of returning to this community, with its old European ambiance and welcoming feeling for family and friends. This is where they want to retire.

Both health and financial problems have hit Gordon and Pat hard over the last year. Six months ago, Gordon found out he had prostate cancer. Now it has metastasized and the tumor has broken through the prostate wall. Things look pretty bleak. He plans to go on disability but can't afford the high cost of converting his employer's group life insurance to an individual policy to protect Pat. He has another $200,000 policy he bought before the onset of the cancer. He would like to keep this policy but isn't sure if he and Pat will be able to pay the premium if he isn't working.

Pat is HIV-positive and fortunately asymptomatic. He has never had an opportunistic infection and is still able to work. Gordon is HIV-negative.

Gordon and Pat know friends with AIDS who have sold, or viaticated, their life insurance policies. But they did not realize that people with cancer or any other terminal illness could do the same thing. They don't have a clue how the viatication process works or know any of its implications, but they would like to learn more.

VIATICAL SETTLEMENTS

With certain types of permanent life insurance—variable, universal, and whole life—it is possible to borrow the cash value from an existing policy. But there is another way to obtain funds from life insurance: **viatication,** or **viatical settlement**. Viatical settlements are contracts in which a terminally ill person receives cash in exchange for turning over the death benefits in his or her life insurance policy to another person/company that is supplying the cash. The individual selling the policy is called a **viator**. The amount of cash the viator receives will be less than the death benefit.

Although the viatical settlement industry is only a decade old, it has grown at an astronomical rate. In 1989, when the concept was first introduced, there were only three companies operating in the field. Today, there are hundreds. Performance among these companies varies dramatically.

Viatical settlements have been steeped in controversy since their inception. People tend to have strong feelings about the viatical settlement industry, whether positive or negative. Some critics have likened the industry to a vulture preying on the dying, while advocates take a pragmatic approach and point out that viatical settlements have helped to ease the increasing debtor position of the HIV community.

However you look at it, viatication has almost single-handedly played the role of replacing savings for the weakening economic base of those who are HIV-positive and, in large part, the gay community. This industry has been responsible for placing millions, perhaps even billions, of dollars directly into the hands of the gay community and bolstering its economic position.

Viaticating your life insurance policy is similar to selling any other asset, such as a car. When you sell your car, you deliver the title to the purchaser. Once the sale is complete, the new owner has all the rights and responsibilities associated with that car. If the oil needs to be changed or any repairs need to be done, it is the responsibility of the new owner. The same holds true with a viatical settlement. In order to sell the policy, you transfer ownership to the purchaser, which in turn names itself beneficiary. From that point on, the purchaser has all the rights in the policy and is responsible for any maintenance on that policy, such as the premium payments. Likewise, the viatical settlement company cannot come back to you and demand repayment of the settlement if your health improves. The sale is final.

There are a number of caveats to keep in mind if you are contemplating the sale of your life insurance. The purpose of this chapter is to make you aware of them and give you the knowledge you need to determine whether or not a viatical settlement is right for you. We will start by taking a look at the basic facts about viatical settlements.

WHAT YOU NEED TO KNOW ABOUT VIATICAL SETTLEMENTS

What Types of Insurance Can Be Sold?

Almost any type of life insurance can be sold, including, in most cases, group life insurance, as long as the insurance company is financially sound. In rare cases, some types of policies cannot be viaticated. One example is a life insurance policy issued by a fraternal organization. Another example is a policy that is attached to your health insurance, since the life insurance policy cannot be separated from the health insurance policy without disrupting your benefits.

Group policies are more difficult to viaticate than individual policies because the process requires the successful coordination of several different parties: the life insurance carrier, the employer, the third-party administrator, and the viatical settlement company. In addition, since viatical settlement companies have less control over the maintenance of group policies, not all of them will buy group insurance. If you are still working and want to sell your group insurance, be very clear how much information you are willing to divulge to your employer. Not all employers maintain a workable environment for the terminally ill. You don't need more stress.

Individual policies tend to be easier to viaticate simply because there are fewer entities to coordinate in the sale of the policy, and maintenance of the policy after the sale is completed is simple. Because of this, viatical providers generally look more favorably on individually owned insurance.

Restrictions and Exclusions

Some critical contractual restrictions that are time-sensitive are included in a viatical settlement. The two most important restrictions in the viatical settlement process are the **contestability period** and **suicide exclusion**. These clauses run for two years from the date the policy became effective.

The **contestability** clause states that the insurance carrier has the right to contest the validity of the insured's application for life insurance during this two-year period. Although this language really applies to individual policies where the insured responds to a medical questionnaire, the language is included in group policies to cover any life insurance provided by the group where medical questions are asked. This is sometimes the case when the individual is allowed to purchase additional life insurance in the group environment.

The **suicide exclusion** clause states that the life insurance carrier will not pay any life insurance benefits if the insured commits suicide within two years of the policy's effective date. Although this may sound like a morbid element to include in a life insurance contract, it actually has sound logic from a historical perspective. During the Depression, a large number of people took out life insurance coverage and committed suicide to provide family security.

Viatical settlement companies assume a lot of risk when purchasing life insurance policies and they will not assume unnecessary risk. As long as these clauses are active, most viatical settlement companies will not offer a settlement. In many group insurance cases, insurance carriers will attempt to create a new policy issue date upon conversion request from group to individual coverage rather than maintain the original date of issue as listed on the group policy. This is an unfair practice because the insurance carrier is trying to restart a suicide clause that may have expired.

California and New York have enacted regulations to prevent insurance carriers from creating loopholes to extend the effective contestability and suicide exclusion periods. The laws state that the original group policy effective date of the life insurance policy must be applied to the converted policy. If the individual converting the policy has been employed more than two years, these clauses expire. If the individual has been employed less than two years, the remaining time effective under these clauses is two years minus the lapsed period of time of active employment.

Although there are other complicating factors, a simple rule of thumb is that a converted policy that has an effective date more than two years old is easier to viaticate than its group counterpart with a more recent effective date. But beware! Conversions are expensive and should not be undertaken for the purpose of viatication unless you receive verification that a viatical funder will purchase the policy upon conversion.

Who Buys Insurance Rights?

Technically, in unregulated states, you can sell your policy to any interested investor. The most common sources of funds for viatical settlements, however, are maintained under the umbrella of the viatical settlement companies. Viatical settlement companies receive their capital from a number of different sources: institutional funds, funds from public offerings, and pooled resources from individual investors. The viatical settlement industry, unfortunately, is not very well regulated. And the investment side of the viatical settlement industry, as of this writing, isn't regulated at all.

Regulatory Guidelines

The viatical settlement industry is regulated on a state-by-state basis by the state's department of insurance, but less than half of the states have enacted regulatory requirements. Regulation was instituted to create guidelines and thresholds for settlements fair to the consumer and to protect consumer confidentiality.

In states where licensing is required, a viatical settlement should take place only through a duly licensed viatical settlement company. As of January 1998, the states that had regulation included California, Connecticut, Florida, Illinois, Indiana, Kansas, Louisiana, Maine, Michigan, New Mexico, New York, North Carolina, North Dakota, Oregon, Texas, Virginia, Washington, and Wisconsin. You can obtain an updated list from the National Association of Insurance Commissioners (NAIC).

If you live in an unregulated state, your ability to seek recourse for unfair settlements or treatment can be compromised. In those states, contract law governs the transaction and the buyer should beware. A simple solution to this problem is to work with companies who have been licensed in states where the regulatory environment is most strict. As of this writing those states are New York, Florida, and Washington, or check www.viatical-expert.net for the latest news on protecting yourself.

An inherent conflict of interest is built into the viatical settlement business. The viatical provider makes a profit when the viator dies. The viator, on the other hand, wants to live. The longer the viator lives beyond the proscribed time frame, the lower the provider's profit.

Unregistered companies sometimes offer higher payouts than registered companies. This creates a tremendous temptation to work with unlicensed companies. There are many reasons not to succumb to this temptation, the main reason being the potential tax liability. Educate and protect yourself—only do business with licensed firms. Viaticating a life insurance policy through an unlicensed company in a state that has active licensing requirements could have a disastrous impact on the tax consequences of your settlement.

HOW TO OBTAIN
A VIATICAL SETTLEMENT

Getting the Best Deal

In her book *Cash for the Final Days: A Financial Guide for the Terminally Ill*, Gloria Wolk recommends running an auction either between two brokers, or between a small number of licensed viatical settlement companies, or between a broker and a licensed funding company.

The National Association of Insurance Commissioners (NAIC) defines a broker as a person (legal term for individual or entity) who, on behalf of the viator and for a fee or commission, offers to or attempts to negotiate a viatical settlement between a viator and one or more viatical settlement providers irrespective of the manner in which the viatical settlement is compensated. It goes on to say that the broker has a fiduciary responsibility to only the viator and to act on the viator's instructions. Having said that, some states have different definitions of broker, which can mean the broker is an agent for the viatical settlement company.

If you think you can best represent yourself, apply to three to six licensed funding companies that you have independently researched. If you choose to use a broker, ask questions about how the firm operates and if it has multiple sources with which to seek settlements. More important, ask the broker to supply you with a listing of the offers the firm has received to ensure that it has "shopped" your file. If the broker tells you that it's not in your interest to shop, that it takes too long or costs too much to get other offers, find another provider or broker. Your goal is to get the highest offer from a legitimate provider.

The amount of the settlement offer is determined by a number of factors:

- Overall health of the viator
- Type of policy and annual premium
- If there is a disability premium waiver
- Expiration of the death benefit
- The viatical provider's cost of funds
- Interpretation of the physician doing your medical evaluation

Working with Brokers

Brokers do not work for free. If Gordon were to sell his $200,000 policy for 50 percent, he would receive $100,000. If the broker were to receive a 6 percent commission, then Gordon would be paying a substantial cost for their services. The broker's $6,000 fee ($100,000 times 6 percent) is really 12 percent of the amount he receives ($6,000 divided by $100,000). Larson, who provides guidelines for working with brokers in his book *Gay Money*, suggests that you can negotiate the fee to as low as 1 percent. He recommends the following steps when working with a broker or brokers:

1. Tell the broker to give you in writing the names of all companies, with phone numbers and contact people, as well as the opening and final bid from all companies contacted.
2. Request and receive from the broker the amount of commission and dollar amount the broker will receive from each company. The broker should receive a commission based on actual dollar amount received. This will help provide an incentive to the broker to seek higher offers.
3. Request that the broker agrees to true competitive bidding.
4. Require that the amount and percentage of the broker commission be stated up front, in writing in the purchase agreement.

If you are wondering why you should use a broker, consider this: Finding licensed companies, obtaining and submitting your medical records, and baring your medical history can be strenuous work that you might find too exhausting. The broker can take the burden of shopping the viatical market off your shoulders. It's your choice.

Protecting Your Privacy

Although there are no guarantees, the best way to protect your privacy is to do business only with firms that are registered and licensed and to ask a lot of questions.

Licensed firms must comply with a level of confidentiality that is much greater than that for unlicensed companies. This can be critical if your policy is viaticated through a company that utilizes pooled money from private investors. With many of these companies, multiple investors have an ownership interest in your policy and often have access to much information about you that should remain confidential. If this type of company has been licensed, the state department of insurance may have investigated the company and determined that it has created adequate safeguards to protect your confidentiality.

Gordon does not want to receive any phone calls from investors asking him if he is still alive, nor does he want to pay unnecessary taxes. Wolk's *Cash for the Final Days* provides a detailed list of what to look out for when viaticating your insurance, as well as detailed instructions on how to do it.

What Happens after I Receive a Settlement?

Once you receive money from a viatical settlement, the company needs to know when and how to collect on the policy. This is done through some form of tracking mechanism. Some companies have you submit a notification card every month. If you skip a month, they will call a person listed by you as a contact. Other companies use less invasive methods. When you talk to the viatical settlement company or broker, ask how they track.

Should I Wait to Viaticate My Life Insurance?

There is sound logic to waiting until the appropriate time to viaticate your life insurance policy. Remember, the shorter your life expectancy is considered to be, the higher the settlement. Waiting too long, of course, would not be wise if you are not enjoying good enough health to utilize your settlement.

If you are holding off taking medications because you think that will result in a larger viatical offer for you, don't do it. Viatical settlement companies factor in drug treatment whether you are taking the medications or not. Protect yourself and get the medical care.

TAXES AND VIATICAL SETTLEMENTS

Payments made under a viatical settlement agreement to a terminally ill individual are excluded from gross income. Payments to a chronically ill individual are only excluded from taxes if the payment is for actual costs incurred that have not been covered by insurance.

A "terminally ill individual" is defined as a person who has been certified by a doctor as having an illness or physical condition that reasonably can be expected to result in death within 24 months. A "chronically ill individual" is someone who has been certified by a health care professional as unable to perform at least two activities of daily living for a period of 90 days. Activities of Daily Living as explained in Appendix I include eating, toileting, transferring, bathing, dressing, and continence or requires substantial supervision due to severe cognitive impairment.

A viatical service provider is defined as any person (individual or entity) regularly engaged in the trade or business of purchasing, or taking assignments of, life insurance on the lives of terminally ill individuals if the person is licensed for those purposes in the state in which the insured resides.

In states where licensing is a requirement, any settlement through an unlicensed source will be automatically taxed. You should not assume that you will escape the IRS, as viatical companies can be audited. The IRS can request that insurance companies provide them with a list of viaticated policies, and banks can be asked by the IRS to turn over records of sums transferred from insurance companies.

In addition, the law states that your life expectancy be such that it can be reasonably assumed as less than 24 months when reviewed by a certified physician. The viatical provider is not required to provide this assessment. As a matter of fact, there is some question as to who, if anyone, is required to provide this assessment. If this assessment becomes necessary to provide tax protection under the law, it appears that any certified physician retained to review the medical records can supply the assessment, which the IRS may require be submitted with your tax return.

What about state taxes? Of course, they will vary state by state. Some states, usually those that regulate the industry, treat viatication as a tax-exempt transaction.

The bottom line is that you should seek tax advice from your CPA or tax attorney before proceeding with a viatical settlement. You should also have the contract reviewed by an attorney familiar with viatical settlements.

How Will the IRS Know
I Have Received a Settlement?

The IRS form called the 1099-LTC must be submitted by the provider funding your settlement. This form was created so that the IRS can ascertain whether the provider was registered to engage in viatical settlements in your state of residence. If the provider was not, you can be sure that you will have a tax liability to the federal government.

What Else Should I Know
about Taxes and Viatical Settlements?

If you are receiving entitlement benefits (Social Security, Medicaid or Medi-Cal, Medicare, etc.) and you get a large sum of money for your life insurance policy, your benefits could be reduced. In addition, you must be very careful whose account the payment goes into. If the funds are to go into an account other than yours, check with your tax advisor on the tax treatment. Some viators have had the payments from a viatical settlement paid to their partner's or other family member's account. If you do this, also be sure you have a power of attorney for the account so that you have access to the money.

Another strategy to consider if you are receiving entitlement benefits or will be receiving them is a **special needs trust**. This type of trust is set up by a partner or other third party and is exempt from Medicaid restrictions. These trusts have been helpful for people who are on Medicaid or Medi-Cal and who want to sell their life insurance. The trusts are also effective for partners who want to make sure that their disabled child will not have to run though all of their inheritance before qualifying for Medicaid. If you think you are a candidate for this type of trust, discuss this area with your attorney.

Earnings on viatical settlement proceeds are taxable. For example, if Gordon receives a $42,000 settlement and invests it in a money market account, the interest earned on the account is taxable income to the person whose Social Security number is on the account.

IS A VIATICAL SETTLEMENT RIGHT FOR YOU?

Viatical settlements are not the starting point when you need cash. You should consider at least six other strategies before you viaticate your life insurance. You (or your retained broker) should investigate all your alternatives to determine which best suits your needs.

One of the alternatives is to add an **accelerated death benefit (ADB)** rider to your life insurance policy. The ADB rider enables you to receive a payment for your insurance from the insurance company rather than through a viatical settlement. The amount of payment is generally between 50 and 100 percent of the face value, depending upon the company and the specifics of the rider. Some companies add the rider free, others charge. Accelerated death benefits tend to be much more restrictive than viatication. Typically, you cannot accelerate your policy unless your life expectancy is assessed to be less than a year (in many cases, less than six months). But the advantage is that you are often allowed to maintain the remaining portion of the policy which has not been accelerated for your heir(s) and which can then be viaticated.

In the right situation, the ADB payment can be better than a viatical settlement for the following reasons:

- ADB riders pay faster than viatical settlements.
- Because life insurance companies are highly regulated, they must maintain privacy and pay on time.
- Viatical settlements are only paid to a terminally ill person, but some ADB riders can pay for other medical needs such as continuous life support, long-term care, or organ transplants.
- With an ADB rider you can retain part of the policy for your heir(s), or to viaticate, if desired.
- ADB riders pay a stated amount per the rider, while viatical settlements can be heavily discounted and are negotiable.
- Since ADB payments are not an investment, the insurance company need not determine if you are still alive and there will be no tracking.

If you are buying a life insurance policy and your broker doesn't mention the ADB rider, ask about it. Many brokers are not even aware it exists. Some insurance brokers won't mention it because there is no money to be made. Ask! If your broker or agent can't give you a straight answer, find another broker or agent.

If your insurance broker recommends that you viaticate the insurance policy that he or she sold you without fully disclosing the commission, run, don't walk, to the nearest exit. Many insurance companies consider this an unethical practice and will terminate the broker's contract. Unethical brokers may not mention the ADB rider because they want to receive a fee for the introduction of the insured to the viatical settlement company. (New York forbids viatical providers from paying fees or commissions to any person who provides medical, legal, or financial services to the viator.)

If you are considering viaticating a policy, ask the insurance company if it will add the ADB rider to an existing policy before you viaticate. Some companies will do this.

There are five other strategies to consider before viaticating all of your insurance:

1. If you have a permanent policy—variable, universal, or whole life—consider using the cash value in the policy as a loan. The loan value will be subtracted from the death benefit when you die.

2. Before viaticating your insurance, talk to your beneficiary. She or he may be able to lend you the money by using your policy as collateral.

3. If your beneficiary doesn't have the money to lend you, consider asking your employer for a loan. The policy can be used as collateral plus interest. Your employer is protected and makes a profit. If you are uncomfortable doing this, ask a friend to talk to the human resources department in your company. Some employers may have the accelerated death benefit rider on their life insurance plan. Ask.

4. If your beneficiary doesn't have the money and your employer isn't the answer, consider asking family members. They may be able to borrow the money and lend it to you. Parents or grandparents might be willing to take an equity loan or reverse mortgage for you. Your life insurance protects them and replaces the funds that were lent to you.

5. If you have a large policy, consider splitting it into smaller policies. Since there is no change in the risk covered for the insurance company, they will usually accommodate this request. For example, Gordon has a $200,000 policy which he can split into four $50,000 policies. This way, the portion he doesn't viaticate can go to Pat or can be viaticated later when Gordon's life expectancy is shorter. Remember, the shorter the life expectancy, the higher the payment. If a cure for his cancer is found, Gordon has the other $50,000 policies.

The main reason for considering these strategies is to protect your beneficiary. If you can get the funds and still keep your insurance intact, you are ahead.

Step-by-Step Instructions for Gordon

1. Gordon decides he should use a broker to help him sell his insurance. He calls the department of insurance in his state for a list of brokers and viatical settlement companies.
2. Gordon completes a general questionnaire for viatical settlements that includes the details of his medical history and life insurance policy information.
3. Gordon, or his representative, looks into converting his employer's group life insurance to an individual policy when he goes out on disability, and finds out if there is a remaining contestability and suicide exclusion on the policy.
4. Gordon learns that he can sell his group life insurance without converting it to an individual policy.
5. Gordon, or his representative, contacts his insurance company to find out if it will provide or add an ADB rider to the existing policy. The company declines.
6. Gordon learns that he has a disability premium waiver feature on his $200,000 personal policy. He will be able to keep the insurance without paying premiums once he is disabled.
7. Gordon requests that the insurance company split his policy into four $50,000 policies with the premium paid by the disability premium waiver.
8. Gordon signs a medical release authorizing his physician and other health providers to release medical information to the viatical settlement companies.
9. Gordon requests written offers from the various sources that his broker has contacted.
10. Gordon requests that his broker go back to the funders with the second and third highest settlement offers to investigate an increase in their offers. Since one offered more, the origi-

nal highest bidder raised its settlement offer for fear of losing the deal.

11. Gordon requests the closing papers from the source with the
highest offer.

12. Before signing the contract, he sees an attorney familiar with
gay issues and viatical settlements to review the contract. He
also asks his CPA how the viatical settlement will be taxed.

13. The settlement proceeds are deposited from the funder in
an escrow account and are paid to Gordon two or three days
after the transaction is completed.

14. The viatical settlement company pays Gordon the viaticum
(the settlement), which he puts into a money market account until he and Pat need the proceeds. The funds will
help pay for Gordon's care expenses. Gordon and Pat also
book a trip to Sitges, where they can spend quality time with
each other.

SUMMARY

In the right situation, a viatical settlement may provide you with
critically needed funds. Traditionally, viatical settlements have been
associated with HIV/AIDS. The industry is broadening its reach
and opening this resource to people with other life-threatening illnesses and to seniors. Before selling the rights to your insurance
policy, consider the alternatives: borrowing from the policy if it has
cash value; selling assets; borrowing money from friends, relatives,
or employers with your insurance as protection for the lender; accelerated death benefits; and splitting the policy into smaller units.

If you are receiving government benefits, always evaluate how
accepting a large cash sum will affect your benefits. And last but not
least, talk to your attorney and tax advisor.

CHAPTER 15

Job Reentry

Work is life, you know, and without it, there's nothing but fear
and insecurity. —John Lennon

As you may remember, we met Larry and Owen in chapter 13. They are in the midst of the Lazarus effect—both of them thought they would be dead by this time, but because of advances in medicine they have survived their illnesses. Now they are grappling with economic issues they didn't expect to face.

Owen, 48 years old, has not had a job for five years due to his health. Because the company he worked for prior to his illness was small, his employer provided only a five-year benefit on his long-term disability insurance, and it's about to expire. Since he has been on medical cocktails to treat his HIV, he has been feeling fit and ready to go back to work, but he knows that his computer skills have fallen behind.

Now that he sees himself living a long life, he is worried that he and Larry will not have enough money to retire. Between his Social Security benefits and private disability insurance, he has been bringing in almost $1,800 per month. His Social Security payments are barely enough to live on.

A good friend recently asked if Owen would help start a new business using his expertise as a marketing consultant. Although Owen wants to work, he doesn't know how much he can earn before his Social Security benefits stop. He also isn't sure what other issues may arise when he returns to work, or even what steps to take when starting to look for a job. He would also like to know how to answer interview questions about his illness without losing job opportunities.

LOOKING AHEAD

In this chapter, we will examine the ground rules for working while disabled on Social Security. We will also review the job reentry process. Since Social Security payments play a large part in the lives of people with disabling illnesses, we will examine how the Social Security Administration calculates what Owen can earn before losing benefits. We will also see what incentives SSA offers to help Owen get back into the workforce before benefits stop.

Owen's other major concern about going back to work is health-related. How effective can he be at work? How will stress affect his health? In this chapter, we address these questions as well.

WORKING WHILE DISABLED

If you are collecting benefits, the SSA has a vested interest in helping you return to work. The AIDS Benefits Counselors (ABC) organization in San Francisco suggests you should answer these four important questions if you are considering returning to work full-time:

- What are your existing income resources?
- How are your medical costs handled?
- How will your benefits be affected if you work while disabled?
- How much stress can you handle without a relapse?

One of the biggest obstacles to returning to work is the cost of health care. Before you accept a job, be sure that the benefits package offered is as good as Medicare, Medicaid/Medi-Cal, or the program you have on disability. You cannot be too careful in this area. The key in returning to work is benefits, benefits, and benefits.

If you are collecting private disability insurance, check for residual benefits, benefits that are paid even if you go back to work. Some plans pay for a percentage loss of income and others pay even if you change your occupation. If you do not have residual or partial benefits in your contract and return to work, your private insurance will stop payments. Ask questions of the insurance carrier, your broker, and your benefits counselor before making a move. Review chapters 8 and 9.

Few people realize that the Social Security Administration administers two programs: SSI and SSDI. **Supplemental Security Income (SSI)** is a needs-based program that issues a check on the first of the month. **Social Security Disability Insurance (SSDI)** is a benefit that is paid for by your payroll taxes from the years prior to your disability. SSDI benefits are paid monthly directly to you or to your bank account by direct deposit. Since Owen had a corporate job before his illness, he and his employer were paying FICA taxes. He is only receiving SSDI. Had he not been paying his Social Security taxes, he might be collecting SSI.

What You Need to Know about SSDI

If you are collecting SSDI only and want to return to work, there are a few things to keep in mind. The SSA defines disability as the inability to work for at least one year. If you are just starting to collect SSDI benefits, it's not a good idea to work during the first year you are on the program. Once you have been disabled for a year, the SSA has programs to encourage you to test your ability to work.

The SSA gives you a nine-month period of time called the **Trial Work Period (TWP)** to try working without losing your benefits. During this time, you can earn any amount of money. Each month in which your gross income amounts to more than $200 counts as one month of TWP. The nine months of work need not be consecutive. For example, you can work six months, stop, and then work a year later for three months. If your earnings are consistently below $500 per month, the SSA will continue your benefits at the end of the nine months worked.

If your earnings are over $500 per month after the nine months, SSA considers that you have **Substantial Gainful Activity (SGA)**. If your earnings are consistently over $500, the SSA may do a work-related review of your claim, decide to suspend your money benefit, and put you on the **Extended Period of Eligibility (EPE)** for thirty-three months following the cessation of benefits. During this time, if your earnings drop below $500 per month you automatically go back on benefits without having to reapply for that month or period of months. At the end of the thirty-three months, if your earnings are less than $500 you will be back on benefits and your claim will continue as long as you are disabled and unable to earn more than $500 per month.

If you are earning more than $500 per month at the end of thirty-three months, your claim ends. If you are disabled after EPE ends, you must reapply for benefits. However, if you reapply any-time within five years of the end of your claim, you are not subject to the five-month no-pay period for Social Security or the waiting period for Medicare as you are on the initial claim.

Gross earnings can be reduced by **Impairment-Related Work Expenses (IRWE)**. IRWE is the total of certain impairment-related items and services that an individual needs in order to work. (The SSA provides two publications as resources: "The Red Book on Work Incentives," publication no. 64-030, and "Working while Disabled," publication no. 05-10095. The "Red Book" pro-vides examples of expenses that are deductible and includes such categories as transportation, medical devices, work-related equip-ment and assistance, prostheses, residential modifications, rou-tine drugs, and nonmedical appliances and devices. For example, if your doctor says that you need massage for your neuropathy and you pay for the massage, this is an IRWE.) IRWE is deducted from gross earnings in calculating your SGA, even if the services are also needed for nonwork activities. You can deduct IRWE only if you paid for the items or services and if you will not be reimbursed.

What You Need to Know about SSI

SSI is paid on the first of the month. It pays a flat rate that is the same in all states. Currently, in a state that has no state supplement, the basic amount for an individual would be $494. In California, the single rate is $650. To determine how much your SSI check will be, take your gross earnings (before taxes) and subtract $65. Sometimes you are allowed to deduct another $20 as a general income exclusion. Then deduct any IRWEs, as discussed previously. Divide the remainder by two. The resulting dollar amount is your **Countable Income**. When your countable income is equal to or greater than your SSI check, you have reached the break-even point and your benefits stop.

Let's assume you are receiving a monthly income of $485. If you subtract $85 ($65 plus $20) and then divide the remainder by two, you have the amount that will be subtracted from your SSI check. When the resulting number is zero or less, your SSI check will stop.

What You Need to Know
if You Receive Both SSI and SSDI
Get help!

Two sets of rules apply, one for your SSI check and one for your SSDI check. You have to apply the rules for each program to that portion of your benefit check. The actual calculation can become complicated because everyone's situation is different and you must put both calculations together. Do not go this alone. This area is complex and confusing. Help is available. (Appendix K provides a list of organizations and hotline numbers to call for referrals to benefits counseling services.)

Other Important Things to Know about Social Security

The SSA is required to do a periodic **Continuing Disability Review (CDR)**. The purpose of the CDR is to determine if the disability is continuing and includes a medical review of your file. (A work-related review differs from a CDR in that wages alone can determine the end of a claim.) CDRs are done periodically based on your claim: every three years for mental-health–based claims, five years for severe HIV symptoms, and seven years for claims based on infections or conditions that would likely result in permanent disability or death.

The best way to prepare for a CDR is to see your treating physician regularly. Report all of your symptoms even if you feel perfectly well. Report all of your symptoms since your last visit, not just how you have been feeling for the last few days. Also, report all adverse effects of returning to work, including fatigue and other frequent symptoms.

With regard to income, it is important to keep records of all the money you earn from working. Keeping a calendar listing the dates worked and the amounts earned is a good idea. Virtually all programs require that you notify them when you start earning income. Reporting income does not necessarily affect your benefits. See your program's rules on working while disabled for the specifics.

If you are self-employed or expect to be self-employed, you must write the SSA a letter stating what you anticipate your earnings will be. They will take your expected income, minus business expenses, and divide it by 12 to determine your monthly income. If you have detailed records of all your income and expenses, they will accept that information if you can back it up with the documents. If you can, you are always better off providing income information to the SSA rather than having them calculate it for you. In calculating TWP and EPE as well as SSI and SSDI benefits, the SSA will count any month in which you worked forty or more self-employed hours.

YOUR JOB-HUNTING CAMPAIGN

Career Counseling

After realizing that he can test the waters, Owen decides to begin a job search. One of his concerns is his ability to handle stress in a job. As an account executive for a PR firm, he was under considerable pressure. It has been quite some time since he prepared a résumé or had a job interview, and the mechanics of conducting a job search seem overwhelming to him.

Owen has many questions. Will he be welcome on the job? Will the employer think he is dependable? Will a small employer be worried about increased insurance costs because of his medical history? How much overtime can he handle? Will the work distract him from taking his medications? How much must he tell the employer and what questions does he *not* have to answer?

One of the most important questions that Owen should consider is, "What is the most appropriate work for me as someone living with AIDS/HIV?" Owen decides to go to a career counselor who will help him identify work that is meaningful to him, has activities he enjoys, and allows him to make a contribution.

A career assessment is an integral health care component for anyone living with AIDS/HIV who is thinking of returning to work. A career assessment can help the person to find a satisfying and enjoyable career, and one that matches his or her personality instead of working against it. All these factors minimize stress. John Ozella, a career counselor in San Francisco, describes career counseling as a process for "helping clients match their work to their personality. The goal is to minimize or eliminate the 'split' that individuals experience whenever the person whom they project themselves to be in the work setting is significantly different from their 'real, at home' selves."

Ozella says that work affects our physical and emotional health, especially since it takes up over half of our waking hours. By matching work to your personality, a career counselor can help you lead a more satisfying life and enhance your emotional and physical health.

In the process of doing the career assessment, Owen decides against self-employment. At first, self-employment looked attractive because of the flexibility it offers. But Owen decided that the extensive marketing, promotion, and other activities necessary to run a business would be just too stressful for him at this point in his life.

With the career counselor's help, Owen concludes that he can best work with his energy level and stress tolerance with temporary employment. Testing his ability to work can help him determine if he is really ready to give up his disability benefits. It will also help him convince future job interviewers of his stamina.

Owen decides to seek part-time employment. First, he starts to work for a small firm. His gross income, minus his medication bills, is under $500 per month. After several months he signs up with a temporary employment agency and earns considerably more than $500 per month.

After a few months at his first foray into the working world, Owen takes a break and goes back to school to bone up on his skills. He and his doctor feel that he is working too much and he should take it easy for a while. He continues to collect his SSDI benefits.

During his "relapse," he decides to get serious about job-hunting. When he is ready, he would like to find a job with a large corporation that has a full package of health benefits.

Step-by-Step Instructions for Owen

1. Owen decides that it's time to start working in earnest if he wants to afford retirement. He calls the Centers for Disease Control and Prevention's hotline (800-342-2437) for a referral to a benefits counseling service in his area, and a counselor explains how the job reentry process works.
2. Owen works full time through a temporary agency for several

months during his "trial work period." He discovers that full-time work is just too much because he is exhausted at the end of the day.

3. Owen goes to a career counselor recommended by his friends in the community. The career counselor does a career assessment to help Owen determine a career that offers less stress and better matches his personality.

4. While still receiving disability benefits, Owen returns to school to complete his master's degree for his new career and to improve his computer skills.

5. After finishing school, he joins another temporary employment agency to try his hand at working part time again. He keeps his earnings under $500 per month so that he can keep his benefits until he is ready to go full time.

Job Hunting

Looking for a job is similar to running a successful business or military campaign. It takes a mission and purpose, organization, discipline, goals, and objectives. To succeed without becoming an emotional wreck, you need to be aware of the difference between the factors that you can control and those you cannot. For example, the number of appointments you have during a week is out of your control, but calling a certain number of people is manageable. Getting a job by a target date isn't something you can control, but asking twelve or fifteen people for a job by the target date is. You can manage your activity and your behavior. Let's examine some of the steps in your campaign.

1. **Get a work space.** Set up a regular work space for your job-hunting campaign. Think of yourself as being in the business of job hunting. The space you set up is your "office" even if it is a table in the corner. It's where you go to do your work.

2. **Schedule time regularly.** Use a calendar and schedule your time. Work on a schedule based on a fixed time period or a set

number of calls you must make before you stop. Whatever time period you set, be consistent. Stop when the period is over or you'll fudge the next time. At the end of the day, evaluate what you accomplished and then prepare a list for the next day.

3. **Divide the task into small pieces.** Breaking your job-hunting campaign into manageable pieces keeps it from becoming overwhelming. If your goal is to call eighty employers a month, aim for calling twenty a week or four in one day. If your goal is to spend twenty hours a week looking for a job, stop after four hours a day. Check off items on your list as you complete them—and make it fun by crossing them off with brightly colored highlighters.

4. **Compile an inventory of names and talk to many prospects.** Prepare the list of who you will call in advance. The more names on your list, the less desperate you will feel. Talk to as many employers as you can, even if you think you have a job in the works. The more people you talk to, the more confidence and knowledge you gain. If you have just one interview lined up or one name to call, you are never out of business.

5. **Do informational interviews.** This will help you identify what's really going on out there and will help you formulate your campaign.

6. **Use a script.** Prepare what you will say in advance. If you have a script, you will have a framework.

7. **Follow up brilliantly** after appointments. Send thank-you letters and call back. People make decisions on first impressions and remember last impressions.

8. **Remember that "no" is okay.** "No" is not the end of the world, it's just a decision. It is not about you as a human being. Go back and ask again. Job hunting is about relationships. If you get turned down again, chalk it up as information and ask for a referral: "Who else should I talk to?"

9. **Keep records of what you've accomplished.** Track

the people you called and the results you got. You are in
business, you are selling a product—your services—and
the prospective employers are the customers. Think like a
businessperson.

10. **Make mistakes.** Reward yourself every time you make a
mistake. You learn more from mistakes and failures than
from successes.

11. **Join a support group.** Job hunting is hard work. If you
can't find a support group to join, then form one.

12. **Learn more.** Get books from the library on how to organize
a job hunt, conduct interviews, and prepare a résumé. The
more you know, the better you will be at it. Information is
not power—information *used* is power.

13. **Have fun.** Your disability benefits provide you with the time
to find what you want. Owen is doing it.

In his book *Selling the Invisible: A Field Guide to Modern Marketing*, Harry Beckwith writes that people with little time are apt to
make snap judgments and then base their decisions on them. You,
as a smart marketer of your services, must be aware of this ten-
dency. What first impression do you make? What's the first thing
you say? How do you differentiate yourself? How well do you follow up? If you think like a businessperson, you will see that your
job-hunting job is really a marketing campaign.

The Interview

When you look for a job, you will be asked all kinds of questions. Do
you have to answer them? Knowing which questions an employer
may ask can help you think ahead about your answers. Ask yourself,
"Is this question relevant to how I will be able to perform my job?"
If an employer persists and asks you a question that you know is illegal, it's your choice whether to answer or not. Do you really want to
work for a firm that tolerates this behavior? Is this the corporate
culture you would want to be in? (Appendix H provides a list of the

questions you don't have to answer under the fair employment practices laws.)

If an illegal question is on the application, you can leave it blank or write "N.A." (not applicable). Answering the question may not be advisable because it could create a problem for you in the future.

If you are in the interview, it's more difficult to not answer a question. One strategy is to answer the question they should have asked. Betty Kohlenberg, a vocational counselor in San Francisco, suggests the following response: "You asked about my health. I expect you're wanting to know if I can be here reliably. I haven't missed a day of work in years, with the exception of the flu I had a few years ago." Before you start answering questions in a confrontational manner, call the Equal Employment Opportunity Commission for more information. Or call your local human rights commission for guidelines in your area.

SUMMARY

Returning to work after a period of disability can be stressful. First ask yourself if you can do it. Then ask if what you will be doing is right for you. If you don't know, work with a career counselor. In fact, work with a career counselor even if you think you know what you want to do. Stress is not your friend; it could result in a relapse. Work with someone who could help you identify your strong areas and guide you on your search.

If you are giving up government benefits, you must be very careful that they are being replaced or that you are compensated enough to replace them. If you are unsure, contact Positive Resources in San Francisco, the AIDS Project of Los Angeles, or call the hotlines listed in the Appendix.

When job hunting, remember to think benefits, benefits, and benefits.

CHAPTER 16

When the
Shadows Lengthen

Let us go in; the fog is rising. —Emily Dickinson

On a Saturday morning, Molly received word that John, her father, had had a fatal heart attack. His friends found him on the floor with the lights and TV set still on. It must have been over quickly.

Molly flew back East to arrange the funeral and close the estate with her sister Sharon. Even though the funeral was simple—one hearse, one car for the family, and a plain pine box in accordance with her dad's religion—the funeral home still had to be paid $5,275. Because there was almost no money in the bank account, the funeral home agreed to take the proceeds from John's $10,000 life insurance policy and give Molly and Sharon the balance.

Molly and Sharon found another policy in their dad's safe deposit box for $25,000, payable to their mother, who had died two years earlier. (Fortunately, both their names were listed on the safe deposit box as cosigners, so they could get to the contents before the bank sealed the box.)

Molly and Sharon had to break into their dad's desk to find his important papers. They also found dozens of keys with no clue to what they were for, and photo albums with no indication of who was who in the pictures. They did the best they could and were able to close their father's estate amicably.

Now Molly's partner, Jackie, is dying from cancer. Molly doesn't want a repeat of her experience with her dad. Jackie's cancer has metastasized in her lungs and is spreading. Time is running out, and Molly wants to know exactly what to do to prepare for the inevitable.

Prior to her illness, Jackie and her business partner, Valerie, had developed a niche market in the gay community, and their insurance business was booming. Jackie was so busy that she was unable to stay current with her personal paperwork. All of Jackie's personal documents will need to be updated.

Another concern is Craig, Jackie's stepbrother, who has been jealous of her success. He feels that Molly has no right to Jackie's property because she is a lesbian. Molly and Jackie are worried that he will challenge Molly's right to inherit her property.

To take care of her emotional well-being, Molly has been going to a cancer support group and seeing her therapist. It's the financial part that she wants to make sure is in order.

LOOKING AHEAD

Molly and Jackie do not want to close out their lives like Molly's father, suddenly, without preparation. Even though Jackie has a terminal illness, it's just as likely that Molly could have an auto accident and die first, so they both want to be prepared. Who knows when time runs out?

Financial security boils down to having enough money when you want and need it, and having the ability to access it. When people die, they do not leave a neat package behind, no matter how much they love you or you love them. This chapter gives you the information you need to adequately prepare for the financial consequences of a partner's death. Dealing with these issues ahead of time will allow you to have more energy to direct where you really need it—to tend to your emotional needs during this intense period of loss and transition.

The first part of the chapter gives you an overview of the

documents and questions you should review. It includes a thorough checklist. The latter part of the chapter covers ways to protect yourself from relatives who might challenge your right to inherit property.

GENERAL PRINCIPLES IN PLANNING

When doing financial and estate planning for someone who is dying, it is essential that their estate plan be fully coordinated in that beneficiary designations, legal documents, and property titles are meeting the intentions of the ill person. If you aren't working with a financial advisor who specializes in financial planning for the terminally ill, contact the Institute for Certified Financial Planners for referrals to planners in your geographic area (800-282-PLAN or www.ICFP.org).

Several goals should be kept in mind. The beneficiary distributions should follow the rest of your plan. You want to eliminate the need for probate as much as possible since, as we learned in chapter 3, probate is expensive and time-consuming. Another goal should be to reduce income and estate taxes wherever possible. (If the ill partner has accumulated a substantial IRA, 401(k), or retirement plan, review chapter 12 for helpful information.)

Molly should make sure that when Jackie is no longer able to manage her own financial affairs and medical care, a durable power of attorney is put into effect. As you will recall from chapter 10, a DPA gives Molly the authority to act on Jackie's behalf. Molly should also have a DPA designating someone to be her attorney-in-fact (to act in her place) should she be unavailable for any reason.

Molly and all her advisors should keep in mind that the situation is urgent and can get very emotional. The people you retain to help with estate planning must be sensitive and patient. Your advisors should be willing to meet anywhere (the nursing home, the hospital, or in the home) when necessary. Who should be on the estate planning team? This will depend on the situation. Consider the following:

- Your partner and family members
- Accountant
- Financial planner
- Attorney
- Trustee
- Insurance agent
- Stockbroker
- Business partner and/or manager

It is essential that the estate planning team include an attorney who specializes in estate planning for the terminally ill and who is familiar with lesbian and gay issues in your state.

When Molly's dad died, all his papers were locked in a desk drawer but no one had the key. First and foremost, Molly should check with Jackie to learn where all her papers and keys are, so that everything will be in order.

Pick an anniversary date that is significant to both of you and review your documents with your attorney, making sure that they are current for your present distribution needs. It is very important that all your documents, beneficiary designations, and titles to real property agree with each other.

DOCUMENTS TO REVIEW

What documents should be reviewed? In a word, everything! First, let's consider business documents.

It is important that the estate planning team understand which assets should be sold, distributed, or allowed to continue. Jackie wants her business to continue with Valerie at the helm. She also wants the residual income on prior insurance sales to continue to Molly. In order for that to happen, the following documents should be current:

- Partnership agreements
- Buy/sell and shareholder agreements

- Domestic partnership agreements
- Property equity share agreements
- Promissory notes
- Leases

There are other business-related questions to consider. Who will mind the store? If Valerie won't be available to generate business, deal with clients, and provide full service, is there another qualified manager? What steps have been taken to retain employees and who is monitoring the business to see how it is doing?

Personal documents as well as business contracts need to be reviewed and may have to be revised. Jackie's will and amendments (also called codicils) to the will, as well as trusts and powers of attorney, must be checked for accuracy with today's needs. Unless you regularly review your estate and financial situation with advisors who know about lesbian and gay issues, it is very easy to let the documents fall behind. Like the shoemaker with holes in his shoes, Jackie, the inveterate insurance advisor, had not taken care of some of her own paperwork in quite a while. The time to check *your* situation is now.

All beneficiary designations will need to be checked because they supersede the will. Beneficiary designations are found on life insurance policies, annuities, and retirement plans (IRAs, 401(k)s, pension and profit sharing plans, etc.). An old life policy that Jackie got when she was in college lists the beneficiary as her stepmother, but she wants the proceeds to go to Molly. Since her stepmother is deceased, the proceeds now will go to her stepmother's estate and eventually to Craig, who hates everything Jackie stands for. The proceeds won't go to Molly. Molly can correct the beneficiary designations herself with a properly drafted durable power of attorney for financial care, naming her as attorney-in-fact.

Pay-on-death (POD) and transfer-on-death (TOD) beneficiary designations on securities, brokerage accounts, mutual funds, and bank accounts will need to be checked and coordinated with the estate plan. As you will recall from chapters 3 and 10, these designations allow property to be transferred at death easily and without cost because they do not pass through probate. If Molly waits until after Jackie dies, it could take years before she has access to the funds in those accounts.

If Jackie is healthy enough to sign the DPA for Molly, then she should also sign the power-of-attorney forms for all of her bank, investment, and securities accounts, as those institutions will have their own forms. It is best to fill out the form provided by each of those institutions to avoid litigation. If a financial institution receives a form prepared by an attorney, they may send it to their legal department before accepting it. Avoid delays by using their forms.

Other important areas to deal with are medical and disability insurance, Medicare, and medical bills. Molly cannot let Jackie's health and life insurance lapse. Here are some additional questions to ask:

- Are accelerated benefits available with life insurance policies?
- Is viatical settlement appropriate?
- Are there any open property or business transactions?

Molly or her attorney will have to check that all property ownership titles are current. Assets that will need to be checked include:

- Deeds to real estate property
- Bank, brokerage, and mutual fund accounts
- Securities
- Other valuable assets

It is also important to check if any of Molly's property has characteristics that could cause a future problem. You or your advisors might want to ask the following questions as you review your estate plans:

- Are there toxic problems related to real estate?
- Does any asset require special attention or skill in management?
- Does a business interest require licensing to manage?

- Are there attributes to an asset that might enhance or diminish its value?
- Is there anything about the operation or management of an asset that we need to know?

When Jackie has all this information, her attorney may review and draft new documents. The following documents may have to be changed or drafted. The rules on many of these are specific to your state.

- Wills
- Trusts and trustees, how assets will be distributed, and tax consequences
- Durable powers of attorney for management of property and personal affairs
- Durable powers of attorney for health care (if this document is more than a few years old it should be reexecuted)
- Living will, or whatever it is called in your state, if valid

Other documents that might be reviewed include Jackie's income tax returns, financial statements, and gift tax returns.

It is important for Molly and her advisors to ask about the existence of other assets that Jackie has that might not be obvious. For example, other property might have been forgotten in storage—jewelry, art, furniture, stamp and other collections. Jackie had a coin collection that her father had left her many years before. She had put it in a safe deposit box and forgotten about it. If Jackie had died without telling Molly, the box would have been sealed and the contents would have gone into her taxable estate. With the knowledge of the box and its contents, Molly has time to make other arrangements and relocate the items. Other assets you should ask about include:

- Expected inheritances
- Beneficial interests in trusts

- Totten accounts
- Powers of appointment
- Annuities
- Copyrights
- Patents
- Mineral rights
- Stock options

Here is a checklist to help you deal with this difficult time in the most painless way possible.

GENERAL PERSONAL INFORMATION

_____ Birth certificate
_____ Citizenship papers
_____ Divorce/separation papers
_____ Domestic partnership/Living-together/
Cohabitation agreement
_____ Equity share/property agreements
_____ Burial instructions, cemetery plot deeds, prepaid
cremation documents
_____ Anatomical gift/organ donor statement

PERSONAL ASSETS

_____ Safe deposit box and keys
_____ Safe and combination

BANKING INFORMATION

_____ Bank account statements
_____ Checks
_____ Credit union account information
_____ U.S. savings bonds
_____ Credit cards and account statements

PERSONAL FINANCIAL INFORMATION

_____ Automobile title

_____ Real estate deeds or other titles of ownership

_____ Mortgage documents

_____ Trust agreements

_____ Loans outstanding or promissory notes
(debts owed to the deceased)

_____ Deferred compensation agreement documents

_____ Buy/sell or partnership agreements

_____ Rental and lease agreements

_____ Lawsuit or pending legal action documents

_____ Income tax returns from prior years

_____ Federal and state gift tax returns

_____ Property and school tax returns

_____ Appraisal or valuables inventory

INVESTMENT INFORMATION

_____ Brokerage account information

_____ Stock certificates not held in an account

_____ Retirement plan statements

_____ Annuity policy documents and statements

_____ Bearer bonds

_____ Investment club agreements

INSURANCE DOCUMENTS

_____ Life insurance policy documents

_____ Mortgage insurance policy

_____ Group life and retirement policies
(booklets and certificates)

_____ Veterans Administration insurance papers

_____ Travel insurance policies

DEALING WITH CHALLENGES FROM RELATIVES

There is always a very real possibility that relatives who are not happy with your lifestyle will create a nightmare for you. It is important for Molly and Jackie to prepare for a challenge from Jackie's relatives, especially Craig.

One way to prepare for a challenge is to ask your estate planning attorney to memorialize the execution of the estate plan. Jackie was videotaped to prove that she was competent. Molly's attorney even went a step further; she acquired affidavits from everyone who witnessed the execution of the estate plan. If you have a large estate, are making major changes, are creating a large charitable gift, or have family members who may dislike you or your relationship, ask your attorney about memorializing your estate plan. Discuss your estate plan distribution and strategy with your attorney frequently. Family law is changing and this is a volatile area.

Never retain old wills. If your current will cannot be found and an old one turns up, that's the one that will be enforced.

THE LAST WORD

When time is running out, you have to take care of first things first. Draft your estate plan. Make sure that the assets that are supposed to be in your living trust actually are. The title to trust property should have the name of the trust in the title. Make certain that your trustee is the person you want now and the distribution plan is the way you want it. Next, make sure that beneficiary designations are current on life insurance policies, annuities, investment accounts, and retirement plans. The money will be distributed exactly as the designation says, even if it is out of date. If you plan to make gifts, check with your estate planning team what can be accomplished most easily and will generate major tax benefits.

And finally, *Do it now!*

CHAPTER 17

Summing Up

A journey of a thousand miles begins with a single step.
— Lao-tzu

C ongratulations, you made it!
Change isn't easy. Taking your destiny into your own hands and taking charge of your financial future can be hard, even overwhelming. But if you break financial planning down into smaller steps, you'll be on your way to the financial security you've always dreamed of having.

The four steps are very simple:

1. **Plan, plan, plan.** Legally married couples may have the luxury of not having to plan ahead in the same way you do, but remember, it is really to your advantage to plan. It is the primary step toward achieving the goal of financial security for anyone, gay or straight.
2. **Protect what's yours** with the insurance products and legal documents that are available to you and your partner.
3. **Think community** by using charitable trusts to offset the negative effects of the gay penalty on retirement plans and the loss of the marital deduction.
4. **Use unconventional wisdom and take action.** You and your partner can bounce back from financial disaster by using

the strategies presented in this book to obtain cash for your life insurance, reenter the job market, and plan for your final days.

Do you remember Smokey the Bear's old saying, "Only you can prevent forest fires"? This is just as true when it comes to financial planning. It takes action, and only you can do it. Begin by sitting down with your partner and asking each other the hard questions. Where do we want to be in five years? In ten years? In twenty years? If a truck hit you and you survived, would I be able to take care of you? Would you be able to take care of me? Where will the money come from?

You've got the tools and strategies now. It's really up to you to set your goals and begin. A financial advisor familiar with lesbian and gay family, legal, and financial issues can help guide you through the process.

I wrote this book to show you what's possible when it comes to financial planning, but this book is only a start. Take the ideas in it to your advisors and tell them what you want. When you're done, let me know how it worked out. What creative ideas did you try out? What changes have occurred and how have they affected your relationship? I've been with you on the journey this far, and I'd like to stay with you.

I plan to revise this book based on your feedback and also to keep up to date with changes in tax laws, family definitions, and other laws. Please—take the initiative, share your ideas, and contact me at hllustig@aol.com.

Appendixes

Appendix A
Federal Gift and Estate Tax Rates*

This table is the unified rate schedule for calculating federal estate taxes when an individual dies with a taxable estate. The same table is used for calculating gift taxes.

If you died in 1999 with an estate worth $1,200,000, the federal estate tax would be $345,800 plus 41 percent of the excess over $1,000,000 or $82,000 (41 percent times $200,000) for a total tentative tax of $428,600 ($345,800 plus $82,000). This amount is less the unified credit for 1999 of $211,300. The federal estate tax due would be $211,300 payable within nine months of your death.

	Tax on lower amount plus next column	Rate of tax on excess of lower amount
Under $10,000	$ 0	18%
$10,000–$20,000	1,800	20%
$20,000–$40,000	3,800	22%
$40,000–$60,000	8,200	24%
$60,000–$80,000	13,000	26%
$80,000–$100,000	18,200	28%
$100,000–$150,000	23,800	30%
$150,000–$250,000	38,800	32%
$250,000–$500,000	70,800	34%
$500,000–$750,000	155,800	37%
$750,000–$1,000,000	248,300	39%
$1,000,000–$1,250,000	345,800	41%
$1,250,000–$1,500,000	448,300	43%
$1,500,000–$2,000,000	555,800	45%
$2,000,000–$2,500,000	780,800	49%
$2,500,000–$3,000,000	1,025,800	53%
$3,000,000 to 10,000,000	1,290,800	55%

	Tax on lower amount plus next column	*Rate of tax on excess of lower amount*
$10,000,000 to 21,255,000	$ 5,140,800	60%
$21,255,000 on up . . .	11,875,000	55%

*Less unified credit (defined in chapter 3 and the glossary) of $211,300 in 1999, $220,050 in 2000 and 2001, $229,800 in 2002 and 2003, $287,300 in 2004, $326,300 in 2005 and $345,800 in 2006 and thereafter. (If you had a gift tax exemption after 9/8/76 or your estate exceeds $10,000,000, please see your tax advisor for more information). See Table 3-1 in chapter 3 for estate tax calculation steps.

Source: 1998 Field Guide to Estate Planning, Business Planning, and Employee Benefits.

Appendix B
Financial Aid Tables for Dependent Students

The following tables reflect the minimum level of income or assets the government feels a family needs to maintain itself and is based on the Department of Labor's "low budget standard." The amounts in these tables are used to calculate your estimated family contribution and are used in the worksheets in chapter 5.

B-1
INCOME PROTECTION ALLOWANCE

Family Members Including Student	Allowance
2	$12,260
3	15,260
4	18,850
5	22,240
6	26,010
Each additional	2,940

Source: Don't Miss Out, 23rd ed., 1998, Octameron Associates.

B-2
ADJUSTMENT FOR BUSINESS NET WORTH

Business Net Worth	Adjustment
To $85,000	40% of net worth
$85,001–$260,000	$34,000 + 50% of net worth over $85,000
$260,001–$435,000	$121,500 + 60% of net worth over $260,000
$435,001 or more	$226,500 + 100% of net worth over $435,000

Source: Don't Miss Out, 23rd ed., 1998, Octameron Associates.

B-3
ASSET PROTECTION ALLOWANCE
(DEPENDENT STUDENTS)

Age of Older Parent	One Parent Family	Two Parent Family
40–44	$39,400	$25,100
45–49	$44,600	$28,000
50–54	$50,900	$31,600
55–59	$58,100	$35,700
60–64	$69,000	$40,900
65 Plus	$75,500	$44,400

Source: Don't Miss Out, 23rd ed., 1998, Octameron Associates.

B-4
PARENT'S CONTRIBUTION

Adjusted Available Income (AAI)	Parent Contribution
To Minus $3,409	($750) (Negative Figure)
($3,409) to $11,000	22% of AAI
$11,001 to $13,700	$2,420 + 25% of AAI over $11,000
$13,701 to $16,500	$3,095 + 29% of AAI over $13,700
$16,501 to $19,300	$3,907 + 34% of AAI over $16,500
$19,301 to $22,100	$4,859 + 40% of AAI over $19,300
$22,101 to More	$5,979 + 47% of AAI over $22,100

Source: Don't Miss Out, 23rd ed., 1998, Octameron Associates.

Appendix C
Financial Self-assessment Quiz*

This quiz can be used to help determine your risk tolerance rating.

Score

1. Investment
I do not need a high level of income from my investments.

5. strongly agree   4. agree   3. disagree   2. strongly disagree   _____

2. Large Expenses
I have set aside savings to cover major expenses like purchasing a home, college tuition, or financial emergency.

5. strongly agree   4. agree   3. disagree   2. strongly disagree   _____

3. Inflation
I am concerned about the effects of inflation on my investments.

5. strongly agree   4. agree   3. disagree   2. strongly disagree   _____

RISK TOLERANCE

4. Volatility
I can tolerate sharp ups and downs in the short-term value of my investments in return for potential long-term gains.

5. strongly agree   4. agree   3. disagree   2. strongly disagree   _____

5. Risk versus Reward
I prefer an investment that has a 50% chance of losing 5% and a 50% chance of gaining 20% in one year rather than an investment that will assure a 5% return in one year.

5. strongly agree   4. agree   3. disagree   2. strongly disagree   _____

6. Decline in Value
I am comfortable holding on to an investment even though it drops sharply in value.

5. strongly agree   4. agree   3. disagree   2. strongly disagree   _____

7. **Equity Investing**
   I am willing to take the risks associated with stocks in order to earn a potential return greater than the rate of inflation.

   5. strongly agree   4. agree   3. disagree   2. strongly disagree   _____

8. **Knowledge of Risk**
   I consider myself knowledgeable about the risks and the potential returns associated with investing in stocks and other types of securities.

   5. strongly agree   4. agree   3. disagree   2. strongly disagree   _____

TIME HORIZON

9. **Your Personal Timeline**
   In how many years do you plan to utilize the results of your investment strategy?

   5. more than 15   4. more than 10   3. more than 5   2. less than 5 _____

10. **Long-term Investing**
    I am comfortable with an investment that may take ten years to provide the returns I expect.

    5. strongly agree   4. agree   3. disagree   2. strongly disagree   _____

    Total score   _____

If your total score is:	You may be a(n):
45–50	Aggressive investor
39–44	Moderately aggressive investor
33–38	Moderate investor
27–32	Moderately conservative investor
20–26	Conservative investor

Appendix D
Types of Term Insurance

Term insurance will pay the face amount of a policy at the death of the insured. There is no accumulation of cash value and there is no continuation of the policy after the premium stops. This type of policy is very much like auto or fire insurance in that when you stop paying the premium, the policy ends.

This insurance tends to start out inexpensive when the insured is young and increase in cost as the insured gets older. The older you are, the closer you are to dying, the higher the price.

Group insurance is generally term insurance. When people leave their employer, and they haven't converted the group term to an individual permanent policy, the insurance protection ends.

There are five basic types of term insurance:

1. **Annual renewable.** This type of policy is renewable every year at an increasing price regardless of the insured's health. Convertible term policies mean that this type of term insurance can be changed for another policy issued by the same insurance company.

2. **Decreasing term.** This type of term insurance has a decreasing death benefit but a level premium. Traditionally this policy has been used to pay off mortgages, so it has been called mortgage insurance. If you're going to buy this type of insurance consider having the death benefit paid to your partner instead of the mortgage lender. In this way she or he can decide whether to pay off the mortgage or not.

   If you have a life-threatening illness and the mortgage provider offers you some form of credit life without medical questions, take it.

3. **Level term.** The death benefit and the premium in this type of insurance remain level for a period of time—five, ten, or fifteen years—and then jump to a significantly higher level for another period of years. At the end of the time period the policy ends unless it is renewed. There is no cash accumulation buildup in the policy and there is none at the end of the time period and, therefore, no refund.

4. **Reentry term.** This type of insurance allows the insured to reduce the premium after five or ten years if certain medical requirements are met. Generally a new physical examination is required. This could

become a problem as one ages or becomes very busy. If the medical requirements are not met, the policy continues at a guaranteed price that is always higher. (Any death benefit that is guaranteed has a higher price tag because the insurance company must take people who ordinarily wouldn't qualify.)

Reentry term can sound very appealing when it's presented. Beware—this product can become very costly if you keep it for a long period of time; the only way to "win" with any term insurance is to die.

Insurance companies know that as we age, health tends to deteriorate. Requalifying for insurance that you already have can become very tiresome. As time passes it is easy to put off another insurance decision. If you don't meet the reentry requirements because of procrastination, or if your health is no longer as good as it used to be when the policy was first bought, the price goes up. Converting to a permanent policy may make more sense.

5. **Group insurance.** This is generally term insurance. The first $50,000 is income-tax-free; anything over that amount will be taxed. You will receive a 1099 for the cost of your group life amount that exceeds $50,000.

When you leave your employer, you should have the option of continuing your group insurance as an individual policy on your own. If you have a medical history that would prevent you from purchasing a new policy, take the option and continue the life insurance. If you are healthy, it is always cheaper to buy the coverage you may need on the open market rather than through a group conversion.

Insurance companies really like term insurance. They make lots of money on term because it's often not in force when people need it the most: when they die. (For many older people the cost becomes too prohibitive and they drop the insurance.)

Term insurance, however, does fill a very important role. When you need more insurance and cannot afford a permanent policy, buy as much term as you can. Then convert it to a permanent policy that offers wealth-building opportunities with tax-deferred dollars, when you can afford it.

Appendix E
Permanent Life Insurance Alternatives

There are basically six types of permanent insurance. The key difference is when the death benefit is paid and how the difference between the premium and the actual cost of insurance is being used. The way to approach this is determined by your financial goals and your tolerance for investment risk.

1. **Whole life insurance.** This type of policy offers coverage for the insured's whole life. It has also been called ordinary life or straight life. The premium and the death benefit remain level for the life of the insured, which is usually calculated to age 95 or 100. At the end of the policy or when the insured surrenders the policy there could be a cash value. The cash value is a guaranteed amount written into the policy; because it is guaranteed its investment yield is very low. This type of policy, as an investment, is very safe. If the policy has dividends, the dividends can be used to accumulate additional cash value or buy more insurance, or may be paid out in cash every year.

   Because whole life has a guaranteed death benefit, a guaranteed price, and guaranteed cash values, it is generally the most expensive form of permanent insurance.

   Growth rates are relatively low since whole life does not participate in stock market growth. If you are planning to use this insurance to accumulate wealth, ask your agent or broker to show you other forms of permanent insurance with the same premium level. But if you want a policy that only provides guarantees, this is the best way to go.

2. **Universal life insurance.** This type of policy is also known as interest-sensitive life insurance. One way to think of this is to imagine that you have a CD wrapped in a life insurance blanket. The policy owner picks the death benefit, which can increase over time as the cash value in the policy increases in value, or can remain level no matter how much the cash value increases. Once the premium is paid, sales charges and expenses are subtracted, the balance of the premium is added to the cash value and a current interest rate is earned. The rate of interest depends on how the underlying bonds of the insurance

company are performing. The rate received is reduced by certain costs of the policy and the insurance company.

3. **Variable whole life insurance.** This type of policy looks like a traditional whole life policy, with two major differences. The death benefit and the cash value of the policy are not guaranteed and are flexible. The premium, minus certain policy costs, is invested in separate accounts of the insurance company. These accounts look and perform a lot like mutual funds, but are part of the life insurance contract. Since this type of insurance is considered a security, the company is required to provide you with a current prospectus describing the policy.

4. **Variable universal life insurance.** This is probably the most flexible type of insurance available today. It is a combination of universal life and variable life. It's like a universal life policy in that it has a flexible premium, flexible death benefit, and flexible withdrawal privileges, and it is also like a variable life policy in that you can choose how and where to invest the cash accumulation in the policy. In many VUL policies the death benefit is calculated like term insurance but is priced at a rate cheaper than regular term insurance. This insurance is considered a security and requires a prospectus.

5. **Survivorship life insurance.** This type of insurance is sometimes called second-to-die life insurance or joint and survivor life insurance, as it insures two lives and pays *only* at the *second person's* death.

   This policy may be used if one of the two people is uninsurable and if that person's insurance needs can be tied to a second person's need for insurance. This can be a very effective product when one partner is uninsurable and both partners want to provide for children.

6. **First-to-die life insurance.** This type of policy insures two lives and pays the death benefit when the *first person* dies. It can be term, whole, universal, variable life, or variable universal life. Some companies have a rider that enables the survivor to continue the policy.

   Unlike term insurance, permanent insurance can provide significant investment opportunities for the buyer if properly structured. The cash in these policies grows on a tax-deferred basis, and can be withdrawn as loans on a tax-free basis. Variable life polices provide the buyer with the opportunity to invest in a tax-sheltered environment.

Appendix F
Steps You Can Take to Improve Results
on Your Insurance Physical Examination

The following steps will help you ensure maximum possible physical condition for your examination:

1. Your exam should be done when you are under the least pressure and completely rested. For most people, this means in the morning. If at all possible, an eight-to-twelve-hour fast prior to the appointment is recommended.
2. Get a good night's sleep!
3. Do not drink coffee for twenty-four hours prior to your exam (decaffeinated is okay).
4. Do not smoke for at least three hours prior to your exam.
5. Do not drink any alcohol for two days prior to your exam.
6. Avoid salt for three to four days before the exam; this should have a beneficial effect on blood pressure readings.
7. Plan your food intake carefully for several days prior to your exam. Avoid rich, high-fat foods or those with large amounts of sugar.
8. Drink plenty of water for one to two days prior to the appointment.
9. Arrive at the exam a few minutes early—a short period of relaxation does wonders for traffic tension and blood pressure.
10. Refresh your memory on dates of past medical histories, as well as the names of doctors involved—a recently issued life insurance policy may be helpful. The insurance company will write to your personal physicians for your medical history.
11. Allocate enough time for the appointment so that you do not feel pressured. You should plan at least 30 minutes for a full exam, plus another 30 minutes if chest X-rays and EKGs are included.

Appendix G
States That Have Adopted the Uniform
Transfer-on-Death Security Registration Act*

The states listed below permit transfer-on-death beneficiary designations on securities.

Alabama	Maryland	Oklahoma
Alaska	Minnesota	Oregon
Arizona	Mississippi	Pennsylvania
Arkansas	Missouri	South Dakota
Colorado	Montana	Tennessee
Connecticut	Nebraska	Texas
Delaware	Nevada	Utah
Florida	New Hampshire	Virginia
Idaho	New Jersey	Washington
Illinois	New Mexico	West Virginia
Iowa	North Dakota	Wisconsin
Kansas	Ohio	Wyoming

*Per *The Nolo News*, Nolo Press, Fall 1998.

Appendix H
Job-Hunting Legal Questions

In the following list are questions a perspective employer may and may not ask you when you are applying for a job. They are based on the fair employment practices law.

NATIONAL ORIGIN/CITIZENSHIP
- *Employers may ask:* if you are you legally authorized to work in the United States. An employer may ask for documentation evidencing identity and employment eligibility under federal immigration laws.
- *Employers may not ask:* about your birthplace, citizenship, the birthplace of your parents or other close relatives, language, national origin, or whether your parents are naturalized or U.S.-born.

RACE/ETHNICITY
- *Employers may not ask:* any questions about your race or ethnicity, nor may they ask questions which may attempt to ascertain national origin or ancestry, e.g., color of eyes, hair, or skin.

PHOTOGRAPH
- *Employers may not ask:* for a photograph to accompany an application.

SEX (GENDER)
- *Employers may ask:* questions regarding gender if they are related to a bona fide occupational qualification that has been ruled to be a legitimate requirement for a particular position, but this is a very narrow exception.
- *Employers may not ask:* about your maiden name, marital status if only asked of one gender, or whether you have children, plan to have children, or have child-care arrangements.

SEXUAL ORIENTATION
- *Employers may not ask:* about your sexuality (gay, bisexual, lesbian, heterosexual) or marital status as a way to ascertain sexual orientation.

DISABILITY

- Once an offer of employment has been made, an employer may condition that offer on the results of a medical examination conducted solely for the purpose of determining whether the employee, with or without reasonable accommodation, is capable of performing the essential functions of the job.
- *Employers may not ask:* if you have a physical or mental disability, or about the nature or severity of your disability. You cannot be asked if you are an alcoholic, or a drug addict, or if you have HIV/AIDS.

EDUCATION/EXPERIENCE/REFERENCES

- *Employers may ask:* about your academic, vocational, professional, educational, and work experience. The latter can include verified volunteer work. Reference questions are okay.
- *Employers may not ask:* questions about education designed to determine how old you are, nor about the nature or character of organizations you belong to. (If you put the name of an organization on a résumé, an employer may be legally able to ask what the organization is.)

LIE DETECTOR TEST

- It is unlawful to require or administer a lie detector test as a condition of employment or continued employment.

AGE

- Generally the only proper question is, "Are you under nineteen, yes or no?" Questions about age may be allowed if necessary to satisfy state or federal law or if age is a bona fide occupational qualification for the position. (For example, serving alcohol in restaurants or bars may have state-mandated age requirements.)

CRIMINAL RECORD

- *Employers may ask* the following series of questions, which can only be answered yes or no:

    1. Have you ever been convicted of a felony?
    2. Have you been convicted of a misdemeanor within the past

five years (other than a first conviction for any of the following misdemeanors: drunkenness, simple assault, speeding, minor traffic violations, or disturbances of the peace)?

3. Have you completed a period of incarceration within the past five years? *(If you are in this category, get legal guidance.)*

- *Employers may not ask:* about arrests if there was no conviction, convictions over five years old, first convictions for misdemeanors of drunkenness, simple assault, speeding, minor traffic violations, or disturbances of the peace. *(If you are in this situation or suspect you are, get legal advice in writing.)*

RELIGIOUS CREED

- *Employers may ask* questions only on a very limited basis and only if they directly pertain to the job (e.g., religious instructor at a Jewish community center).
- *Employers may not ask:* about your religious denomination, practices, obligations, or what religious holidays you observe.

Appendix I
Activities of Daily Living (ADLs)

The following definitions are for the activities of daily living that are used in federally qualified long-term care insurance policies and certificates. (Federal law or regulations may supersede these definitions.)

1. **Dressing:** Putting on and taking off all items of clothing and any necessary braces, fasteners, or artificial limbs.
2. **Toileting:** Getting to and from the toilet, getting on or off the toilet, and performing associated personal hygiene.
3. **Transferring:** The ability to move into or out of bed, or a chair or wheelchair.
4. **Eating:** Feeding oneself by getting food into the body from a receptacle (such as a plate, cup, or table) or by feeding tube or intravenously.
5. **Bathing:** Washing oneself by sponge bath or in a tub or shower, including the act of getting into and out of a tub or shower.
6. **Continence:** The ability to maintain control of bowel and bladder function; or when unable to maintain control of bowel or bladder function, the ability to perform associated personal hygiene (including caring for a catheter or colostomy bag).

Appendix J
Helpful Phone Numbers

If you need health insurance and have been unable to obtain it, contact the high-risk pool for your state. These programs are only available in your state of residence, are expensive, and can be your last resort.

If you are collecting Social Security and/or private disability and want to return to the job market or are leaving the job market because of ill health, contact the hotline numbers for benefits counseling in your area. They are free and are there for you.

If you plan to viaticate your life insurance policy, check the consumer advocacy Web site listed below. State regulation is sporadic and changing.

STATE HIGH-RISK POOL PLANS FOR MEDICALLY UNINSURABLE RESIDENTS°

Alabama	Comprehensive Health Insurance Association	800-404-2386
California	Major Risk Medical Insurance Program (MRMIP)	800-289-6574
Colorado	Colorado Uninsurable Health Insurance Plan (CUHIP)	303-894-7499
Connecticut	Health Reinsurance Association (HRA)	800-842-0004°°
Illinois	Illinois Comprehensive Health Insurance Plan (ICHIP)	800-367-6410
Indiana	Indiana Comprehensive Health Insurance Association (ICHIA)	800-552-7921
Iowa	Iowa Comprehensive Health Association (ICHA)	317-581-4100
Kansas	Kansas Health Insurance Association	800-255-6065°°
Louisiana	Louisiana Health Insurance Association	800-736-0947
Minnesota	Minnesota Comprehensive Health Association (MCHA)	800-531-6674

°If your state is not listed, please call your state's department of insurance. Not all states have these programs.

°°In-state phone number.

Missouri	Missouri Health Insurance Pool (MHIP)	800-843-6447
Nebraska	Comprehensive Health Insurance Pool (CHIP)	800-356-3485
New Mexico	New Mexico Comprehensive Health Insurance Pool (NMCHIP)	800-432-0750
North Dakota	Comprehensive Health Association of North Dakota	800-737-0016
Oregon	Oregon Medical Insurance Pool (OMIP)	800-777-3168
South Carolina	South Carolina High-Risk Insurance Pool (SCHIP)	800-868-2500
Tennessee	Tennessee Comprehensive Health Insurance Pool (TCHIP)	615-741-8642
Texas	Health Risk Pool	888-398-3927
Utah	Comprehensive Health Insurance Pool (HIP)	800-624-6519**
Wyoming	Wyoming Health Insurance Pool (WHIP)	800-438-5768

BENEFITS COUNSELING

California	AIDS Benefits Counselors (ABC)/Positive Resource	415-598-9845
	AIDS Hotline	800-367-2437
	AIDS Project of Los Angeles (APLA)	213-993-1472
Massachusetts	Disability Law Center (Boston)	800-872-9992
New York	Gay Men's Health Crisis	212-367-1500
National	AIDS Hotline	800-863-2437
	Centers for Disease Control and Prevention	800-342-2437

VIATICAL SETTLEMENT RESOURCES

Consumer Advocacy	www.viatical-expert.net
Viatical Association of America	800-842-9811
National Viatical Association	800-741-9465

**In-state phone number.

MAJOR CREDIT BUREAUS

Experian
P.O. Box 2104
Allen, TX 75013-2104
Phone: 888-397-3742
www.experian.com

Trans Union
800-888-4213
P.O. Box 390
Springfield, MA 19064-0390
www.transunion.com

Equifax
P.O. Box 105873
Atlanta, GA 30348
800-997-2493
www.equifax.com

Glossary

Accelerated death benefit (ADB). A pre-death benefit paid to a terminally ill person insured by an insurance company.

Annuitant. The person who receives the benefits from an annuity.

Annuity. A contract between an insurance company and an individual in which the company agrees to pay a stream of equal payments at predetermined intervals, such as monthly. Annuities can be either fixed or variable for a specific period.

Asset. Anything owned that has a monetary value.

Asset allocation. The assignment of investment funds to broad categories of assets, such as stocks, bonds, domestic, international, tax-deferred.

Balanced fund. A type of mutual fund that tends to be a blend of equity investments and bond investments. Each mutual fund defines its own mix of investments.

Beneficiary. The person or institution designated to receive the income, death proceeds, or assets of a trust, insurance policy, estate, annuity, qualified retirement plan, and so on.

Bond. A type of security that represents a loan from the purchaser of the investment to the issuing organization. Bonds may be issued by private companies or governments. The issuer promises to repay the loan at a specified time at a specified interest rate.

Broker-dealer. A member organization of the National Association of Security Dealers (NASD) or any major stock exchange that provides the only conduits through which Registered Representatives can buy or sell securities. (Registered Representatives can include stockbrokers, financial planners, investment advisors, and so on.)

Build-up.   The cash accumulation inside a life insurance policy.

Cash surrender value.   The amount of money payable to an investor in exchange for a life insurance policy that has not matured yet.

Cash value.   The accumulation of cash within a permanent insurance policy such as whole life, variable life, or universal life.

Chapter 7.   A form of bankruptcy in which nonexempt property is sold and used for debt repayment and in which the remaining balance of debt is discharged.

Chapter 13.   A form of bankruptcy in which debt is paid off over a period of time under the supervision of a trustee of the United States Bankruptcy Court.

Charitable lead trust (CLT).   A trust under which a donor (grantor) places funds to pay out either an annuity (fixed periodic payment) or percentage of the fair market value of the trust assets to a charity and the remainder interest (proceeds) to the grantor or some other noncharitable beneficiary at the end of the life of the trust.

Charitable remainder annuity trust (CRAT).   A trust under which a *fixed amount* of at least 5 percent of the initial fair market value of trust assets is paid to a noncharitable beneficiary, with the proceeds (remainder interest) going to a charity at the end of the life of the trust. Payments to the noncharitable beneficiary may be for a period not to exceed twenty years or for life.

Charitable remainder unitrust (CRUT).   A trust under which a *fixed percentage* of the net fair market value is paid at least annually to a noncharitable beneficiary, with the proceeds (remainder interest) of the trust going to a charity at the end of the life of the trust. The percentage must be at least 5 percent and payments to the noncharitable beneficiary may be for a term not to exceed twenty years or for life.

COBRA.   A benefit under the Consolidated Omnibus Budget Reconciliation Act of 1985, which requires employers of twenty or more people to allow employees to continue health insurance benefits for eighteen months after their employment terminates for any reason except gross misconduct.

Conservatorship.   A court proceeding to appoint and supervise a manager (the conservator) for the financial and/or personal care of an adult (the conservatee) who is unable to care for himself or herself.

Consumer price index (CPI).   Government-sponsored index of changes in prices for consumer goods and services, including food and beverages, transportation, housing, medical care, and entertainment. Used as a measure of inflation.

Cost basis.   The cost of property for calculating capital gains or profit. Generally what you paid for the property plus additions or improvements. Also called tax cost.

Death benefit.   The amount received by a beneficiary, also known as face amount or face value, when death benefit is paid by a life insurance policy.

Decedent.   A deceased person.

Disability premium waiver (DPW).   A rider that excuses the premium payment on a life insurance policy when an insured is disabled for at least six months.

Discharge.   The release of debts during a Chapter 7 bankruptcy.

Dollar-cost averaging (DCA).   Investing a fixed sum at regular intervals. Since more shares are purchased when prices are low than when they are high, the result is an average cost that is lower than the average share price.

Durable power of attorney (DPA).   A written document in which the principal designates another person to act on his or her behalf in matters requiring legal action. This document remains effective even after the person becomes legally incompetent. It allows *you* to choose who will act for you should you become unable to act on your own behalf.

Durable power of attorney for medical care (DPAMC).   A written document in which you authorize another person to make binding health care decisions for you should you become unable to do so. Also known as a durable power of attorney for health care (DPAHC). The name of this document may be different in your state.

Estate planning.   Traditionally, estate planning has meant preparing for the orderly and efficient transfer of assets at death. Today, it has come to mean the accumulation and distribution of an estate during one's lifetime as well as at death.

Estate taxes.   Taxes imposed by the federal government and some states on the estate of a person who has died. Federal estate taxes are due within nine months of the date of death.

Evidence of Insurability. Information about the health, occupation, lifestyle, habits, income, net worth, and other insurance of an applicant for insurance.

Extended period of eligibility (EPE). Permits the reinstatement of Social Security Disability Insurance (SSDI) benefits, without a new application, disability determination, or waiting period, for people whose cash payments were previously stopped because of substantial gainful activity (SGA).

Face amount. The amount of life insurance stated on the face of the policy; the amount that is paid at the death of the insured less any policy loans or withdrawals made.

Gift taxes. Taxes imposed by the federal government upon an individual's transfers of money or property by gift. Individuals are allowed an annual exemption of $10,000 per person for gifts to any number of people.

Graded death benefit life insurance. Life insurance designed for people with a serious illness; it pays a lower amount in the early years of the policy. These policies generally have no medical questions, do not require blood or urine tests, and do not require statements from health care providers.

Growth fund. A type of mutual fund that can invest in securities that the fund's managers feel will appreciate in value, although this type of fund can be volatile. Each mutual fund has its *own* definition for what its growth fund is.

Guardian. The person who has the care of the person or the property of a minor.

Impaired risk. People who apply for life or health insurance with a serious medical history. Also called substandard risk.

Impairment-related work expenses (IRWE). Applies to all SSDI and SSI beneficiaries who are not blind and who are working while receiving Social Security benefits. It provides that people who are working with a disability can deduct certain expenses necessary to work (transportation, drugs, devices, attendant care services, etc.) from earned income.

Income fund. A type of mutual fund that invests in bonds, other debt securities, or high-dividend paying stocks.

Income in respect of a decedent (IRD). Income that a decedent was entitled to receive as part of gross income that has not been included in taxable income for the year of his or her death.

Incontestability period. The two-year period in which an insurance contract can be voided for cause by an insurer.

Individual retirement account (IRA). A retirement fund where an individual may contribute up to $2,000 per year; contributions may be deductible; earnings are nontaxable until withdrawn; funds cannot be withdrawn until age 59½, but must commence by age 70½. Also called a traditional IRA as opposed to a Roth IRA.

Inheritance taxes. Taxes imposed by some states on the passing of property from the deceased person's estate to heirs.

Insurable interest. An insurable interest arises from the relationship of the party obtaining life insurance on an insured providing there is a reasonable economic benefit from the continuance of the insured's life or continuation of love and affection.

Irrevocable life insurance trust (ILIT). One of the most basic tools of estate planning, a trust funded by life insurance to keep that insurance out of the estate.

Lapse. When a life insurance policy premium has not been paid beyond the grace period, it lapses or ceases to exist.

Lazarus effect. In the New Testament, Lazarus died and was restored to life. People with AIDS who thought they were going to die but are now alive because of the medicines they are taking are said to be like Lazarus.

Living will. A legal document that allows an individual to state in advance his or her unwillingness to be subjected to life-prolonging medical procedures once there is no chance of recovery. Almost all states have some form of this document. It may also be called a directive to physicians or health care proxy or may be part of the durable power of attorney for medical care, depending on where you live. This document has also been called a die-with-dignity will.

Long-term disability insurance (LTD). Generally refers to group long-term disability insurance. It usually has a six-month waiting period before benefits start and continues benefits to age 65.

Marital deduction. Federal tax provision under which unlimited amounts of property can be passed between spouses in a legally recognized marriage during lifetime or at death without payment of gift taxes during lifetime or estate taxes at death. The marital deduction is *not* available to lesbian or gay couples.

Medicaid.   A health care assistance program administered jointly by the federal and state governments. Each state operates its own program following federal guidelines; some states offer minimal services while others offer expanded services. Medicaid may pay for nursing care for the destitute; benefits and requirements differ by state. (In California Medicaid is called Medi-Cal.)

Medical Information Bureau (MIB).   A nonprofit trade association of seven hundred life insurance companies that provides a confidential exchange of underwriting information among its members as a safeguard against fraud.

Medicare.   Two-part health insurance program under the Social Security Administration's Health Care Financing Administration (HCFA) for eligible disabled and retired people. Part A provides hospital insurance and Part B covers physician services, laboratory tests, and X-rays.

OBRA.   Provision under the Omnibus Budget Reconciliation Act of 1989 that allows employees to continue health insurance benefits for an additional eleven months beyond COBRA's eighteen months if the person electing COBRA has an approved Social Security disability.

Payable-on-death (POD).   Beneficiary designation on bank or savings and loan accounts that transfers property at death directly to the designee with proof of death of the depositor without going through probate.

Personal asset.   Property you own that is personal in nature, such as your home, furnishings, skis, art, auto, jewelry.

Policy loan.   Funds borrowed from a life insurance company using the cash value in a policy as collateral.

Portfolio.   A collection of investment assets, such as stocks and bonds, held by an individual, corporation, or trust. Also, all assets held by a mutual fund at any specific time.

Power of attorney (POA).   A written document executed by an individual called the principal, authorizing another person, called the attorney-in-fact or agent, to act on that individual's behalf. A *general* power of attorney enables the attorney-in-fact to discharge virtually all of your legal obligations and should be considered very carefully before you sign it. A *special* power of attorney has limitations on what the attorney-in-fact can do.

Premium.   The payment required to keep an insurance policy in force.

Probate.   A court-supervised legal proceeding during which the will is proved, decedent's assets are collected, debts and taxes are paid, the balance of property distributed in accordance with the will or the laws of intestacy succession. Probate has no effect on property distributed by means of title, beneficiary designations, or in trusts.

Real property.   Land and any buildings on it.

Revocable living trust.   A trust that is established during a person's lifetime that can be revoked. This trust does not avoid federal estate taxes although it passes outside of probate and, hence, can reduce state transfer taxes and expenses at death. A grantor who lacks legal capacity cannot revoke a living trust.

Rider.   A provision in an insurance contract that changes the benefits.

Roth IRA.   Type of retirement account that permits individuals to make nondeductible contributions of up to $2,000 per year; contributions can be made beyond age 70½, and funds accumulate tax-free and can be distributed tax-free if they have remained in the Roth IRA for at least five years and the owner is over the age of 59½ or has died. There are special distribution rules for first-time home buyers or disability.

Rule of 72.   The number 72 divided by the growth rate or the interest rate of an investment will give the number of years it will take the investment to double in value if the interest or dividends are reinvested. When the number 72 is divided by the inflation rate the result will be the number of years it takes one dollar to be worth 50 percent of current value.

Section 1035 exchange.   See *Tax-free exchange*.

Social Security Disability Insurance (SSDI). Monthly payment of $1 to $1,400 for people who have paid FICA taxes in 20 of the last 40 months. Must meet SSA definition of disability, which generally means being unable to perform duties of any job, remaining disabled for at least a year, or having a condition resulting in death within 12 months. SSDI has a 5-month waiting period, benefit is adjusted for age, and after 24 months the recipient will automatically receive Medicare.

Sole ownership.   To have or hold property under one person's name only.

STD.   Short-term disability income. An employee group benefit that pays disability insurance up to six months or until long-term disability insurance benefits start.

Stepped-up basis.   The increase in tax cost or "basis" of property in an estate to its fair market value at the date of death of the owner.

Stock.   A type of security that represents ownership of an interest in a corporation. A stock owner is called a shareholder, as people own shares of stock. Shareholders make money if their stock earns dividends or if the value of the stock goes up and they sell the stock at a profit.

Substandard risk. People who apply for life or health insurance with a serious medical history, also called impaired risk.

Substantial gainful activity (SGA). The performance of work duties over a reasonable period of time for pay or profit, generally defined for SSDI and SSI as averaging $500 per month for nonblind individuals. (The SGA level for individuals who are blind changes from year to year and, as of this writing, is $1,000 per month.)

Supplemental Security Income (SSI). A needs-based disability income cash payment, received on the first of the month. To be eligible for SSI a person must have little or no income or resources, be considered medically disabled, and be unable to work for at least a year.

Tax credit. Dollar-for-dollar offset directly against taxes.

Tax-free exchange. When property is exchanged for "like-kind" property, gain or loss need not be recognized, as the taxpayer is essentially in the same position as she or he was prior to the transaction. Real estate transactions can be structured as tax-free exchanges. When life insurance or annuity contracts are exchanged for other life insurance or annuity contracts the tax-free exchange is called a Section 1035 exchange (after the governing portion of the Internal Revenue Code).

Tax shelter. An investment that produces relatively large current deductions that can be used to offset other taxable income.

Tenants in common. One form of joint ownership whereby, on death of one tenant in common, the share owned passes to the other by will or intestacy law.

Transfer-on-death (TOD). Beneficiary designation on stocks, bonds, mutual funds, or brokerage accounts that transfers property at death directly to designee with proof of death without going through probate. In some states the department of motor vehicles has a TOD designation for cars.

Trial work period (TWP). A period of nine months (not necessarily consecutive), over a sixty-month rolling period, that enables a Social Security Disability Insurance beneficiary the opportunity to test if she or he has the ability to work. Earnings for TWP are defined as $200 or more or forty hours per month if self-employed.

Unified credit.   The amount that offsets a portion of federal gift and estate tax. The Taxpayer Relief Act of 1997 increases this amount from $211,300 in 1999 to $220,050 in 2000 and 2001, $229,800 in 2002 and 2003, $287,300 in 2004, $326,300 in 2005, and $345,800 in 2006 and thereafter. This amount corresponds with the Unified Credit Exemption Equivalent.

Unified credit exemption equivalent.   The maximum estate size that can pass without federal gift and estate taxes. The Taxpayer Relief Act of 1997 increases this amount from $650,000 in 1999 to $1,000,000 in 2006 and thereafter. This amount corresponds with the Unified Credit.

Viatical provider.   The viatical settlement company or investor providing the funds for a viatical settlement. The viatical provider may also be referred to as the viatical benefactor or the viatical funder.

Viatical settlement (viatication).   The sale or assignment of all or part of the ownership of, or the beneficial interest in, an existing individual life insurance policy or the interest in a group policy.

Viatical settlement broker.   A person ("person" is defined as a legal entity such as a corporation, individual, partnership, limited liability corporation, etc.) that on the behalf of a viator and for a fee, commission, or other valuable consideration, offers or attempts to negotiate viatical settlement contracts between a viator and one or more viatical settlement providers. Irrespective of the manner in which the viatical settlement broker is compensated, a viatical settlement broker is deemed to represent only the viator and owes a fiduciary responsibility to the viator to act according to the viator's instructions and in the best interest of the viator.

Viaticate.   To sell a life insurance policy or an interest in a group policy to a third party when the insured has a catastrophic, life-threatening, or chronic illness or condition.

Viaticum.   The payment in a viatical settlement contract.

Viator.   The owner of a life insurance policy or a certificate holder under a group policy insuring the life of an individual with a catastrophic, life-threatening, or chronic illness or condition who enters or seeks to enter into a viatical settlement contract.

Waiver of premiums.   A rider that excuses the premium payment on a life insurance policy when an insured person is disabled for at least six months.

Bibliography

Baldwin, Ben G. *The New Life Insurance Investment Advisor: Achieving Financial Security for You & Your Family through Today's Insurance Products.* rev. ed. Chicago: Irwin Professional Publishing, 1994.

Beckwith, Harry. *Selling the Invisible: A Field Guide to Modern Marketing.* New York: Warner Books, 1997.

Berkery, Peter M., Jr. *Personal Financial Planning for Gays and Lesbians: Our Guide to Prudent Decision Making.* Chicago: Irwin Professional Publishing, 1996.

Cady, Donald F. *1998 Field Guide to Estate Planning, Business Planning & Employee Benefits.* Cincinnati, Ohio: National Underwriter, 1998.

Dominguez, Joe, and Vicki Robin. *Your Money or Your Life: Transforming Your Relationship with Money and Achieving Financial Independence.* New York: Viking Penguin, 1992.

Elkin, Larry M. *Financial Self-defense for Unmarried Couples: How to Gain Financial Protection Denied by Law.* New York: Doubleday Currency, 1995.

"Estate Planning for the Unmarried Adult, Tax Management Estates, Gifts and Trusts Portfolios, Tax Management Inc." Washington, D.C.: The Bureau of National Affairs, 1997.

A Guide to Social Security and SSI Disability Benefits for People with HIV Infection. Publication No. 05-10020.

Hammond, Bob. *Life after Debt.* 2d ed. Franklin Lakes, New Jersey: Career Press, 1996.

———. *Life without Debt.* Franklin Lakes, New Jersey: Career Press, 1996.

Hayden Curry, Denis Clifford, and Robin Leonard. *A Legal Guide for*

Lesbian and Gay Couples. 9th national ed. Berkeley, California: Nolo Press, 1996.

Hertz, Frederick. *Legal Affairs: Essential Advice for Same-Sex Couples.* New York: Henry Holt, 1998.

Hoyt, Christopher R. "How to Structure Charitable Bequests from Donor Retirement Plan Accounts." Paper presented at the Fifth Annual Planned Giving Conference, San Francisco, 1997.

Jorgensen, James. *It's Never Too Late to Get Rich: Secrets of Building a Nest Egg at Any Age.* Dearborn, Michigan: Dearborn Financial Publishing, 1994.

Larson, Per. *Gay Money: Your Personal Guide to Same-Sex Strategies for Financial Security, Strength, and Success.* New York: Dell, 1997.

Leider, Anna, and Robert Leider. *Don't Miss Out: The Ambitious Student's Guide to Financial Aid.* Alexandria, Virginia: Octameron Associates, 1998.

Leimberg, Stephen R., et al. *The Tools & Techniques of Estate Planning.* 10th ed. Cincinnati, Ohio: National Underwriter, 1995.

LeShan, Lawrence. *Cancer as a Turning Point.* New York: Viking Penguin, 1990.

Mellan, Olivia. *Money Harmony: Resolving Money Conflicts in Your Life and Relationships.* New York: Walker, 1994.

Miner, Deborah A., et al. *Tax Facts 1 on Life Insurance.* Cincinnati, Ohio: National Underwriter, 1997.

Randolph, Mary. *Eight Ways to Avoid Probate.* Berkeley, California: Nolo Press, 1996.

"The Red Book on Work Incentives," publication no. 64-030. Washington, D.C.: Social Security Administration, 1995.

Rowland, Mary. *Best Practices for Financial Advisors.* Princeton, New Jersey: Bloomberg Press, 1997.

Ryan, Paula Langguth. *Bounce Back from Bankruptcy: A Step-by-Step Guide to Getting Back on Your Financial Feet.* Tracy's Landing, Maryland: Pellingham Casper Communications, 1996.

Scott, David. *Wall Street Words: An Essential A to Z for Today's Investor.* Boston: Houghton Mifflin, 1997.

Silver, Don. *Baby Boomer Retirement: 65 Simple Ways to Protect Your Future.* Los Angeles: Adams-Hall, 1994.

Thompson, Karen, and Julie Andrzejewski. *Why Can't Sharon Kowalski Come Home?* Minneapolis, Minnesota: Spinsters Ink, 1988.

Westhem, Andrew D., and Donald Jay Korn. *Protecting What's Yours: How to Safeguard Your Assets and Maintain Your Personal Wealth*. Secaucus, New Jersey: Birch Lane Press, 1995.

"What You Need to Know about Financing Your Children's Education." New York: American Express Financial Advisors, 1996.

Who Writes What in Life & Health Insurance. Cincinnati, Ohio: National Underwriter, 1997.

Wolk, Gloria. *Cash for the Final Days: A Financial Guide for the Terminally Ill*. Laguna Hills, California: Bailkin Books, 1997.

Index

ABOUT THE AUTHOR

HAROLD L. LUSTIG, M.B.A., has been a financial planner and advisor for over twenty-two years, specializing in financial and estate planning for the gay and lesbian community for the past seven years. His clients include professionals, business owners, retirees, singles, and couples ranging in age from their early twenties to mid-eighties. He is a Chartered Life Underwriter, and a Chartered Financial Consultant. He has an independent financial planning practice in San Francisco and is an Associate Investment Advisor and Registered Representative with Multi-Financial Securities Corporation, Denver, Colorado.

Lustig has been a contributing editor and columnist for *Q San Francisco* and his articles about financial planning have appeared in the *San Francisco Bay Area Reporter* and *Pension Review*.

Formerly president of his own financial planning firm, Lustig has been affiliated with American Express Financial Advisors, New England Life, Phoenix Home Life, Equitable Life Assurance Society of the U.S., and Nathan and Lewis Associates.

Lustig is the former dean of the Huebner School in New York City. He has taught numerous seminars on the topics of retirement planning, investment planning, and planned giving for educational institutions and corporations, including McDonald's, Learning Annex, and the San Francisco Center for Performing Arts.

Harold Lustig was born in New York City and currently makes his home in San Francisco with his wife, Clarinda Cole Lustig.